Paper I

Tax administration

ATII
STUDY
TEXT

©
BPP Taxation Courses
1996

Finance Act 1996 Edition for ATII Qualifying Examinations in November 1996 and May 1997

Published by

BPP Taxation Courses
Faraday House
48 Old Gloucester Street
London
WC1N 3AD

Printed in England by
DACOSTA PRINT
35/37 Queensland Road
London N7 7AH
(0171) 700 1000

Contents

Introduction

Syllabus

Paper I of the Chartered Institute of Taxation examination is entitled 'Tax administration, professional responsibilities and ethics'. The syllabus is as follows:

1. The administration of income tax, capital gains tax and corporation tax under the Taxes Management Act 1970 including the activities, rights and powers of the Inland Revenue Enquiry Branch, Special Offices and Special Investigation Section.

2. The reporting and payment obligations for corporation tax under the 'Pay and File' regime and, generally, under the Taxes Act.

3. The administration of National Insurance Contributions, including enforcement and appeal provisions.

4. The regulations governing the operation of the Pay As You Earn scheme for the deduction of income tax and national insurance contributions from emoluments.

5. The regulations governing the Construction Industry Tax Deduction Scheme.

6. The administration of inheritance tax under Part VIII of the Inheritance Tax Act 1984.

7. The administration of value added tax including regulations covering the documents and records to be provided and retained; the role and powers of Customs and Excise including the charging of interest and penalties; and appeals to Value Added Tax tribunals.

8. The Ethical Rules of the Institute.

9. The Practice Guidelines published by the Institute.

These last two items are dealt with in a separate text entitled Ethical rules, practice guidelines and professional conduct.

The form of Paper I

Paper I is a two and a quarter hour paper which is in three parts:

Part A Ethical rules, practice guidelines and professional conduct

Part B Direct tax administration

Part C Indirect tax administration

Twelve questions are set of 15 marks each, four in each part, of which seven are to be answered. At least two questions must be answered from Part A.

About this study text

The text is divided into two parts, reflecting the syllabus for Parts B and C of Paper 1:

Part 1 Direct tax administration

Part 2 Indirect tax administration

At the end of each session you will find a quiz. You should always attempt the quiz before proceeding to the next session, as it will provide an indication of whether you have understood the material just covered. If it appears that you have not grasped certain of the principles involved you should re-study the appropriate part of the session before moving on to the next.

There is a comprehensive index at the end of this study text.

If you have already studied the FA 1995 Paper I study text you may prefer to read only the new and updated items. To assist you, these items are highlighted in the text. It is recommended that you also re-work all examples and each quiz.

Past questions

Details of Parts B and C of previous Paper I examinations are given below.

May 1994

Part B

Q5   Discussion of deduction of tax under Construction Industry Tax Deduction Scheme and of conditions to be satisfied before Revenue will issue a sub-contractor's certificate.

Q6   Discussion of Group Relief under Pay and File.

Q7   Explanation of IHT reporting requirements for gifts into a discretionary trust, calculation of interest on late paid IHT, explanation of penalty position for late IHT returns and explanation of CGT reporting requirements.

Q8   Discussion of the statutory clearances which may be obtained from the Inland Revenue.

Part C

Q9   Calculation and explanation of VAT penalty for errors in returns.

Q10 Discussion of unauthorised issue of VAT invoices, use of computers in accounting for VAT and a person's right to rely on Customs and Excise leaflets.

Q11 Explanation of VAT registration, Customs and Excise refusal of retrospective grouping and Customs request for security.

Q12 Discussion of Customs and Excise control visits and powers available to Customs and Excise to enable them to police VAT.

November 1994

Part B

Q5   1.   Review of time limits for submission of returns and payment of tax under self assessment.

    2.   Interest on overdue tax calculation, self assessment rules.

Q6   Discussion of the interest and penalties arising in respect of unreported chargeable gains.

Q7   Advice to a client on the national insurance implications of being an employee, a director and a self-employed individual.

Q8   1.   Review of Revenue procedures following an 'error or mistake' claim.

    2.   Appeal procedures against the Revenue decision.

Part C

Q9   1.   Outline of the VAT penalties in relation to serious misdeclaration or neglect and persistent misdeclaration.

    2.   Advice concerning disclosure of previous underdeclaration.

Q10 Review of the VAT aspects arising on the purchase of a business from a VAT registered trader.

Q11 Calculation of default surcharge and consideration of reasonable excuse.

Q12 Explanation of the record keeping requirements of the second-hand car scheme.

May 1995

Part B

Q5   Letter outlining the PAYE implications for a UK company of using the personnel of an Isle of Man company for a 9 month period and of employing a Swiss national for 5 years, where that employee will only spend 2 months per annum in the UK.

Q6   Explanation of interest and penalties which may be imposed on a company in respect of failure to notify chargeability, failure to make a return and late payment of tax. Consideration of effect of carry back of both losses and of surplus ACT on the interest and penalties.

Q7   Letter explaining to a sole trader the interest and penalty position as a result of a failure to notify chargeability on commencement of self employment and the late payment of tax and NIC. Also explaining the interest and penalty position on the late payment of tax and NIC in respect of an employee's wages.

Q8   Notes for a talk explaining to a local society of solicitors how self assessment will affect the administration of partnership taxation.

Part C

Q9   Explanation of the penalty regimes applying to late registration, tax evasion involving dishonest conduct and late submission of returns or late payment of tax.

Q10   VAT consequences of overseas company making supplies in the UK, including the potential need to appoint a tax representative; tax refund procedure for non-EC businesses.

Q11   Explanation of cash accounting, annual accounting and the farmers' flat rate scheme.

Q12   Procedure for dealing with disputes, including rights of appeal.

November 1995

Part B

Q5   Description of the PAYE system as it applies to different methods of providing emoluments.

Q6   1.   Outline of time limits under the Pay and File system and provisions for failing to comply.

      2.   Statement of circumstances where returns can be made in round £000's.

Q7   Description of the conditions and procedures to apply to obtain MIRAS relief.

Q8   Calculation of amounts needed to complete forms CT61 - quarterly accounting for ACT and income tax - and the interest and penalties payable on amounts paid late.

Part C

Q9   Statement of the circumstances and conditions for use of Customs power to enter premises and inspect or remove records.

Q10   Letter to client concerning an appeal against Customs direction for a client's business to be aggregated with that of his wife.

Q11   Statement of when a repayment supplement is made for VAT overpaid and a calculation of the amount due. Calculation of default interest payable where Customs establish that an over repayment has been made.

Q12   Description of what constitutes a valid document to support a right to input tax credit and what information it should contain.

Part 1
Direct tax administration

Contents

SESSION 1
THE INLAND REVENUE

By the end of this session you will be able to:

- appreciate the general structure of the Inland Revenue

- understand the Revenue's powers to issue tax returns and other notices requiring information, together with the limits on those powers

- explain the Revenue's rules for giving technical guidance which can be relied on and the role of clearance procedures

- outline the Revenue's approach to back duty investigations, their powers to extend the 6 year time limit for raising assessments and to charge penalties

- explain the role of the Special Compliance Office and the various specialist departments

- describe the procedure at an appeal hearing before the General or Special Commissioners, and the right of appeal to higher courts

References: TMA 1970 unless otherwise stated

1.1   Introduction

1.1.1   The current structure of the Inland Revenue

Direct taxes are administered by the Board of Inland Revenue (also referred to as 'The Commissioners of Inland Revenue'). The general administration is regulated by statute.

s.1

Direct taxes include income tax, capital gains tax, corporation tax and inheritance tax.

The UK is divided into tax districts with an office headed by a District Inspector. Each district collects tax on income and capital gains arising within its area. The Inspector supervises the system of self assessment. Collectors of Tax collect tax when it is paid.

Although the two functions are currently kept separate the Treasury is considering combining them and has enacted legislation which enables 'Collectors' and 'Inspectors' to be interchangeable terms in the legislation.

There are also long-term plans for local tax offices and collection offices to be restructured into new-style taxpayer service offices and taxpayer district offices. The taxpayer service offices will perform the day to day work on PAYE codes, changes to personal reliefs, making 'self assessments' for taxpayers when required, and 'repairing' self assessments while the taxpayer district offices will conduct compliance work, such as enquiries into selected business accounts, PAYE audit, and follow up collection work. In some locations a taxpayer assistance office will provide a counter service for personal callers requiring forms or leaflets or answers to basic queries.

At the start of 1993 there were 631 tax offices and 136 local collection offices spread throughout the UK employing over 50,000 staff so the change will require a lengthy transitional period. There is also an intention to slim down staff numbers as the self assessment system shifts more compliance work onto taxpayers and employers, and away from the Revenue.

There is also a Head Office which combines two main functions: firstly, to give advice on policy to Government Ministers and secondly, to provide a technical and support service to the local offices. Head office is organised into divisions on a subject basis, eg. Business Taxation, Personal Taxation, Financial & Oil.

There is also an independent adjudicator appointed by the Revenue to independently review and make recommendations on complaints by taxpayers made against the Revenue where the normal tribunal system would not be appropriate.

The Inland Revenue is under the ministerial control of the Treasury which, among other functions, promotes tax legislation in Parliament.

1.2 Revenue's powers to obtain information

1.2.1 Tax returns

For the purposes of establishing the amounts on which a person is chargeable to income tax and capital gains tax and the amounts of tax payable for a year of assessment, that person may be required by a notice issued by an Inspector to supply such information as the Inspector requires. This would normally be a return of his income and gains computed in accordance with the Acts specifying the amount from each source.

s.8(1)

If the Revenue decide to enquire into the return, they have a power to request any documents in the taxpayer's possession and any 'accounts or particulars' required to determine the accuracy or completeness of the return. The taxpayer can appeal against the request.

s.19A

Persons who receive income or gains on behalf of others, eg. trustees, may be required to make a return of that income.

ss. 13 & 8A(1)

Employers may be required to make a return of payments to employees (and of their addresses). A trader, and a non-trader in respect of payments for services, may be required to make a return of payments made by him to another person if they exceed £15 in the year. 'Non-trader' includes government departments, public and local authorities and other public bodies. There are other similar rules relating to bank deposit interest and interest paid gross and to rent paid by tenants.

ss.15 & 16

ss.16(8)
ss.17-19

Information may, in certain circumstances, be sought from government departments, public and local authorities and other public bodies in relation to the payment of grants or subsidies out of public funds and business licence holders (eg. taxi drivers).

s.18A

There are a number of rules requiring persons who make specified payments to make a return. These include an employer who pays a 'golden handshake'.

s.148(7) ICTA 1988

1.2.2 General powers to obtain information

An Inspector may by notice require a person to produce documents or furnish particulars relevant to a taxpayer's liability. Where there is an enquiry into a self assessment, the Inspector will use this situation to require the information and documents needed to conclude the enquiry. Otherwise the Inspector will need to use his powers under ss20 - 20D TMA 1970. However, in exercising these powers the Inspector must have the authority of the Board and also the consent of a Commissioner.

s.19A

ss.20 - 20D

The General or Special Commissioner giving consent to the issue of the notice may not take part in any appeal proceedings in which the information required by the notice is likely to be given.

s.20(7AB) & (7AC)

The Inspector must give the person to whom the notice applies a written summary of his reasons for applying for consent to the giving of the notice. It is not necessary for the Inspector to divulge any information which might identify any person who has provided information which has been taken into account in applying for the notice. In addition, the Inspector need not disclose any information if the Commissioner is satisfied that the Inspector has reasonable grounds for believing that its disclosure would prejudice the assessment or collection of tax.

s.20(8E)-(8H)

Such a notice:

(a)   may be addressed to the taxpayer (or any other person in respect of a named taxpayer);

(b)   must relate to documents etc. specified or described in the notice; and

(c)   may require the person to whom it is addressed to produce the documents etc. so specified or described if they are in his possession or power.

An Inspector, authorised by the Board and with the consent of a Special Commissioner, may issue a notice to a third party, requiring the production of documents, without naming the taxpayer in whose affairs the Revenue are interested. However, the Inspector will have to satisfy a Special Commissioner prior to his giving consent that: *s.20(8A)*

(a)   the notice relates to a taxpayer or class of taxpayers whose identity is unknown to the Inspector;

(b)   there are reasonable grounds for believing that the taxpayer/class of taxpayers to whom the notice relates may have failed or may fail to comply with the Taxes Acts;

(c)   serious prejudice to the assessment or collection of tax is a likely result of such failure;

(d)   the information sought by the Inspector is not readily available from another source.

A person on whom such a notice is served has the right to object within 30 days after the date of the notice that it would be onerous for him to comply with it. As a last resort, the matter can be referred back to the Special Commissioner.   *s.20(8B)*

'Documents' do not include personal records or journalistic material as defined under sections 12 and 13 respectively of the Police and Criminal Evidence Act 1984. *Furthermore* notices issued by an Inspector cannot require the production of documents less than thirty days after the date of the notice. The thirty day period can be waived by the Board, and not an Inspector, directly issuing the notice. The Inspector is specifically empowered to make copies of the documents.   *s.20(8C)*
     s.20(8D)
     s.20(2)
     s.20(8D)

The Board can only issue a notice direct to a taxpayer if they have reasonable grounds for believing that the taxpayer either has or may fail to comply with the Taxes Act. Even then that failure must be likely to seriously prejudice the proper assessment or collection of tax.   *s.20(7A)*

The Revenue can require information relevant to the taxpayer's liability to a tax of an EC member state other than the UK, as if it was a liability to UK tax.   *s.125 FA 1990*

1.2.3   Working papers of auditors, tax accountants etc

There are exempting provisions relating to the working papers of auditors, tax accountants, lawyers, etc. The Revenue explain in SP 5/90 how these provisions apply in respect of 'third party' notices in relation to accountants' working papers. In practice the Revenue may prefer to enforce production of documents by amending a self assessment on enquiry and leaving the taxpayer to appeal if he disputes the amendment. On appeal the Commissioners are empowered to issue a notice ordering the appellant to produce relevant papers or particulars in his possession (see para 1.6.3).   *s.20B(8)-(14)*

     SI 1994/1812,
     1811

1.2.4   Documents held by tax accountants

With the approval of a circuit judge, an Inspector or officer authorised by the Board may require a tax accountant to produce any documents in his possession relating to the tax liability of *any client*. But the tax accountant is only subject to this power if he has first been convicted of a tax offence or has had awarded against him a penalty for knowingly assisting in or inducing the delivery of an incorrect tax return. 'Documents' do not include personal records or journalistic material and at least 30 days will be allowed to comply with the notice.   *s.20A*

1.2.5 Restriction on Revenue's powers

The Revenue's powers under ss.20 and 20A are restricted by s.20B. Before an Inspector can issue a notice under s.20 or s.20A he must allow the person to whom the notice would be addressed a reasonable opportunity to deliver the documents voluntarily. A notice cannot require the delivery of documents relating to the conduct of a pending tax appeal of either the taxpayer (s.20) or of the tax accountant's client (s.20A). An Inspector cannot (but the Board can) give a s.20 or s.20A notice to a solicitor, advocate or barrister. Even where a notice is issued by the Board, such persons are entitled to claim professional privilege.

s.20B

The Inspector must give a copy of any notice issued to a third party to the taxpayer. Where the Inspector has reasonable grounds for suspecting the taxpayer of fraud, he can apply to a General or Special Commissioner for a direction not to supply a copy to the taxpayer. Furthermore, third party notices cannot require an auditor to deliver his audit working papers nor require a tax adviser to disclose communications between himself, his client or any other of the client's tax advisers regarding the giving or receiving of tax advice. This protection does not extend to the documents of a tax accountant which contain information on returns and accounts, which he has assisted the taxpayer in preparing for or delivering to the Inland Revenue.

s.20BB

1.2.6 Entry of premises

A person who intentionally falsifies, conceals or destroys a document he was required to deliver under a s.20 or s.20A notice, or was given an opportunity to deliver voluntarily, is guilty of a criminal offence which carries a maximum two year prison sentence or a fine or both. With approval of a circuit judge, an Inspector may also enter premises, search them and seize documents required as evidence for the purposes of tax proceedings provided there are reasonable grounds for suspecting any form of fraud.

s.20C
CIR v Rossminster Ltd (1980) STC 42

For warrants issued under s.20C, the Revenue's power to enter and seize is restricted to cases of serious fraud. The Revenue's conduct during the 'raid' is prescribed by statute concerning such matters as the number of officers to be present, the production of a copy of the warrant to the occupier and the furnishing of a list describing all the things seized. Where documents are removed, an officer of the Board, on request, will provide the occupier or the person who had custody of the documents with a record of what has been removed. There is provision for original documents to be returned if a copy would suffice and for supervised access to documents while held by the Revenue.

s.20CC

These rules are generally aimed at providing reasonable safeguards for the taxpayer. The Revenue's powers are however extended in one respect, which is to permit an officer of the Board to search any person on the premises who is believed to be in possession of documents, etc. which may be required as evidence.

1.2.7 Information from Banks and Building Societies

The Revenue have wide powers to require banks and building societies by notice in writing to supply virtually any information relevant to tax except records from which the identity of a net-paid investor could be ascertained. All details held on gross-paid investors relevant to whether they should be paid gross, must be supplied by the bank or building society when required. These broad powers attracted some criticism when discussed in parliament and an undertaking was given that the Revenue would not use them for 'fishing expeditions' and would restrict themselves to checking whether gross certificates had been properly given (ie. not given by taxpayers liable to tax).

SI 1990/2231
Regs 13- 15
SI 1990/2232
Regs 10 - 12
H C debates (16 July 1990)
vol 176 col 804

1.2.8 Summary

Once notice has been given, the Revenue will require the taxpayer to make a return of his income. A person must make a return if required by the Revenue to do so.

Various persons may be required to provide the Revenue with information relevant to a taxpayer's liability, eg. trustees, employers, banks.

An Inspector may by notice require the production of documents, but he needs the authority of the Board and the consent of a Commissioner before such a notice can be issued. If there is an enquiry in progress, the Inspector can require the taxpayer to produce the relevant papers although the taxpayer has a right of appeal.

In certain circumstances, a tax accountant can be ordered to produce documents in his possession relating to the tax liability of any client.

1.3   Technical advice to taxpayers

1.3.1   Technical guidance

For many years the Revenue's Head Office would give detailed technical guidance on tax matters where possible but by the early 1980s this policy was restricted due mainly to insufficient manpower. Accordingly the Revenue announced in May 1986 that Head Office would only respond to requests for information or guidance from practitioners if the enquiry involved recent legislation or changes in practice.

ICAEW TR 621

In October 1990 this policy was relaxed to some extent. Staff at Head Office have been told that 'they should be prepared when they can to answer requests for guidance on the Revenue's interpretation of tax law, not only where they involve the interpretation of recent legislation, Statements of Practice and other published information, but also in cases where there is a major public interest in developments in an industry or in the financial sector but where the operation of the law is uncertain'. This is more generous than the previous practice, of course, but still falls short of full assistance. In fact, understandably, the instruction to staff prohibits advising on tax planning or advising on the arrangement of a person's tax affairs.

ICAEW TR 818 and TR 830

The Revenue, following principles set out in a recent tax case, advise that where the enquirer wishes to rely on the guidance sought he must:

R v CIR ex parte MFK Underwriting Agencies Ltd (1989) STC 873

(a)   put all his cards face upwards on the table;

(b)   indicate the guidance sought;

(c)   make it plain that it is fully considered guidance that is being sought;

(d)   indicate the use which it is intended to make of the guidance, and in particular whether he proposes to tell others of it.

There are a number of specific statutory provisions whereby a taxpayer can obtain a clearance from the Revenue to establish their view of, typically, a transaction he intends to undertake in advance of the undertaking (see para 1.1.5 below).

To be binding on the Revenue, their decision must be reasonable and all facts must have been adequately disclosed. This has been discussed in Part A of this study text.

R v CIR ex parte Matrix Securities Ltd (1994) STC 272

The Revenue intend, as part of the new system for self assessment applying for 1996/97 and later (see session 2), to allow a new formal procedure under which taxpayers can seek binding rulings on completed transactions ("post transaction rulings") from the Revenue before completing their tax returns. A pilot scheme is already running.

1.3.2   Clearances

The Taxes Acts provide a clearance procedure in certain circumstances where the taxpayer may be caught out by anti avoidance legislation or where special reliefs may be due. A clearance procedure is provided in the following circumstances:

(a)   capital gains tax reconstructions;

s.138 TCGA 1992

(b)   companies purchasing their own shares;

s.225 ICTA 1988

(c)   company demergers;

s.215 ICTA 1988

(d)   transactions in securities.

s.707 ICTA 1988

(e)   artificial transactions in land.

s.776(11) ICTA
1988

To obtain clearance, the taxpayer must apply in writing to the Board of Inland Revenue giving details of the proposed transaction. The Board is obliged to notify its decision within 30 days of receiving the application, or within 30 days of receiving any additional information which has been requested. If the Board has requested further information but this is not supplied, the application lapses.

The application must provide the following information:

(a)   tax district and reference numbers of parties to the transaction;

(b)   full details of the transaction (including any preparatory transactions or reorganisations already effected;

(c)   the purpose of the transaction and the commercial reasons for it; and

(d)   copies of the latest accounts of each company involved in the transaction.

Where clearance is given by the Revenue, it is only valid in relation to the particular transaction for which clearance was obtained and only if it has been carried out within any time limit set.

If full details had not been given to the Revenue when the clearance was obtained, or the details were inaccurate or misleading the clearance will be invalid. Otherwise, a taxpayer may rely on a statutory clearance which has been given.

In certain circumstances the Revenue may also be willing to give an informal advance clearance.

The Revenue are considering the feasibility of introducing a more general system of 'pre transaction rulings'.

1.4 Unpaid taxes

1.4.1 Recovery of unpaid tax

The Revenue enjoy extensive powers enabling them to recover amounts of tax which remain unpaid. The Revenue are empowered to levy distraint, as well as being able to sue in the Magistrates' Court (where the tax unpaid does not exceed £2,000) and the County Court (amounts up to £5,000). The case may be taken to the High Court where the unpaid amount is greater than £5,000.

ss.61-68
SI 1991/1625

Leave to appeal against the decision of the County Court involving recovery of tax under s.66 TMA 1970 must be obtained from the County Court judge or the Court of Appeal if the value does not exceed £5,000.

SI 1991/1877

The Insolvency Act 1986 abolished the Crown's preferential creditor status in the case of taxes assessed on the taxpayer. However, that preferential status is retained where the taxpayer acts as agent for the Revenue, eg. PAYE, NIC, payments to sub-contractors.

In order to comply with the Insolvency Act 1986 where a third party has seized the taxpayer's goods under distraint proceedings, the Revenue's preferential status for PAYE etc. is limited to sums due for the twelve months prior to the date of seizure.

1.4.2 Arrears of tax arising through official error

Steps were first taken in 1971 to grant relief to those taxpayers who are suddenly faced with a demand for payment of arrears of tax which have built up due to departmental error. By concession, and subject to certain conditions, the whole or part of those arrears may be waived.

ESC A19

The main condition which must be fulfilled is that the arrears resulted from a failure of the department to make proper and timely use of information supplied by the taxpayer about his income and personal circumstances, so that he could reasonably believe that his affairs were in order.

With effect from 26 April 1994, the scope of ESC A19 is extended to cover the failure of the Revenue to make proper and timely use of information supplied by the DSS in respect of a taxpayer's retirement or widow's pension.

The proportion of the arrears remitted under this concession is determined by reference to the size of the taxpayer's income. The aim is to recognise the degree of hardship which would be suffered by the taxpayer in meeting the arrears. The current income scales have applied to notifications made after 17 February 1993 and apply separately to husband and wife. The existence of the income scales does not prevent special consideration being given to a taxpayer whose income is in excess of the relevant limit if he has exceptional family responsibilities.

1.4.3 Summary

The Revenue are likely to recover unpaid tax through the courts.

Depending on the level of their income, taxpayers may be given complete or partial relief where arrears of tax build up because of official error. The income limits are occasionally revised.

1.5 Investigations

1.5.1 Introduction

If a taxpayer evades tax by failing to declare his full income, or by claiming reliefs, etc. to which he is not entitled or otherwise, the Revenue may:

(a)   prosecute;

(b)   claim penalties (see later);

(c)   make assessments (with interest) to recover the tax which should have been paid.

In practice prosecution is rare, and recovery of the tax with interest plus penalties is more common.

A taxpayer who discovers (or is informed by his adviser) that he has made an incorrect return should in his own interest inform the Revenue without delay of the true position. He has no assurance of immunity but the Revenue are more likely to be lenient if he volunteers the information.

If the taxpayer entrusts the preparation of his return to an agent, it is the taxpayer's duty not only to provide information to the agent on request but also to volunteer any relevant information needed to complete his return. When a taxpayer signs his return it is his return although prepared by an agent. The taxpayer, even if unaware of it, is liable for the negligent conduct of his agent.

Clixby v Pountney (1967) 44 TC 515

1.5.2 The Inland Revenue departments

The majority of investigations are carried out in the local tax office by an Inspector. However, the more serious cases are likely to be dealt with by a specialist office. The Special Compliance Office is the executive agency which includes a number of specialist departments. The Revenue have published a series of codes of practice for the different types of work carried on by the Special Compliance Office. The role of the specialist departments is dealt with in this section.

Enquiry Branch (EB)

The more serious cases of tax evasion will be handled by an investigator from EB. In addition to substantial financial settlements, EB may seek a criminal prosecution. As a result, the investigations handled by EB will be run on much more formal lines than those being worked in the local office.

There are several EB offices nationwide, staffed by both Inspectors and qualified accountants. Cases are referred to EB by local tax districts, PAYE audit teams and also Special Office (see below). In addition, it may well be that one EB investigation leads to another.

Examples of the type of cases handled by EB are:

(a)   cases of evasion involving an accountant or solicitor (either where he is suspected of evasion himself or of promoting it amongst his clients); and

(b)   cases where it is thought likely that the tax evaded is 'substantial'; and

(c)   particularly serious offences involving forgery or conspiracy.

An EB investigation will start with an initial meeting between the EB Inspector and the taxpayer. If the taxpayer refuses to attend such a meeting EB may resort to their statutory powers to enable them to obtain relevant documents and records.

s.20

At the initial meeting the EB Inspector will explain to the taxpayer the Board of Inland Revenue's practice in cases of fraud. Formerly the Inspector would read the 'Hansard Extract', the text of a reply in parliament in 1944 by the then Chancellor of the Exchequer to a question by an MP concerning Revenue practice. In recent years many taxpayers have been perplexed by the wording so it was changed to the following:

HC written answer 18 October 1990 (vol 177 col 882) (see also IRPR 90)

(a)   The Board may accept a money settlement instead of instituting criminal proceedings in respect of fraud alleged to have been committed by a taxpayer.

(b)   They can give no undertaking that they will accept a money settlement and refrain from instituting criminal proceedings even if the case is one in which the taxpayer has made full confession and has given full facilities for investigation of the facts. They reserve to themselves full discretion in all cases as to the course they pursue.

(c)   But in considering whether to accept a money settlement or to institute criminal proceedings, it is their practice to be influenced by the fact that the taxpayer has made a full confession and has given full facilities for investigation into his affairs and for examination of such books, papers, documents or information as the Board may consider necessary.

This has not changed the Revenue's practice, only updated the wording to everyday English. The agent will be relieved to hear the Inspector quoting Hansard, or its new version, as it invariably means that a criminal prosecution is unlikely unless the taxpayer continues to act fraudulently. If the Inspector deliberately omits Hansard the taxpayer should seek the advice of a solicitor before proceeding.

The money settlement referred to in the 'Hansard extract' is discounted for factors such as disclosure.

As an alternative to the EB Inspector giving out the 'Hansard Extract' he may instead give a formal caution.

The reading of the caution is an indicator that EB is considering criminal proceedings. The taxpayer may be best advised to say nothing further until a solicitor has been engaged.

Special Office (SO)

SO is normally concerned with areas of tax avoidance and tax evasion not normally investigated by the local tax office. SO will, for example, often look at particular persons or industries. SO has often been involved in the larger Schedule E investigations and, increasingly, in cases with an international angle.

Cases taken up by SO will normally give rise to a substantial financial settlement.

The Board's Investigation Office (BIO)

The BIO is concerned with prosecution in cases of fraud, including fraudulent claims to personal allowances, subcontractor frauds or substantial PAYE frauds.

Special Investigation Section (SIS)

The SIS is concerned with counteracting artificial avoidance schemes.

1.5.3   The conduct of an investigation

Usually the Inspector will seek an initial interview with the taxpayer and his agent in a straightforward case of suspected fraud. This might typically be a trader who has suppressed takings and has attracted the Inspector's attention by reporting a gross profit percentage lower than expected.

In a case of suspected tax evasion, the Revenue adopt two approaches to quantifying omissions. One is to construct a *business economics model* from information provided at interview by the taxpayer; the other is to construct *capital statements*. The latter are a comparison of the taxpayer's net worth at the beginning and end of a period with any known increases in wealth, eg. surplus income or legacies received. What cannot be explained is treated as undeclared income.

Example

	£	£	£
Opening assets			580,000
Opening liabilities			(120,000)
			460,000
Closing assets		685,000	
Closing liabilities		(141,000)	544,000
Increase in capital			84,000
Declared income		45,000	
Specific expenses	16,000		
General living expenses	26,000	(42,000)	
Surplus income			(3,000)
Unexplained			£81,000

In a case such as this there is room for argument over estimated figures such as living expenses. But 'betting winnings' are not accepted as an explanation of increased net worth unless specific evidence is available.

When advising a client who is the subject of an in-depth investigation, the tax adviser should obtain all bank statements, building society pass books etc. so that these can be carefully scrutinized for receipts of capital, which would affect the net worth calculations. Receipts of income should be cross-checked to previous tax returns. Where possible all receipts and payments should be identified.

The starting point for an in-depth investigation in the case of a 'cash' business is often the Revenue's comparison of actual gross margins on purchases with the Revenue's list of 'norms' for different types of businesses. Obviously not all businesses will comply with these estimated margins, and actual margins should be calculated on several high selling items. Enquiries should be made as to the possible reasons for the reduction in margins (eg. shoplifting, obsolete stock, dishonest employees, goods for own use, etc.).

The client should be asked about his life style so that an accurate picture of his annual expenditure can be established. If the client normally draws cash from the business, to finance his day to day expenditure, how is this recorded? Is what was recorded sufficient to cover his living expenses?

When the tax adviser's investigations are completed and the client has provided adequate explanations on all items raised, a meeting between the Inspector, the client and the tax adviser should be arranged so that either the Revenue's allegations can be entirely refuted or so that a settlement, on the best possible terms for the client, may be obtained.

1.5.4 Extended time limit (ETL) assessments

The Revenue cannot normally raise assessments for years prior to 1996/97 more than six years after the end of the relevant year of assessment. For 1996/97 onwards the time limit for 'assessment' is five years after 31 January following the year of assessment. In certain cases, these time limits may however be extended.

For the purpose of correcting a loss of tax attributable to the fraudulent or negligent conduct of a person or his agent the five (or six) year time limits referred to above are extended to 20 years. Thus if fraudulent or negligent conduct is involved, the taxpayer can be assessed for 1983/84 at any time up to 5 April 2004 or for 1996/97 at any time up to 31 January 2018.

s.36(1)

'Fraudulent or negligent conduct' is not defined. 'Neglect' was defined for statutory purposes as 'negligence or a failure to give any notice, make any return or to produce or furnish any document or other information required by or under the Taxes Acts' but the definition is now repealed. Fraud is a common law concept requiring conscious untruth.

Derry v Peek (1889) 14 AC 337

If an assessment is raised on partnership trading profits under these rules due to the fraudulent or negligent conduct of one of the individual partners, it can also be raised on the other partners regardless of their conduct.

s.36(2)

If an assessment is raised in these circumstances the taxpayer can claim any relief or allowance to which he would be entitled for the year of assessment concerned but for the time limit for the claim having expired.

s.36(3)

An assessment can be raised to recover the tax attributable to the fraudulent or negligent conduct (before he died!) of a deceased person. However, assessments can only be made on the personal representatives for years of assessment which end in the six year period prior to the death. Such assessments for years prior to 1996/97 must be made before the end of the third year of assessment following the year of assessment in which he died. Thus, if a taxpayer dies on 2 February 1994, assessments for a year no earlier than 1987/88 can be made provided they are issued no later than 5 April 1997. The time limit is slightly extended for assessing 1996/97 or later years. An assessment can be made within three years of 31 January following the end of the year of assessment.

s.40(2)

In all these situations, it is important to realise that there is no practical difference between 'fraud' and 'neglect' and the Inspector does not have to apply to a General or Special Commissioner for leave to raise an ETL assessment.

1.5.5 Penalties

A person who fails to give due notice of liability to tax under s.7 is liable to a maximum penalty of 100% of the tax ultimately payable on the undisclosed income and which remains unpaid on 31 January following the year of assessment.

s.7(8)

A person who fails to deliver a return after receiving notice to do so is liable to an initial penalty of up to £300 and then a further daily penalty of £60 while the failure continues following the award of the initial penalty.

s.93

If the failure to comply with the notice continues beyond 31 January following the end of the year of assessment concerned, the taxpayer becomes liable to an additional penalty of the amount of the tax due on the income correctly reported on the return.

A person who fraudulently or negligently delivers an incorrect return is liable to an initial penalty of up to £300 and then a further penalty not exceeding the amount of tax unpaid as a result of the incorrect return following the award of the penalty.

s.95

The above penalties can be mitigated by the Revenue.

A person who *assists* in or *induces* the making of a return which he knows to be incorrect is liable to a penalty of up to £3,000. If he is a tax accountant the Revenue may then require him to produce specified documents in his possession relating to the tax liabilities of any of his clients. This result also follows if a tax accountant is convicted of a tax offence (paragraph 1.2.4). A tax accountant is any person who assists others in the preparation of their returns.

s.99

s.20A

s.20D(2)

An individual who fraudulently or negligently furnishes a form R85 to a bank or building society to certify that he is not liable to pay income tax and can therefore receive interest gross, is liable to a penalty not exceeding £3,000. A penalty will not apply where a form was furnished in good faith, but the individual turned out in the event to be liable to tax. It will only apply where an individual knowingly makes a false declaration or deliberately fails to inform the bank or building society when he becomes liable to tax.

s.99A

IRPR 19.3.91 STI (1991) 288

As mentioned earlier, the Revenue practice is to exact penalties rather than to prosecute on criminal charges. Proceedings for penalties are civil not criminal and may be instituted before the Commissioners or in a County Court. If it is shown that a taxpayer discovered that he had made a mistake in the first instance and failed to correct it within a reasonable time, he is deemed to have acted negligently.

Perjury Act 1911
Theft Act 1968
s.17 s.100(5)

The death of a taxpayer does not preclude the possibility of penalty proceedings, which may be commenced or continued (if already begun prior to the taxpayer's death) against his personal representatives. Where the Revenue are successful, the penalty awarded becomes a debt due and payable from the estate of the deceased. This may be contrasted with criminal charges, which terminate on the defendant's demise.

The time limit for commencement of proceedings for recovery of penalties is normally six years from the date on which the penalty was incurred. But in the case of tax related penalties where a taxpayer is still alive the limit is extended to three years after the final determination of the amount of tax covered by the assessment.

s.103

This three year extension does not apply if the penalty is payable by personal representatives and any tax concerned was assessed more than six years after 31 January following the year for which it is charged.

A twenty year time limit applies to a penalty for knowingly assisting in the preparation of incorrect returns.

Penalties for fraudulently or negligently delivering an incorrect return may be remitted at the Revenue's discretion. The following factors are taken into account in determining the extent of mitigation:

(a) *Disclosure*

Up to 20% abatement, depending upon the extent to which the taxpayer makes full and prompt disclosure of any irregularities. However, up to 30% of the penalty may be abated if the taxpayer voluntarily discloses any errors or omissions before being challenged by the Revenue;

Booklet IR73

(b) *Co-operation*

Up to 40% abatement, depending upon the extent to which the taxpayer's behaviour has contributed towards a speedy settlement;

(c) *Gravity*

Up to 40% abatement, depending upon the size of the understatement of income, both in absolute terms and by comparison with the taxpayer's total income.

The Revenue can in most cases determine penalties as they would raise a tax assessment. A notice of determination is served on a taxpayer and he has the right to appeal as though it was a tax assessment. The appeal Commissioners can then confirm, set aside, increase or reduce the determination. Initial penalties for late returns however will continue to be awarded by the appeal Commissioners.

s.100 and ss.100A-100D

In serious cases the Revenue practice is to inform a taxpayer that it has power to accept a pecuniary settlement and that it will be influenced by a full confession. Such a confession if made is admissible as evidence in subsequent proceedings (paragraph 1.5.2).

1.5.6 Summary

Where a taxpayer evades tax, the Revenue will usually attempt to recover all of the unpaid tax, together with interest and penalties.

An Inspector will handle the majority of investigations. More serious cases are dealt with by Enquiry Branch, Special Office, the Board's Investigation Office or Special Investigation Section.

The Revenue adopt two basic approaches to an investigation of a taxpayer's position:

(a)   a reconciliation of the taxpayer's net worth, by reference to his known income (capital statements); and

(b)   where the taxpayer carries on a trade, a comparison of the margin shown in the accounts with the Revenue's expected margin for the type of business (business economics model).

Extended time limit assessments may be made where there has been a loss of tax due to the taxpayer's fraudulent or negligent conduct. ETL assessments can be made up to twenty years after the year concerned or after 31 January following the tax year concerned for 1996/97 onwards.

In the case of a deceased person, no assessment may be made for a year more than six years before the year of death. Moreover, any such assessment may only be made within three years of 31 January following the end of the year in which the taxpayer dies.

Penalties may be chargeable under the provisions of the Taxes Management Act 1970, but an Inspector may be prepared to accept less than the full amount in settlement, depending upon, for example, the degree of co-operation offered by the taxpayer.

1.6 Appeals system

1.6.1 Introduction

Under the self assessment system explained beyond in session 2 many taxpayers will simply 'self-assess', pay their taxes and have very little contact with the Revenue. In a proportion of cases the Revenue will open an 'enquiry' and points of contention may arise.

In cases where agreement cannot be reached an appeal will be heard by the Commissioners. This section deals with hearings before the Commissioners.

1.6.2 Hearings before the Commissioners

The appeal may be either to the *General* Commissioners, who are laymen appointed locally for divisions, or to the *Special* Commissioners who are experts in tax. The General Commissioners are appointed by the Lord Chancellor and receive no remuneration. The Special Commissioners are full-time civil servants and are also appointed by the Lord Chancellor.

s.2
s.4

Appeal *must* be made to the Special Commissioners if an assessment was made by the Board or the issue concerns certain specified provisions of the Taxes Acts eg. s.660A ICTA 1988. In any other case, the normal procedure is to appeal to the General Commissioners, but the taxpayer may in his notice of appeal elect to be heard by the Special Commissioners. An Inspector may seek a taxpayer's agreement (or failing that a direction by the General Commissioners) that the election be disregarded but only where the Inspector is satisfied that it is a delay appeal as opposed to a contentious appeal.

s.31(3)
s.31(4)
s.46
IRPR 26.2.90

Where an appeal under self-assessment contains a question that would be heard by a specific tribunal were it an appeal against an assessment, the question (but not necessarily the whole appeal) should be heard by that tribunal.

Sch.21 FA1996

It is usual for an appeal to be heard by two Commissioners but there is provision for a hearing by a single Special Commissioner. The panel of Commissioners (or the single Special Commissioner) is referred to as a Tribunal.

s.44(5)
s.45

The General Commissioners of each Division appoint a Clerk (and possibly an assistant Clerk) to assist them.

s.3

In special circumstances there is an appeal to the Lands Tribunal or to a Board of Referees.

s.47

A taxpayer who has given notice of appeal may only withdraw it with the agreement of the Revenue, made or confirmed in writing. But if the taxpayer gives notice that he wishes to withdraw his appeal and the Revenue fails within 30 days to notify him of its disagreement, it is deemed to have agreed. A taxpayer may within 30 days of making an agreement to withdraw his appeal, withdraw from that agreement. It is a question of fact whether negotiations between the taxpayer and the Revenue have reached the stage of 'agreement'.

s.54

When agreement has been reached on the withdrawal of an appeal, no further assessment can be made, ie. the original assessment becomes binding on both parties. For that reason the Revenue do not in practice give their agreement until matters outstanding have been settled.

The Board may permit an appeal to be made out of time if there was reasonable excuse for failing to give notice within the time limit and application is made within a reasonable time thereafter.

s.49

1.6.3 Appeal procedure

The procedural rules for hearings by the General or Special Commissioners have been changed with effect from 1 September 1994, and are now governed by statutory instrument. The rules for both sets of Commissioners are broadly similar.

SI 1994/1811
SI 1994 1812

The Clerk to the Commissioners fixes a date for the hearing and gives at least 28 days notice of it to the taxpayer. Where several cases involve a single issue, the cases may be linked and all heard together. This can even apply to cases being heard over different Commissioners' divisions. The Tribunal may adjourn the hearing as it deems necessary until the appeal has been determined but in its decision should consider what is fair between the parties.

s.50

Packe v Johnson (1991) STC 1 (ChD)

The taxpayer's appeal to the General Commissioners was adjourned at the taxpayer's request. At the second hearing he failed to appear but sent a letter requesting a further adjournment. The letter stated that his accounts had been supplied to the Inspector. The Commissioners refused the adjournment and confirmed the assessments stating that no evidence had been supplied to justify varying the assessments. The taxpayer appealed.

Held: the Commissioners were at fault in refusing an adjournment. They had denied the taxpayer an opportunity to put the accounts before them, and to put his case forward on the basis of those accounts. There had been a miscarriage of justice and the appeal was allowed.

The Revenue is usually represented by the Inspector (or other official). The taxpayer may appear in person but cannot be compelled to appear at all. However, the burden of proof rests on him and it would therefore be imprudent of him not to appear or be represented in any way.

The taxpayer may be represented by a barrister, a solicitor, or by an accountant who is a member of an incorporated society. Interestingly, members of the Chartered Institute of Taxation do not yet have a right to be heard but in practice they will generally be accepted. The Institute has attempted to obtain this right as some members are not otherwise professionally qualified to represent a taxpayer before the Tribunal.

The taxpayer cannot be compelled to give evidence. The Tribunal may join any other person as a party to the proceedings, and may call any other person to attend and give evidence on oath and to produce documents. An agent or employee of the taxpayer or a person employed in confidence on his affairs may refuse to be sworn or to answer questions to which he objects. The Tribunal can impose a penalty not exceeding £1,000 for refusing to comply when required to do so.

s.52

As already explained (paragraph 1.2.2), at any time before the conclusion of an enquiry into a self assessment the Revenue may compel the taxpayer to produce documents in his possession or power or to provide particulars relevant for the purposes of the appeal. The Revenue may take copies of any documents so produced. But the taxpayer can appeal against the demand to the Commissioners by arguing that the documents are not reasonably required by the Revenue for the purpose of the enquiry.

The Revenue are empowered to gain access to records held on computer, if they would normally be entitled to inspect those records.

s.127 FA 1988

The Tribunal may give a 'direction' before or during a hearing if it thinks it fit or if it feels that it will assist in the making of a determination. The onus rests on the taxpayer to show that he has been overcharged by the assessment or self assessment. But if the Revenue allege fraud or neglect the burden of establishing these grounds rests on them.

s.50(6)

There are no preliminary written pleadings. There are rules of procedure, but they are intended to avoid formality. The normal procedure is:

(a) the Clerk to the Commissioners calls the case for hearing;

(b) the hearing will be in private if it is before the General Commissioners. Hearings before the Special Commissioners are in public, unless any party to the proceedings applies for the hearing to be in private (consent of a Special Commissioner is required if the application is by the Revenue);

(c) the taxpayer or his representative 'opens' his case and calls his witnesses for examination, cross-examination by the Revenue and re-examination. (in a case of alleged fraud or neglect the Revenue go first);

(d) when the taxpayer's case is concluded the Inspector makes his submission in answer to it, and calls his witnesses for examination, cross-examination and re-examination;

(e) at any time during the hearing the Tribunal may put their own questions to the parties or their witnesses;

(f) the taxpayer or his representative has a right of final reply;

(g) the Tribunal announces its decision. It may be a majority decision, and in the event of a tie the presiding Commissioner has the casting vote. The Tribunal may reserve its decision, and must send notice of its decision to all parties once made. Decisions by the Special Commissioners must be accompanied by a statement of the facts found.

Any party to the hearing may ask the Tribunal for a review of its decision, or the Tribunal may carry out a review on its own initiative, on the following grounds:

(a) the determination was wrongly made owing to an administrative error; or

(b) a party who was entitled to be heard failed to appear, but had good reason for this failure; or

(c) accounts or other information had been sent to the Clerk or the Inspector but had not been received by the Tribunal until after the hearing.

An application for review must be made in writing within 14 days of the determination of the original hearing. All parties to the hearing may be heard at the review.

A decision of the Tribunal cannot bind a person affected by it who is not a party to the proceedings. There is no clear rule as to whether such a person ought to be joined as a party, it is left to the discretion of the Tribunal, although the taxpayer or the Revenue may request that the third party should be joined. As an example, a decision on the value at which a trader is deemed on closing down to dispose of his stock may affect the purchaser (see s.100 ICTA 1988).

CIR v Barr (1955) 36 TC 455

The Special Commissioners are empowered to award costs where either party has acted wholly unreasonably in making, pursuing or resisting an appeal. As the General Commissioners are denied this power, taxpayers can avoid the risk of an award of costs against them by choosing them to hear their appeal.

s.56C

The Presiding Special Commissioner is empowered to select decisions of the Special Commissioners for general publication (in an anonymised form, if necessary). They are labelled numerically eg. the 65th reported case is SpC 65. These reported decisions will not be binding on the Special Commissioners but will be a useful indicator of their views on important questions of tax law. Previously, the decisions of Commissioners on cases that went no higher were only known to the Revenue and taxpayers were therefore occasionally at a disadvantage compared to the Inspectors in knowing whether to pursue a particular legal point before the Commissioners.

s.56D

The Revenue published an "Interpretation" in October 1995 on the status of Special Commissioner decisions. Although in their view the decisions do not create a binding precedent, the conclusions reached may be relevant to other cases particularly where the SpC decision has not been appealed. Where an SpC decision is or may be subject to an appeal, it should be ignored in considering other cases pending the possible appeal.

The Lord Chancellor has also been empowered to change the name of the General and Special Commissioners to make it clear to the layman that they are independent tax tribunals and not to be confused with the 'Commissioners of Inland Revenue'. A change is not planned for the present, though.

s.75 F (No. 2)A 1992

1.6.4 Appeal from the Commissioners

Either party may appeal from a decision of the General Commissioners on a point of law to the High Court. He must give notice in writing to the Clerk to the Commissioners within 30 days after the determination, requiring a case to be stated for the opinion of the High Court.

s.56

The 'case stated' is a summary of the findings of fact and the conclusions of the Commissioners on relevant points of law. The Commissioners' draft case is referred to the parties who agree upon whatever alterations or additions are considered necessary to present an adequate summary to the High Court. The appellant can if necessary apply for an order of mandamus (compelling the Commissioners to carry out their duties) and the High Court also has power to send the case back for amendment.

From the date of receiving a case stated the taxpayer has 30 days to submit it to the High Court. In a recent case this mandatory time limit was not complied with and the Revenue argued successfully that the court had therefore no jurisdiction to hear the appeal.

s.56(4) Brassington v Gurthrie (1992) STC 47

Appeals may also be made from decisions by the Special Commissioners on a point of law to the High Court. There is no requirement for a 'case stated', since the Special Commissioners' decision is accompanied by a statement of the facts found.

s.56(a)

Meanwhile tax must be paid in accordance with the determination of the Tribunal. If the High Court decides that too much tax has been paid it is repaid with interest. If the High Court decides that too little tax has been paid the Inspector issues a notice of the amount which then becomes payable within 30 days and interest will run from this date to payment. The High Court may only reverse or alter a determination of the Commissioners on a point of law. But if on the facts stated the court concludes that 'the true and only reasonable conclusion contradicts the determination' it may set it aside (see case below).

s.56(9) s.56A(8) & (9)

Edwards v Bairstow & Harrison (1955) 36 TC 207 (HL)

In 1946, an employee of a spinning firm and a director of a leather manufacturing company purchased a cotton spinning plant intending to sell it at a profit. Eventually, the plant was sold in five separate lots in a 16 month period. The General Commissioners found that the transaction was isolated, and not an adventure in the nature of trade assessable under Schedule D Case I.

Held: the decision of the General Commissioners was overturned since the only reasonable conclusion that could be drawn from the facts was that the transaction was an adventure in the nature of trade.

In general the answers to primary questions such as what transactions took place are treated as facts which the court cannot disturb. But inferences drawn from primary facts are on the borderline. A determination that certain transactions were carrying on a trade has been treated as fact. But a determination that a body was or was not established for charitable purposes only has been treated as law. The meaning of words in a statute is obviously a point of law.

An appellant may withdraw his appeal. But the High Court cannot make an order for the withdrawal of an appeal on terms agreed between the parties. The High Court may award costs.

From the High Court either party may appeal to the Court of Appeal and thence, with leave, to the House of Lords. Alternatively if the High Court was bound by a decision of the Court of Appeal which the appellant wishes to have reviewed he can, if the judge certifies that the case raises a point of general public importance, appeal direct to the House of Lords from the High Court.

Administration of Justice Act 1969 ss.12, 13 & 16

It is possible to appeal directly to the Court of Appeal from a decision of the Special Commissioners. The appeal may be referred to the Court of Appeal if:

SI 1987/1422

(a)   the parties consent; and

(b)   the determination involves a fully argued point of law relating to statutory construction; and

(c)   a single judge of the Court of Appeal has given leave.

In Scotland, appeal is to the Inner House of the Court of Session and thence to the House of Lords. In Northern Ireland, appeal is to the Special Commissioners or a county court in Northern Ireland and cases stated are heard by the Court of Appeal in Northern Ireland.

1.6.5   Summary

Where an appeal cannot be determined by agreement between the Inspector and the taxpayer, the case will be listed for hearing before the Commissioners (Special or General, depending on the case).

Subject to a right of appeal to the Tribunal, the taxpayer may be compelled by the Revenue to produce documents or to provide any particulars relevant to an enquiry into a self assessment. The Revenue may take copies of any such documents produced.

The Revenue must show that there has been fraud or neglect on the part of the taxpayer, if that is their contention. Otherwise, it is for the taxpayer to prove that he is overcharged by the self assessment as amended by the Revenue.

There is a right of appeal from the Tribunal to the High Court on a point of law. The appellant must give notice in writing within 30 days requiring a case to be stated for the opinion of the High Court which in turn must be transmitted to the High Court within 30 days. Appeals against Special Commissioners' decisions no longer require a case stated.

From the High Court, there lies a right of appeal to the Court of Appeal and thereafter, with leave, to the House of Lords.

QUESTIONS

1. What is the time limit for issuing an assessment to make good loss of tax in 1992/93, due to the negligent conduct of the taxpayer?

2. To what penalty is a person liable, if he knowingly assists in or induces the making of an incorrect return?

3. An appeal from the Commissioners to the High Court is only possible on a point of ....?

SOLUTIONS

1.   5 April 2013.   (1.5.4)

2.   Up to £3,000.   (1.5.5)

3.   A point of law.   (1.6.4)

ADMINISTRATION UNDER SELF ASSESSMENT

By the end of this session, in relation to the new self assessment regime applying from 1996/97 for income tax and CGT, you will be able to:

- understand the duty to notify liability to income tax and capital gains tax

- appreciate the role of the tax return and the need to retain records

- describe how an individual has to self assess his income tax and CGT liability for a year

- outline the way reliefs are claimed

- explain how an individual pays his income tax and CGT liability including the right to pay CGT by instalments

- understand the Revenue's powers to enquire into assessments, determine assessments and make discovery assessments

- appreciate the Schedule E and PAYE aspects of self assessment

References: TMA 1970 unless otherwise stated

2.1 Introduction

Self-assessment of income tax and capital gains tax marks the introduction of a new system of personal tax compliance under which a far greater burden is placed on the taxpayer and his advisers. In some respects the new provisions are similar to the corporation tax 'Pay and File' rules (see session 4).

The introduction of self-assessment involves very substantial re-drafting of the Taxes Management Act 1970. As part of this major revision of the personal tax compliance regime, previous references to 'inspector' will be replaced by 'officer of the Board'.

References in this section to income tax include (where appropriate) Class 4 NIC.

Except where otherwise stated, self assessment rules apply for the tax year 1996/97 and subsequent years.

The Finance Acts 1994 to 1996 have introduced amendments to TMA 1970, most of which will not take effect until 1996/97. The statutory references in the margin in this session are to the TMA as amended.

2.2   Notification of liability to income tax and CGT

Although introduced as part of the self assessment changes, the rules for notifying liability have changed with effect from 1995/96.

Individuals and trustees who are chargeable to income tax or capital gains tax for any year of assessment and who have not received a tax return are required to give notice of chargeability to an officer of the Board within six months from the end of the tax year ie. by 5 October 1996 for 1995/96. The former time limit for notifying chargeability was 12 months.

s.7(1) & (2) TMA 1970

A person who has no chargeable gains and who is not liable to higher rate tax does not have to give notice of chargeability if all his income:

s.7(3)-(7)

(a)   is/has been subject to PAYE;

(b)   is from a source where that income could not be liable to tax under a self-assessment;

(c)   has had (or is treated as having had) income tax deducted at source; or

(d)   is chargeable to tax under Schedule F (ie. a qualifying distribution).

The maximum mitigable penalty where notice of chargeability is not given is 100% of the tax assessed which is not paid on or before the 31 January next following the tax year; ie. for 1995/96, by January 1997.

s.7(8)

There is a potential problem where an employee receives a benefit (particularly a new benefit) but, as will invariably be the case, the Revenue do not send him a revised notice of coding before the 5 October deadline. The employee cannot be sure that the benefit has been brought within PAYE thereby removing his requirement to complete a tax return. To create certainty for such employees, the Revenue state (in SP 1/96) that employees receiving a copy of form P11D from their employers can assume that the Revenue have been informed of the items shown on the form. As long as the employee is satisfied that the information is complete and correct and has no reason to believe the Revenue have not received their copy he can assume he need take no further action (see section 2.7 for further aspects of Schedule E).

2.3 Tax returns and keeping records

2.3.1 Tax returns for individuals

With effect from 1996/97 there will be a fundamental change in the design of the personal tax return. In April 1997 taxpayers will be sent a Tax Form and a number of Schedules depending on their known sources of income, together with a Tax Return Guide and various notes relating to the individual schedules. Taxpayers with new sources of income may have to ask their tax offices for further schedules.

The current draft of the Tax Form contains the following parts:

Part 1   General summary of income and gains

Part 2   Deductions and reliefs for the same tax year

Part 3   Allowances for the same tax year

Part 4   Either a request for the Revenue to calculate the tax or a final figure for the current year and a figure for payments on account for the following year as calculated by the taxpayer

Part 5   Taxpayer's instructions if tax overpaid or underpaid

Part 6   Personal details - address, telephone number, NI number etc

Part 7   Space for additional information

Part 8   Declaration and statement of which further schedules are included

If the taxpayer wishes to calculate his own tax, there is a tear out working sheet in the Tax Return Guide which the taxpayer does not need to submit but should keep in case the Revenue 'need to see it'.

Most taxpayers are likely to have to complete one or more appropriate additional schedules and these are cross-referenced to the Tax Return and the working sheet. At present there are nine draft schedules:

Schedule 1   Employment income

Schedule 2   Share schemes

Schedule 3   Self employment

Schedule 4   Partnership income

Schedule 5   Income from land and property in the UK

Schedule 6   Foreign income and gains

Schedule 7   Income from trusts and settlements

Schedule 8   Capital gains

Schedule 9   Non-residence and non-domicile

All such documents require information relating to, and reflect the taxable position after, claims to reliefs and allowances and after taking into account tax deducted at source and tax credits applicable to items in the return, etc. The system depends on all the figures for the relevant year of assessment being available. Entries on tax returns such as 'per accounts', 'per P11D', 'per PAYE' will not be adequate and any returns containing such entries will be rejected by the Inland Revenue.

The time limit for making a return depends on when it is issued by the officer of the Board. The due filing dates are:

(a) Notice to make a return issued on or before 31 October following the tax year: Return to be delivered by 31 January following the tax year; eg. for 1996/97, by 31 January 1998.

(b) Notice issued after 31 October following the tax year: Return to be delivered not later than three months after notice issued. s.8(1A)

Earlier dates apply where the taxpayer wishes the Revenue to prepare the self assessment on his behalf (see 2.4.1). s.8(1B) & (1C)

A partner in a business will have to include his share of the partnership income, loss, etc (as adjusted for income tax purposes) in his personal tax return.

In outline, the maximum penalties for late delivery of a tax return will be:

(a) Return delivered within six months following the due filing date: £100

(b) Return delivered more than six months but not more than 12 months following the due filing date: £200

(c) Return delivered more than 12 months following the due filing date: £200 + 100% of the tax liability shown in the return s.93

In addition, the General or Special Commissioners can direct that a maximum penalty of £60 per day be imposed where failure to deliver a tax return continues after notice of the direction has been given to the taxpayer. s.93

The fixed penalties of £100/£200 can be set aside by the Commissioners if they are satisfied that the taxpayer had a reasonable excuse for not delivering the return. The tax geared penalty is mitigable by the Revenue or the Commissioners.

2.3.2 Trustees Tax Returns

Provisions similar to those described above, including the same time limits, apply to tax returns made by trustees. Notices to make a return may be given to any one trustee, or to all the trustees, or to some of the trustees, as the officer of the Board thinks fit. s.8A

2.3.3 Partnership Returns and Statements

From 1996/97, partnerships will be required to file separate returns which will have to include 'a partnership statement' (see below). The partnership return will normally be made by the senior partner (or whoever else may be nominated by the partnership), but the Inland Revenue have power to require any, all, or some of the partners (or their nominated successors) to submit the return. s.12AA

Every partnership return will have to include a declaration of the name, residence and tax reference of each partner, as well as the usual declaration that the return is correct and complete to the best of the signatory's knowledge. s.12AA(6)

The normal due filing date for a partnership tax return is 31 January following the tax year to which the return relates or, if later, three months after the notice to make the return was issued by the Revenue. s.12AA(4)

The maximum penalties for late delivery of a partnership tax return will be as shown above, save that there is no tax-geared penalty if the return is more than 12 months late. It should be noted that such penalties apply separately to each partner. s.93A

Partnership Statements: The concept of a partnership statement is new. Each partnership tax return will be incomplete unless it includes a partnership statement.

s.12AB

A partnership statement must show:

(a)   the amount of the adjusted partnership income or loss from each source, and any partnership charges on income, for each period of account ending in the year of assessment to which the partnership return relates; and

(b)   the allocation of such income, losses and charges between each individual partner.

s.12AB(1)

2.3.4   Electronic lodgement of tax returns

From a date yet to be appointed the electronic lodgement of tax returns (including supporting documents), self assessments, partnership statements, particulars and claims will be possible. It was planned that the system would be available for when self assessment came into operation.

s.115A & Sch.3A

The following conditions must be satisfied:

(a)   Only persons approved by the Board of the Inland Revenue will be permitted to transfer information electronically, but it will be possible for such persons to be authorised to act as agents for other firms etc. and transmit their information. There will be a right of appeal to the Special Commissioners where approval is refused or withdrawn.

Sch.3A para 4

(b)   The information must be transmitted using approved hardware and software.

Sch.3A para 5

(c)   A hard copy of the information (signed by the taxpayer etc.) must be made before the information is transmitted electronically and the fact that this has been done must be signified as part of the transmission.

Sch.3A paras 6, 8 & 9

(d)   The information transmitted electronically must be accepted by the Inland Revenue's computer.

Sch.3A para 7

The advantages of electronic lodgement to the Inland Revenue are obvious. However, the procedure is voluntary and the benefits to the taxpayer and his agents are less apparent. The Revenue have indicated that electronic lodgement will not be possible where repayment of tax is claimed because of the requirement to provide proof of payment of tax (such as dividend warrants) before the tax can be repaid.

2.3.5   Accounts submitted with tax returns

Three line accounts

To simplify the reporting requirements of small businesses, 'three line' accounts (ie. income less expenses equals profit) only need be submitted with tax returns. The turnover of the business (or gross rents from property) must be less than £15,000 pa.. This relief is an administrative curiosity and not as helpful as might appear at first sight, as underlying records are required for tax purposes (disallowable items etc.) when producing both a detailed and a three line statement of profit.

Large businesses: rounding in accounts

To reduce the compliance burden at the other end of the scale, large businesses with a turnover of at least £5 million which have used figures rounded to the nearest £1,000 in producing their published accounts will be spared from recomputing their profits to the nearest £1 for tax purposes.

IRPR 18.5.93

2.3.6 Keeping of records

The self assessment provisions contain a formal legal requirement for all taxpayers to keep and retain all records required to enable them to make and deliver a correct tax return. This requirement has effect for the tax year 1996/97 and subsequent years, and the period of retention depends on whether or not the taxpayer is in business.

s.12B

Records must be retained until the later of:

(a) (i) 5 years after the 31 January following the year of assessment where the taxpayer is in business (as a sole trader or partner); or

(ii) 1 year after the 31 January following the year of assessment otherwise; or

(b) provided notice to deliver a return is given before the date in (a):

(i) the time after which enquiries by the Inland Revenue into the return can no longer be commenced; or

(ii) the date any such enquiries have been completed.

Where a person receives a notice to deliver a tax return after the normal record keeping period has expired, he must keep all records in his possession at that time until no enquiries can be raised in respect of the return or until such enquiries have been completed.

s.12B(2A)

The maximum (mitigable) penalty for each failure to keep and retain records is £3,000 per tax year/accounting period.

s.12B(5)

The Inland Revenue has published further guidance and advice on the above rules. In practice penalties will not be sought in respect of record keeping failures that take place before that advice is published and until a reasonable period of time has been allowed for taxpayers and their advisers to assimilate the guidance and make any necessary changes to their record keeping systems and procedures.

IR booklet
SA/BK3

The duty to preserve records can generally be satisfied by retaining copies of original documents except that where a document shows tax deducted or creditable the originals must be kept. However, vouchers that show that domestic or foreign tax has been suffered (ie. dividend or interest certificates and vouchers issued under the sub-contractor's scheme) must be kept in their original form.

ss.12B(4) & (4A)

Record keeping failures will be a factor taken into account in considering the mitigation of penalties for other tax offences, eg. the fraudulent or negligent submission of incorrect accounts giving rise to a penalty under s.95 TMA 1970. Where the record keeping failure is taken into account in this way, a penalty under s.12B TMA 1970 will normally only be sought in serious and exceptional cases where, for example, records have been destroyed deliberately to obstruct an enquiry or there has been a history of serious record keeping failures.

2.4   Self assessments and claims for reliefs

2.4.1   Self assessments

From 1996/97 every personal and trust tax return will contain a self-assessment section in which the taxpayer will normally be expected to calculate his income tax and capital gains tax liability for the year of assessment to which the return relates.

s.9(1)

However, a self-assessment is voluntary, at least to the extent that there is no obligation for the taxpayer to self-assess if the completed return is delivered to an officer of the Board by no later than:

(a)   30 September following the tax year to which it relates; or

(b)   if later, within two months after the notice to make the return was issued.

s.9(2)

Where a tax return is delivered to the Revenue within the above time limits (ie. for 1996/97 normally by 30 September 1997) an officer of the board must make an assessment on the taxpayer's behalf on the basis of the information contained in the return, and must send a copy of the assessment to the taxpayer. Such assessments, even though raised by the Revenue, are to be treated as self-assessments.

s.9(3)

2.4.2   Corrections and amendments

Within nine months of receiving a tax return, the Revenue (acting through an officer of the Board) have the power to amend a taxpayer's self-assessment to correct any obvious errors or mistakes in the return; whether errors of principle, arithmetical mistakes or otherwise.

s.9(4)(a)

Within 12 months of the due filing date (*not* the actual filing date), the taxpayer has the right to give notice to an officer to amend his tax return and self-assessment. Such amendments by taxpayers are not confined to the correction of obvious errors. They may not be made whilst the Revenue are making enquiries into the return (see 2.6.1).

s.9(4)(b)
s.9(5)

The same rules apply to corrections and amendments to partnership statements.

s.12AB(2) & (3)

2.4.3   Claims for reliefs etc

From 1996/97 the basic rule is that all claims and elections which can be made in a tax return must be made in this manner if a return has been issued by the Revenue and claims for any relief, allowance or repayment of tax must be quantified at the time the claim is made. However, this does not apply to claims to carry back loss relief to an earlier year or to claims that can be dealt with into through the PAYE system (eg. by amending a code number).

s.42

s.42(1)-(3)

Where relief for a loss etc. is carried back to an earlier year of assessment:

s.42(3A) & (3B)

(a)   the claim for relief is treated as made in relation to the year in which the loss was actually incurred;

(b)   the account of any tax repayment due is calculated in terms of tax of the earlier years to which the loss is being carried back; and

(c)   any tax repayment etc. is treated as relating to the later year in which the loss was actually incurred.

Thus, a trading loss carried back can only give rise to a repayment supplement from 1 February next following the end of the tax year in which the loss was actually incurred. Similarly rules apply for averaging farming profits and for relating back pension contributions.

Claims and elections which cannot be made in a tax return are governed by separate provisions which are similar to the rules governing the treatment of returns under self assessment. The rules cover:

Schs 1A & 1B

(a)   making the claim;

(b)   keeping supporting records;

(c)   amending the claim;

(d)   giving effect to the claim;

(e)   enquiring into the claim;

(f)   amending the claim after enquiry;

(g)   giving effect to the amendment;

(h)   appealing against amendments.

s.43

The time limit for making a claim is 5 years from 31 January following the year of assessment, unless a different limit is specifically set for the claim (eg. 31 January next but one following the year of assessment of the loss for loss relief claims into under s.380 ICTA 1988).

> Prior to self assessment a large number of reliefs had a 'two year' time limit - meaning generally, two years from the end of the year of assessment. With very few exceptions these have been shortened slightly to be claimed by 31 January approximately 22 months after the end of the year of assessment.

From 1996/97 capital losses will only be allowable for CGT purposes if notified to an officer of the Board and such notification will be treated as a claim for relief for the year in which the loss accrues. Therefore, notification of such losses will have to be made within 5 years from 31 January next following the year of into assessment in which they accrued.

s.16(2A) TCGA 1992

s.43

Losses for 1996/97 and subsequent years (notified as above) are to be treated as relieved against chargeable gains in priority to losses that accrued prior to into 1996/97.

s.113(2) FA 1995

> Prior to self assessment, a claim to a deduction could not be allowed until the Revenue had agreed to it. Occasionally this would require the taxpayer to demonstrate his entitlement beforehand to the Revenue. However, this runs counter to the principle of self assessment. Taxpayers will therefore be allowed to claim a deduction in a self assessment without prior approval by the Revenue provided the necessary conditions for the relief exist.
>
> This is carried a stage further for roll-over relief for capital gains on business assets. For disposals on or after 6 April 1996, individuals will be able to provisionally claim roll-over relief in advance of making the necessary reinvestment.

s.153A TCGA 1992

2.4.4   Error or mistake claims

An error or mistake claim may be made for errors in a return or partnership statement where tax would otherwise be over charged. The time limit is 5 years from 31 January following the year of assessment. The claim may not be made where the tax liability was computed in accordance with practice prevailing at the time the return or statement was made.

s.33 & 33A

2.5 Payment of income tax and capital gains tax

2.5.1 Introduction

In outline, the new self-assessment system will usually result in the taxpayer making three payments of income tax and (where appropriate) one payment of capital gains tax for each year of assessment. The pattern of payments will usually be:

31 January in the year of assessment: 1st payment on account of income tax

31 July after the year of assessment: 2nd payment on account of income tax

31 January after the year of assessment:

Final payment to settle the income tax liability for the year; and

Due payment date re. any CGT liability

It is understood the Inland Revenue will issue payslips/demand notes, but there is no statutory obligation for them to do so and the onus is on the taxpayer to pay the correct amount of tax on the due date.

2.5.2 Payments on account of income tax

Payments on account of income tax will usually be required where the taxpayer is assessed to income tax in the previous year and the assessed amount exceeded the amount of income tax deducted at source; this excess being known as 'the relevant amount'. For this purpose, income tax deducted at source includes tax deducted or treated as deducted, PAYE deductions (including any deductions to be made in a subsequent year re. the current year's income) and tax credits on dividends/distributions.

s.59A(1) & (8)

The normal rule is that the two payments on account for each year of assessment are to be 50% of the relevant amount for the previous year. Any adjustment to the final tax liability of the previous year automatically affects the payments on account of the following year. However, the taxpayer can claim to reduce his payments on account if he expects the relevant amount for the current year to be less than that for the previous year.

s.59A(2)
s.59A(9)
s.59(3)-(5)

Example

This example is new.

Gordon is a self employed builder who paid tax for 1997/98 as follows:

		£
Total amount of income tax assessed		9,200
This included:	Tax deducted by contractors on SC60's	1,700
	Tax deducted on savings income	1,500
He also paid:	Class 4 NIC	1,200
	Class 2 NIC	320
	Capital gains tax	4,800

How much are the payments on account for 1998/99?

Solution

The relevant amount of income tax:

	£
Total income tax assessed for 1997/98	9,200
Less: tax credits for 1997/98 (1,700 + 1,500)	3,200
	£6,000

The relevant amount of Class 4 NIC is £1,200.

Payments on account for 1998/99:

31 January 1999	Income tax £6,000 x ¹/₂	£3,000
	NIC £1,200 x ¹/₂	£600
31 July 1999	As before, income tax	£3,000
	NIC	£600

There is no requirement to make payments on account of capital gains tax.

An officer of the Board may direct that payments on account are not required in a particular case for any year of assessment. Any such direction must be made by no later than 31 January next following the year of assessment.

s.59A(9)

2.5.3 Payments on account for 1996/97

The payments on account rules are modified for 1996/97, the first assessment year. The Inland Revenue will calculate the payments on account due for 1996/97. In most cases the effect of the transitional rules will be that:

(a)   the first payment on account of income tax due on 31 January 1997 will be the same as the tax payable on 1 January 1996 in respect of 1995/96 Schedule A and Schedule D income; and

(b)   the second payment on account due on 31 July 1997 will be the same as the tax payable on 1 July 1996 in respect of 1995/96 Schedule D Case I and II income.

This means that the payments on account for 1996/97 will not include any 1995/96 higher rate tax on taxed investment income.

Example

This example is new.

Tony's income tax, capital gains tax and Class 4 NIC liabilities for 1995/96 have been agreed as follows:

	£
Schedule D Case I	7,400
Class 4 NIC	1,184
Schedule D Case IV interest received gross	1,200
Interest received net	2,380
Schedule A	3,620
UK dividends	1,800
Higher rate tax on income received net	2,692
Capital gains tax	8,600
Total	£28,876

What payments on account will be due for 1996/97?

Solution

	£	31.1.97 £	31.7.97 £
Schedule D Case I	7,400	3,700	3,700
Class 4 NIC	1,184	592	592
Schedule D Case IV	1,200	1,200	-
Interest received net	2,380	-	-
Schedule A	3,620	3,620	-
UK dividends	1,800	-	-
Higher rate	2,692	-	-
CGT	8,600	-	-
	£28,876	£9,112	£4,292

Special rules apply to old partnerships. A partnership assessment will be issued for 1996/97 in the usual manner for all pre-6 April 1994 continuing partnerships. The tax assessed will be due for payment on 1 January and 1 July 1997, subject to any appeal and postponement application. Each partner will be required to include his share of the partnership profits in his personal (self assessment) tax return and will be credited with his share of the 1996/97 tax paid by the firm as though his partnership income had been received under deduction of tax. Therefore, partners will not be expected to make payments on account for 1996/97 in respect of their partnership income.

2.5.4 Payment of income tax and capital gains tax

The basic rule is that the balance of any income tax due for a year of assessment (after deducting payments on account and tax deducted at source), together with any capital gains tax liability for that year, is payable on the 31 January next following the year of assessment.

s.59B(1), (2) & (4)

Example

> This example is new.

Suppose Tony in the above example makes the required payments on account for 1996/97 and then calculates his total income tax and Class 4 NIC liability at £18,000 of which £2,750 had been deducted at source. In addition he calculates that his CGT liability for disposals in 1996/97 is £5,120.

What is the final payment due for 1996/97?

Solution

Income tax and Class 4 NIC: £18,000 - £2,750 - £9,112 - £4,292 = £1,846. CGT = £5,120.

Total payment due on 31 January 1998 (excluding the first payment on account for 1997/98) £1,846 + £5,120 = £6,966

Tax charged in an amended self-assessment is usually payable on the later of: (i) 31 January next following the year of assessment to which it relates; and (ii) the day following 30 days after the making of the revised self assessment.

s.59B(5)

2.5.5   Surcharges on unpaid tax

The following surcharges will normally be imposed in respect of late paid income tax and capital gains tax:

(a)   tax paid within 28 days of due date: 0%

(b)   tax paid more than 28 days but not more than six months after the
        due date: 5%

(c)   tax paid more than six months after the due date: 10%   s.59C(1)-(3)
                                                                                 s.59C(4)

However, no such surcharge applies where the late paid tax liability has attracted a tax-geared penalty on the failure to notify chargeability to tax, or the failure to submit a return, or on the making of an incorrect return (including a partnership return).

The surcharge provisions have also been extended to income tax and capital gains   S.109(2) FA
tax assessments for 1995/96 and earlier years which are made on or after 6 April   1995
1998. Therefore, any tax charged by such an assessment which is not paid within
28 days of the due date will attract a 5% surcharge (10% if paid more than 6 into
months after the due date).

The surcharge rules do not apply to late payments on account of income tax.   s.59C(1)

2.5.6   Interest on overdue tax

Under self assessment, the basic rule is that interest is chargeable on the late   S.86
payment of both payments on account of income tax (under s.59A TMA 1970) and
payments of income tax and capital gains tax (under s.59B TMA 1970). In both   s.86(1)-(3)
cases interest will run from the due and payable date until the actual date of into
payment. The rate of interest is set by regulations made under s.178 FA 1989   SI 1989/1297

Therefore, in respect of:

(a)   tax payable following an amendment to a self assessment made after 31
        January next following the year of assessment;

(b)   tax payable in a discovery assessment (see 2.6.2); and

(c)   tax postponed under an appeal which becomes payable;

interest will usually be charged from 31 January next following the year of assessment until the date of payment.

There are complicated rules governing the calculation of interest where a   s.86(4)-(6)
taxpayer makes a claim to reduce his payments on account and there is still a
final payment to be made. The basic rule is that interest is charged on the
payments on account as if each of those payments had been the lower of:

(a)   the reduced amount, plus 50% of the final income tax liability; and

(b)   the amount which would have been payable had no claim for reduction
        been made.

Where interest has been charged on late interim payments of income tax and the   s.87(7)-(9)
final settlement on 31 January next following the year of assessment produces an
income tax repayment, all or part of the original interest payable is to be
remitted.

The above provisions have general effect for 1996/97 and subsequent years, save   Sch.19 para
that they do not apply to pre-6 April 1994 partnerships until 1997/98.   23(2) FA 1994

The above provisions also apply to income tax and capital gains tax assessments   s.110(2) FA 1995
for 1995/96 and earlier years which are made on or after 6 April 1998.

2.5.7 Repayment supplement

The rules for the payment by the Revenue of repayment supplement will change to reflect the revised payment dates. Interest will be paid on overpayments of:

s.824 ICTA 1988

(a)   payments on account of income tax;

s.824(1) ICTA 1988

(b)   payments of income tax and capital gains tax, including tax deducted at source or tax credits on dividends; and

(c)   penalties.

The repayment will run from the later of the due date and the date of payment, until the date the repayment is made.

The due dates are:

S.824(3) ICTA 1988

(a)   31 January in, and 31 July following, the year of assessment, for payments on account;

(b)   31 January following the year of assessment for payments of tax, including tax deducted and tax credited;

(c)   30 days after the imposition of the penalty.

The rate of repayment supplement remains the same as the rate of interest on overdue tax.

2.5.8 Payment of CGT by instalments

Where the consideration for a disposal of an asset is receivable in instalments over a period exceeding 18 months, the taxpayer has the option to pay the CGT arising from the disposal by instalments.

s.280 TCGA 1992

The Revenue then allow payment of CGT to be spread over the shorter of:

(a)   the period of instalments; and

(b)   eight years.

For disposals prior to 6 April 1996 the taxpayer had to show that paying the tax in one lump sum would cause undue hardship and paying tax by instalments was at the Revenue's discretion.

s.281 TCGA 1992

There is also an instalment option for CGT due on gifts which do not qualify for gift hold-over relief (rather than a claim simply not being made) where the gifted assets are:

(a)   land (or an interest in land);

(b)   shares or securities (quoted or unquoted) out of a controlling holding; and

(c)   shares or securities which are unquoted (and not on the USM) which did not give the transferor control immediately prior to the gift.

Gift relief is discussed in section 4.2 of your Paper IIb: Capital Gains Tax study text.

The instalment option is also available on CGT payable on a gift of such assets where gift relief is restricted. Only the restricted amount qualifies for the instalment option.

The person paying the tax can elect in writing to the Inspector for the option to pay in ten equal yearly instalments, the first due on the date tax would be payable if paid in one lump sum. No time limit for the election is specified so the normal six year or five year limit given by s.43 TMA 1970 would apply. However, in practice the election should be made before the first payment is due.

The outstanding balance bears interest which is added for payment to each instalment.

Example

Michael gifts a country cottage (not his main residence) to his daughter Ethel in May 1997 thereby crystallising a gain of £40,800. Gift hold-over relief is not available and Michael elects to pay the CGT of £14,000 in instalments under s.281 TCGA 1992. Assuming the rate of interest on unpaid tax is 7% the first three payments he will make are as follows:

			£
31 January 1999:	1/10 x £14,000		1,400
31 January 2000:	1/10 x £14,000	1,400	
	7% x (14,000 - 1,400)	882	2,282
31 January 2001:	1/10 x 14,000	1,400	
	7% x (14,000 - 2,800)	784	2,184

The taxpayer has the option to pay off all the outstanding instalments with accrued interest, if he wishes. The outstanding balance and accrued interest become immediately payable if:

(a)   the gift was to a connected person or was a deemed disposal of trust property; and

(b)   the gifted asset is sold for valuable consideration (whether by the donee or someone else).

2.6 Enquiries, determinations and discovery assessments

2.6.1 Enquiries into returns

An officer of the board has a limited period within which to commence enquiries into a return or amendment to a return, where a self assessment has been made (whether by the taxpayer or the Revenue) based on that return or amendment. The officer must give written notice of his intention within the period ending on:

(a) the first anniversary of the due filing date (not the actual filing date); or   s.12AC

(b) if the return is filed after the due filing date, the quarter day following the first anniversary of the actual filing date. The quarter days are 31 January, 30 April, 31 July and 31 October.

Enquiries may also be made into partnership returns (or amendments) upon which a partnership statement is based within the same time limits. A notice under s.12AC TMA 1970 is deemed to incorporate a notice under s.9A TMA, to enquire into each individual partner's tax return.

In the course of his enquiries the officer may require the taxpayer to produce documents, accounts or any other information required. The taxpayer has the right to appeal to the Commissioners.   s.14A

During the course of his enquiries the officer may amend a self assessment if it appears that insufficient tax has otherwise been charged and an immediate amendment is necessary to prevent a loss of tax to the Crown. Once the enquiries are complete, the officer must notify the taxpayer and advise him of the tax that he considers to be due, or the amount that should be included in the partnership statement. The taxpayer then has 30 days within which to amend the self assessment or partnership statement. The taxpayer may also make any other corrections or amendments which he would have made had he not been prevented from so doing by the officer's enquiries (see 2.4.2). The officer then has a further 30 days to make any adjustments he considers necessary.   s.28A(2)
s.28A(5)
s.28B(5)
s.28A(3) &
s.28B(2)
s.28A(4) &
s.28B(3)

At any time during the course of the enquiry into a return, the taxpayer may apply to the Commissioners to require the officer to notify the taxpayer within a specified period that the enquiries are complete, unless the officer can demonstrate that he has reasonable grounds for continuing the enquiry. Once an enquiry has been completed into either a return or a partnership statement, the officer is precluded from making further enquiries.   s.28A(6)
s.9A(3) &
s.12AC(4)

If a return is under enquiry the Revenue may postpone any repayment due as shown in the return until the enquiry is complete. The Revenue have discretion to make a provisional repayment but there is no facility to appeal if the repayment is withheld.   s.59B(4A)

2.6.2 Determinations and discovery assessments

In addition to the Revenue's powers to enquire into returns, they are able to make determinations of tax where no return is submitted, or raise discovery assessments where additional facts come to light.

Determinations

If notice has been served on a taxpayer to submit a return but the return is not submitted by the due filing date, an officer of the board may make a determination of the amounts liable to income tax and capital gains tax. Such a determination must be made to the best of the officer's information and belief, and is then treated as if it were a self assessment. This enables the officer to into make enquiries, seek payment of tax etc.   s.28C

The determination must be made within the period ending 5 years after 31 January following the year of assessment. It may be superseded by a self assessment within 12 months of the date of the determination.

Discovery assessments

If an officer of the board discovers that profits have been omitted from assessment, that any assessment has become insufficient, or that any relief given is, or has become excessive, an assessment may be raised to recover the tax lost. There are conditions limiting the circumstances in which a discovery assessment may be made.

s.29

If the tax lost results from an error in the taxpayer's return but the return was made in accordance with prevailing practice at the time, no discovery assessment may be made.

s.29(2)

A discovery assessment may only be raised where a return has been made if:

(a)   there has been fraudulent or negligent conduct by the taxpayer or his agent; or

s.29(4)

(b)   at the time that enquiries into the return were completed, or could no longer be made, the officer did not have information to make him aware of the loss of tax.

s.29(5)

An officer is assumed to have information contained in the tax return, claims and supporting documents for the year of assessment and the two preceding years, together with any additional information supplied on enquiry.

s.29(6) & (7)

These rules do not prevent the Revenue from raising assessments in cases of genuine discoveries, but prevent assessments from being raised due to the Revenue's failure to make timely use of available information.

2.7   Schedule E and PAYE aspects

2.7.1   Introduction

Under self assessment, it is envisaged that most Schedule E under-payments will continue to be collected through PAYE coding adjustments, rather than by direct payment. Directors and employees whose additional tax liabilities are collected in this manner will be encouraged by the Inland Revenue to file their tax returns by 30 September each year.

For the purposes of the self assessment the tax deducted from Schedule E income is:

(a)   the tax deducted under PAYE during the relevant year of assessment (per form P60); less

(b)   the unpaid tax for earlier years which has been the subject of a coding adjustment for the relevant year; plus

(c)   the tax due for that year which has been included in a PAYE code for a later year.

s.59A

These figures will be shown on the respective Notices of Coding (form P2) issued to employees.

No assessment need be made in respect of income assessable to income tax where the correct amount of tax has been deducted under PAYE. This includes income other than Schedule E income where it is taken into account in the PAYE code, such as untaxed interest. The correct amount of tax is the amount deductible on the assumption that the correct PAYE code is operated throughout the tax year in conjunction with the cumulative PAYE tax tables. However, an employee can require the Inland Revenue to issue a return for any tax year so that he can make a self assessment. Any such request must be made not later than 5 years after 31 into October next following the tax year, ie. for 1996/97, by 31 October 2002.

s.205 ICTA 1988

2.7.2   Employers' Obligations

In order that directors and employees can complete their personal tax returns into correctly it will be necessary for employers to provide:

SI 1995/1284

(a)   each individual employed at the end of the tax year with a form P60 on or before the next following 31 May (no date was specified prior to 1996/97);

s.15
SI 1993 No.744

(b)   each current and former director/employee with details of expenses payments (insofar as not covered by a dispensation) and benefits in kind (including the taxable value of any benefits) provided in the tax year. This information must be provided on or before 5 July next following the tax year.

From 1996/97 the time limit for delivering forms P11D to the Inland Revenue is extended from 5 June to 5 July.

SI 1993 No. 744

Forms P11D for 1996/97 onwards will need to show the following additional detailed information:

(a)   How business entertainment expenses are paid to or for employees, whether the employer carries on a trade, profession or vocation and whether the amount will be disallowed in computing the employer's Schedule D Case I or II profits;

reg.46(1) & (4)

(b)   Where the employer has arranged for some other person to make payments to or provide benefits for his employees, details of such amounts;

reg.46(8)

(c)   Where the employer operates a fixed profit car scheme (FPCS) arrangement, details of any taxable profit, total amount of mileage allowances paid for business travel and the total business mileage for which mileage allowance was paid;

reg.46AA(4)

(d)   Where a third party makes payments to or provides benefits for another person's employees but there is no arrangement with the employer (see above), the third party must notify the amount of such payments or benefits to the employees concerned on or before 5 July next following the end of the tax year. Where the employer knows that such benefits etc. have been provided by a third party, the employer will be required to provide the third party's name and business addrses to the Inland Revenue as part of the employer's year end PAYE obligations.

reg.46AB

s.15(9)(c)

2.8　Summary

Self assessment will affect Tax Returns covering income and gains of 1996/97 and subsequent tax years. Each Return will have space to enable the taxpayer to calculate his own income tax and capital gains tax liability. However, the taxpayer can opt out of self assessment if he delivers the Return by 30 September following the end of the tax year to which it relates. In this case, the Revenue will assess the taxpayer's liability.

The taxpayer will make two payments on account and then a third payment to finalise his income tax liability. The payments on account will be due on 31 January in the year of assessment and 31 July immediately following. The final payment will be due on 31 January following the end of the year of assessment.

Only one payment will be due in respect of capital gains tax, on 31 January after the end of the year of assessment.

Where a Tax Return is not sent to an individual, he is under an obligation to advise the Revenue if he is chargeable to income tax or capital gains tax. From 1995/96, the individual must advise the Revenue of the chargeability within 6 months of the end of the tax year (previously the time limit was 12 months).

QUESTIONS

1.   When will income tax be payable by a sole trader for 1996/97?

2.   When will income tax be payable in respect of a partner in a pre-6 April 1994 partnership for 1996/97?

3.   When will capital gains tax be payable for 1996/97?

4.   Bob does not feel able to self assess his own tax liability for 1996/97. When must he submit his Tax Return by to enable the Revenue to assess the liability for him?

5.   Jane receives a notice to make a return for 1996/97 on 31 December 1997. What will be the maximum penalty if the return is submitted on 31 August 1988?

6.   Jim gifts the lease of his flat in London (not his main residence) to his niece Joanna and the CGT payable is £10,000. Gift relief is not available. Can the tax be paid by instalments?

7.   If the 1996/97 CGT of £10,000 is not paid until 1 July 1998 what interest and surcharge may be imposed? (Assume an interest rate of 6.25% throughout)

SOLUTIONS

1.   31.1.97:   1st payment on account

     31.7.97:   2nd payment on account

     31.1.98:   Final payment   (2.5.1)

2.   1.1.97:   1st instalment of partnership tax (paid by partnership)

     31.1.97:   1st payment on account

     1.7.97:   2nd instalment of partnership tax (paid by partnership)

     31.7.97:   2nd payment on account

     31.1.98:   Final payment   (2.5.3)

3.   31.1.98   (2.5.1)

4.   30.9.97, or, if later, within 2 months after the notice requiring him to
     make the return was made.   (2.4.1)

5.   £100. Return is submitted within 6 months of the due filing date of 3
     months after 31 December 1997 = 31 March 1998.   (2.3.1)

6.   Yes.   (2.5.8)

7.   *Surcharge*

     (Return more than 28 days late, less than 6 months)

     £10,000 x 5% = £500   (2.5.5)

     Interest

     $£10,000 \times \dfrac{151}{365} \times 6.25\% = £258.56$ (2.5.6)

Note: Interest is usually calculated on a daily basis and to the nearest
penny but the Examiner should specify this in the question.

INCOME TAX AND CGT ADMINISTRATION - BEFORE SELF ASSESSMENT

By the end of this session, in relation to the administration rules applying before self assessment, you will be able to:

- understand the pre self assessment assessing procedure, and how a taxpayer could appeal and postpone payment of tax

- outline the pre 1996/97 normal due date for payment of income tax and how interest on overdue tax runs from the reckonable date and could be mitigated by purchase of certificates of tax deposit

- calculate the repayment supplement which may be added to repayments of tax overpaid

- describe how the Revenue may make further assessments for pre 1996/97 years following a discovery and how the taxpayer may claim relief for tax paid by error or mistake

- describe the Revenue's powers to charge penalty interest

References: Pre 1996/97 version of TMA 1970 unless otherwise stated

3.1   Introduction

3.1.1 Background

The self assessment rules as covered in session 2 apply for 1996/97 onwards and are radically different from the assessment rules applying up to and including 1995/96. However, as the old rules may still be examined they are therefore explained in this session.

3.1.2 Tax returns

For the purpose of assessing a person to income tax or capital gains tax, the Inspector could issue a notice requiring him to supply such information as the Inspector required.

This was normally in the form of a Tax Return in which the taxpayer had to report his income and chargeable gains for the tax year computed in accordance with the Acts and specifying the amounts from each source.

The senior partner of a firm was usually required to make a return of the partnership income on behalf of all partners. However, an Inspector could, if he thought fit, require the same information from any of the other partners.

s.9

3.1.3 Requirement to notify liability to income tax

A taxpayer who has neither made, nor been asked to make, a return under s.8 TMA 1970 is obliged to notify the Inspector of both any liability to income tax and each separate source of income within the *6 months* following the year of assessment in respect of which he is chargeable. A similar requirement applies to his capital gains. The time limit was 12 months for 1994/95 and earlier. There are, however, three sources of income which are not required to be notified in this way:

s.7(1)
s.3(6) TCGA 1992

(a)   income which has been subjected to tax under PAYE;

s.7(2)-(5)

(b)   income which has already been assessed or taken into account in determining the taxpayer's liability to income tax; and

(c)   income received under deduction of tax at source in respect of which the taxpayer is *not* liable to higher rate tax. This includes UK dividends.

Where chargeable gains for the tax year 1995/96 do not exceed £6,000 (the annual exemption) and aggregate disposal proceeds do not exceed £12,000 (ie. twice that amount) a statement to that effect is sufficient compliance with the statutory obligation to make a return of gains made, unless the Inspector requires otherwise.

S.7 TMA 1970 is aimed at ensuring that all untaxed income is disclosed eg. where a PAYE taxpayer commences to carry on a trade in his spare time.

There are various penalties for failure to make a return, the submission of an incorrect return or failure to give notice of liability. These are described in paragraph 1.5.5 for 1995/96 and earlier.

3.1.4 Production of information

Except where it relates to the Revenue powers to enquire into a self assessment, paragraph 1.2.2 above explains how the Revenue obtained information prior to the introduction of self assessment.

However, for 1995/96 and earlier years, where there is an assessment under appeal, the Inspector can ask the Commissioners to issue a notice requiring the taxpayer to provide the information necessary to settle the appeal.

3.2   Assessment procedure

3.2.1   Introduction

Under the pre 1996/97 system an assessment is usually made by the Inspector but may be made by the Board. The Inspector, if dissatisfied with the taxpayer's return (paragraph 3.1.2) or if no return has yet been submitted, may make an assessment 'to the best of his judgement'. The notice of assessment sent to the taxpayer must be dated and specify the period within which he may appeal. Once the appeal period has expired (without an appeal) the notice becomes final. The notice once issued can only be varied in accordance with the Taxes Acts, ie. by the Commissioners or by the court on appeal.

s.29(1)

3.2.2   Time limits for assessments

The normal time limit for the making of an assessment is six years after the year of assessment to which it relates. For example, in 1996/97 assessments may be made for 1990/91, but not for any earlier year. In this case, the Revenue need not have any special grounds nor obtain the leave of a Commissioner. If the taxpayer objects that an assessment has been made out of time he may appeal against it.

s.34

It has been held that an assessment is made at the time the Inspector signs a certificate in the appropriate assessment book and not at the time the notice is received by the taxpayer.

Honig v Sarsfield (1986) STC 246 (CA)

Mr Honig died in September 1966. In 1970 the Inspector started an income tax enquiry and issued additional Schedule D assessments for the years 1960/61 to 1966/67 on the executors. The notices of assessment were received for the first time by the executors on 7 April 1970, having been returned twice by the Post Office to the Revenue.

Under s.40(1) TMA 1970 the normal time limit within which an assessment must be made is reduced to three years after the end of the year of assessment in which the taxpayer died, so that the additional assessments had to have been made before 5 April 1970. The executors contended that the assessments were out-of-time.

In front of the Commissioners the Inspector produced the assessment book. This contains the originals of the assessments in essentially the same form as the notices of assessment issued to the taxpayers. This showed that the assessments were issued on 16 March 1970.

Held: an assessment is 'made' when the Inspector signs the certificate in the appropriate assessment book. Since they were made on 16 March 1970 they were within the three year time limit. This was so notwithstanding that the notices had not been received by any of the executors until after the time limit had expired.

The six-year time limit may be extended in the case of fraudulent or negligent conduct on the part of the taxpayer. Special rules also apply to the assessment of the personal representatives of a deceased taxpayer. The rules relating to such cases are dealt with in paragraph 1.5.4 above.

3.2.3   Appeal against assessment

A taxpayer may appeal against an assessment by giving notice of appeal in writing within *30 days* of the date of issue shown on the notice of assessment. The notice of appeal must be given to the Inspector or other officer by whom the notice of assessment was issued.

s.31

The notice of appeal (usually given on form 64-7 (New)) must state the *grounds* of appeal. But these may be stated in general terms. At the hearing the Commissioners may allow the appellant to put forward grounds not stated in his notice if they are satisfied that his omission was not wilful or unreasonable.

s.31(5)

Where a person, having failed to make a return, simply pays the amount of tax charged in an estimated assessment, he is likely to be guilty of negligent conduct if he knows that the tax is insufficient (paragraph 1.5.5).

The appeal procedure is described in greater depth in section 1.6 above.

3.2.4 Postponement of payment of tax

The giving of notice of appeal does not in itself relieve the taxpayer of liability to pay tax on the normal due date unless he obtains a 'determination' of the Commissioners or the agreement of the Inspector that payment of all or a specified amount of the tax may be postponed pending the determination of the appeal.

s.55(2)

If the taxpayer has grounds for believing that he has been overcharged he may apply to the Commissioners for a determination. His application must be in writing, specifying the amount by which he believes he is overcharged and giving his reasons for that belief. It is separate from the notice of appeal although normally made at the same time since the time limit is the same.

s.55(3)

In the ordinary course the taxpayer must make his application to the Commissioners within 30 days of the issue of the notice of assessment. But he is permitted to do so at a later stage if there has been a change in the circumstances of the case.

s.55(3A)

If the Commissioners deal with the matter there will be a formal hearing. It is more usual however for the taxpayer to reach an agreement, made or confirmed in writing, with the Inspector on the postponement of payment of a specified sum. As regards the amount not postponed, the determination or the agreement has the same effect as if a notice of assessment had been issued on the date of the determination or the agreement (hence the tax is due 30 days later, if that is later than the normal due date).

s.55(5)

s.55(7) & (8)

When the appeal itself has been determined, if the Commissioners find that any part of the postponed tax is due the Inspector issues a notice of the amount payable. That amount is then due for payment 30 days after the issue of the notice as if it had been an assessment notice.

s.55(9)

Interest however is still payable from the reckonable date (paragraph 3.3.2).

s.86

3.2.5 Appeals and postponements - practical points

A great many appeals against assessments and applications for postponement of tax result from the Revenue issuing estimated assessments. This is especially true of Schedule D Case III and Schedule A assessments, where often the tax falls due before the relevant accounts and/or returns are received by the Revenue. In this area in particular self-assessment (applying for 1996/97 onwards) will save considerable administrative time.

Whenever a tax adviser receives an assessment in respect of a client, it is essential that it is dealt with swiftly, bearing in mind the 30 day time limit. All items on the assessment should be checked. Where final figures are unavailable, the best possible estimates should be obtained and appeals and postponements based on those estimated figures.

Whenever income tax is due within a year of assessment on income arising in that year, the Inspector will have to make an estimated assessment. This will be subject to appeal and postponement of tax in the normal fashion. Even if there is no appeal, s.29(1A) provides for any necessary adjustment to be made once the true figures are known.

When postponing tax on Schedule D assessments it should be remembered that items which can be deducted from any source of income should first be set against unearned income, thus reducing the amount of tax payable at 1 January .

The Revenue will generally allow relief to be given in a Schedule D Case I or II assessment for fixed RAP and PPS payments even before proof of payment has been furnished. This treatment has apparently been extended to variable payments which the taxpayer claims will be paid. If the premiums are not then subsequently paid, interest will be charged on any tax paid late as a result.

Law Society Gazette 15 April 1992, p12

Once an appeal is lodged and application for postponement made the client should be informed as to how much tax is payable, on which dates and the implications for interest on overdue tax, and any further information required to determine the assessment should be requested. Postponements of tax should thereafter be carefully monitored to ensure that no liability to interest on overdue tax arises, eg. because the reckonable date has been passed.

The appeals procedure now covers Inspectors' determinations of penalties or s.88 interest due.

There are situations where there might be initial uncertainty as to the actual charging provisions to apply in assessing a 'profit'. For example, income from a sale of land could be a trading receipt or a capital gain or even assessable under s.776 ICTA 1988 as Schedule D Case VI income (see paragraph 13.4.2 of your Paper IIa: Personal Tax study text). A recent case held that the Revenue are entitled to raise an assessment under each of any such potential provisions as long as they eventually pursue only one of them.

CIR v Wilkinson (1992) STC 454

3.2.6 Assessment procedure for CGT

The method of assessment depends upon whether the chargeable person concerned is an individual or a company (including an unincorporated association).

Individuals are charged to CGT by reference to net chargeable gains (ie. gains net of losses) arising in the tax year. For example, if Mr Adams has £20,000 net chargeable gains in the year ended 5 April 1996, these gains are charged to CGT for 1995/96.

s.2(2) TCGA 1992

Companies are charged to corporation tax by reference to net chargeable gains arising in an accounting period. The method of computation is described in your Paper IIIb: Corporation Tax study text and the Pay and File system of accounting for corporation tax is covered in session 4.

s.8 TCGA 1992

3.2.7 Summary

The rules described above relate to 1995/96 and earlier (ie. pre-self assessment).

An assessment becomes final once the period allowed for appeal has expired without an appeal being submitted.

Normally an assessment may not be made more than six years after the end of the relevant year of assessment.

Notice of appeal must be given within 30 days of the date of an assessment in writing. The notice must state on what grounds the appeal is made.

If the taxpayer believes that the amount of tax charged by an assessment is excessive, he may, in addition to appealing against the assessment, apply for part or all of the tax to be postponed. The time limit for the postponement application is also 30 days from the date of the assessment.

3.3 Payment of tax and interest

3.3.1 Normal due date for income tax

The date when tax is due for payment under pre-self assessment rules depends on the nature of the income. Here is a summary showing the due date for income tax purposes:

s. 5 ICTA 1988

Income	Normal due date
Schedule A	1 January in tax year
Schedule D Cases I & II	2 equal instalments 1 January in tax year 1 July following
Schedule D Cases III-VI: Unearned	1 January in tax year
Schedule D Cases V & VI: Earned	2 equal instalments 1 January in tax year 1 July following
Schedule E	During tax year under PAYE or 14 days after application by Collector
Income taxed at source	BR: Deducted at source during tax year HR: 1 December following tax year

Note that, with the exception of income taxed at source, lower rate, basic rate and higher rate tax is due at the same time. Prior to 1996/97, only UK dividends were effectively taxed at source at the lower rate. Interest etc was taxed at source at the basic rate if paid net.

3.3.2 Reckonable date and interest on overdue income tax

Interest on overdue tax (which is non-tax allowable) runs from the reckonable date. The way in which the reckonable date is determined depends primarily upon whether the assessment has been appealed. The following rules apply:

s.86

(a) *if no appeal has been made*, the reckonable date is the due date for payment of the tax assessed, ie. the later of the normal due date (as set out in the table above) and 30 days after the date of issue of the assessment;

(b) *if an appeal has been made, and the due date for payment falls before the 'Table date' in s.86*, the reckonable date is the due date.

The Table date for Schedules A and D is 1 July following the tax year concerned. For income subject to deduction of tax at source, the Table date for any higher rate tax liability is 1 June in the following tax year but one (eg. for 1995/96 higher rate liabilities, the Table date is 1 June 1997);

(c) *if an appeal has been made and the due date for payment falls after the s.86 Table date*, the reckonable date is the later of:

(i) the Table date; and

(ii) the date on which the tax would have been payable if there had been no appeal.

The reckonable date for Schedule E assessments is always the due and payable date which is 14 days after the first application by the Collector for payment. However, in practice the Revenue will only seek interest from 14 days after the revised application in cases where the assessment is appealed.

The effect of these rules is that unless the original assessment is itself late, a taxpayer cannot delay payment for more than six months beyond the due date without interest running against him.

At the time of writing, interest is chargeable at 6.25%, this rate being effective from 6 February 1996 (prior to that date the rate was 7%).

Penalty interest (s.88 TMA 1970) is covered in section 3.6.

Example

Notice of assessment is issued on 1 November 1995 for Schedule D Case I tax of £6,000 in respect of 1995/96. On 15 November 1995 the taxpayer gives notice of appeal and also applies for postponement of payment of £2,000 tax. The Inspector replies on 25 November proposing that £1,500 tax be postponed, ie. £750 of the instalment due on 1 January 1996 and £750 of the instalment due on 1 July 1996. On 10 December 1995 the taxpayer replies agreeing to these proposals. His appeal is settled on 20 July 1996 and on that date the Inspector issues a notice showing that the total tax payable is £5,500.

The reckonable date for the first instalment (originally payable on 1 January 1996) is 9 January 1996 (ie. 30 days after agreement is reached); £2,250 is payable on that date and £2,250 on 1 July 1996. The balance of £1,000 (ie. £5,500 less £4,500 paid) is due on 19 August 1996, ie. 30 days after the issue of the notice of determination of the appeal. Interest on £1,000 runs from 1 July 1996.

For Schedule D Case I/Class 4 NIC assessments, the s.86 interest rules apply to Class 4 NIC as they do to Schedule D Case I income tax.

The rate of interest is fixed on a formula basis and changes automatically when the average of base lending rates for the main clearing banks change. The rate is determined by:

SI 1989/1297

(base rate + $2^1/2$%) x (100 - basic rate of income tax)%

rounded down to the nearest one-quarter percent.

Example

If the bank base rate is 6%, the rate of interest on late paid tax is:

$(6+2^1/2)$% x (100 - 25)% = 6.375%

rounded down to the nearest one-quarter percent: ie. 6.25%.

This assumes the rate applies to amounts outstanding before 6 April 1996 when the basic rate was 25%.

3.3.3 Interest: final assessment greater than original assessment

The appeal may result in a determination that the original assessment was inadequate and that more tax has to be paid than the amount which it was agreed should be postponed. In these circumstances the reckonable date for the *entire amount* which has to be paid following the appeal is the reckonable date for the amount postponed.

s.86(3A)

Example

Geoffrey has sundry receipts which have been assessed under Schedule D Case VI. An estimated assessment on the income for 1995/96 is issued on 1 November 1995 showing:

Profits assessed	£12,000
Tax charged @ 25%	£3,000
Due 1 January 1996	

An appeal is lodged and an application to postpone tax of £1,000 is agreed to. The tax not postponed of £2,000 is paid on the due date, 1 January 1996. The appeal is determined and a revised assessment is issued on 1 January 1997 showing:

Profits assessed	£15,000
Tax charged @ 25%	£3,750
Additional tax due £(3,750 - 2,000)	£1,750
Paid 1 March 1997	

Since the reckonable date for the tax is 1 July 1996 (six months after the normal due date) interest is chargeable on £1,750 from 1 July 1996 to 28 February 1997 (inclusive).

Example

A 1995/96 Schedule D Case I assessment is issued on 15 October 1995, for tax of £10,000. The taxpayer appeals and applies for the postponement of £1,000. This is agreed by the Inspector on 15 November 1995. Two instalments of £4,500 are paid on 1 January 1996 and 1 July 1996 respectively. The appeal is settled on 5 September 1996, and on that date the Inspector issues a notice showing total tax payable of £13,000. The balance of £4,000 is paid on 18 September 1996.

Interest will be charged on the £4,000 from 1 July 1996 (the reckonable date) to 17 September 1996 (inclusive):

$$£4,000 \times 79/365 \times 6.25\% = \underline{£54.11}$$

3.3.4 Normal due date for CGT

The normal due date for payment of CGT for 1995/96 and earlier years is the later of:　　　　　　s.7 TCGA 1992

(a) 1 December following the year of assessment; or

(b) 30 days after the notice of assessment is issued.

Where a taxpayer has grounds for believing that an assessment against which he　　s.55
appeals is too high, he may apply for part or all of the tax to be postponed pending the determination of his appeal. Any tax which is not postponed becomes due for payment on the later of:

(a) 1 December following the year of assessment; or

(b) 30 days after the agreement with the Inspector as to the amount to be postponed.

Where the appeal is determined in an amount greater than the non-postponed tax, the excess is actually due for payment on the later of:

(a) 1 December following the year of assessment; or

(b) 30 days after the Inspector issues a notice setting out the tax payable in accordance with the determination of the appeal.

Example

Anthony is assessed to CGT for 1995/96 in the sum of £12,000 on 14 August 1996. He applies for £4,000 to be postponed, and this is agreed by the Inspector on 15 November 1996. The appeal is determined by the Commissioners on 15 March 1997, and the Inspector issues a revised assessment showing tax due of £13,500 on 21 March 1997.

You are required to show the due dates of payment.

Solution

£8,000 is due on 15.12.96   -   30 days after 15.11.96, being later than 1.12.96

£5,500 is due on 20.4.97   -   30 days after 21.3.97, being later than 1.12.96

3.3.5   Reckonable date for CGT

Interest on late paid capital gains tax runs from the reckonable date. The reckonable date is determined in the same way in which it is determined for income tax purposes (see paragraph 3.3.2).

If no appeal has been made against the assessment the reckonable date is the normal due date (see 3.3.4 above).

If an appeal has been made and the due date for payment falls before the 'Table date' in s.86 TMA 1970, the reckonable date is the due date. The Table date for a 1995/96 capital gains tax assessment is 1 June 1997.

If an appeal has been made and the due date for payment falls after the s.86 Table date, the reckonable date is the later of:

(a)   the Table date; and

(b)   the date on which the tax would have been payable if there had been no appeal.

Example

Bernard is assessed to CGT for 1995/96 in the sum of £6,000 on 10 January 1997. His application to postpone £1,500 is accepted by the Inspector on 21 March 1997. The appeal is determined at £7,000 by the Commissioners on 14 July 1997, and Bernard is notified on 20 July 1997.

You are required to state from what date(s) interest runs.

Solution

Non-postponed tax of £4,500

Due date for payment	20 April 1997
Table date	1 June 1997

As the due date for payment falls before the Table date, the reckonable date is the due date for payment so interest will run from 20 April 1997.

Postponed tax, plus increase in the assessment totalling £2,500

Due date for payment	19 August 1997
Table date	1 June 1997

This time the due date for payment is after the Table date and therefore the reckonable date is the later of:

-     the Table date   1 June 1997

-     the date on which the tax would have been payable if there had been no appeal   9 February 1997

The £2,500 is due for payment on 19 August 1997; however interest will run from the reckonable date of 1 June 1997.

At the date of publication interest was chargeable at 6.25%, this rate being effective from 6 February 1996.

s.89(1)

3.3.6 Certificates of tax deposit (CTD)

Where there was likely to be some delay in agreeing tax liabilities with the Revenue, and the uncertainty could result in interest charges, the taxpayer could prevent any liability to interest arising by purchasing certificates of tax deposit. These are deposits with the Collector of Taxes, which may be set against tax liabilities or realised for cash. Interest, which is taxable, accrues up to the due date for payment of the tax, or the date a deposit is withdrawn for cash.

Provided the certificate is dated on or before the relevant reckonable date, a deposit applied towards a liability when it is agreed is treated as settling that liability on the due date. Thus no charge to interest on overdue tax can arise.

3.3.7 Summary

The rules described above relate to 1995/96 and earlier (ie. pre-self assessment).

The normal due date for payment of income tax varies according to the Schedule and Case under which the income is assessed. The normal due date for CGT was 1 December following the tax year.

Interest on overdue income tax or CGT runs from the 'reckonable date', which may either be the due date for payment or some other date specified in s.86 (the 'Table date'). The reckonable date is never more than six months after the normal due date.

If the original assessment was inadequate, the reckonable date for the additional amount payable once the appeal is determined is the same as the reckonable date for the amount originally postponed.

Where there is uncertainty as to the amount of tax which will ultimately become payable, interest on overdue tax could be avoided by the purchase of a certificate of tax deposit.

3.4 Repayment of tax

3.4.1 Claims for repayment

The notes below relate to the system applying for 1995/96 and earlier years. For 1996/97 and later years, the system of self assessment radically alters the previous rules relating to the repayment of tax and repayment supplement.

A taxpayer may not submit a claim for repayment of tax overpaid more than six years after the relevant year of assessment. For example, a claim for repayment of tax overpaid in 1990/91 must be made by 5 April 1997.

By concession, in certain circumstances the Board may make repayments relating to claims made outside of the statutory time limits where an overpayment has arisen because of an error by the Revenue and where there is no dispute or doubt as to the facts.

ESC B41

The Revenue have streamlined the repayment system by allocating repayment taxpayers to tax offices specialising in processing repayments. A claim for repayment for £50 or more of tax deducted on most forms of savings income can be made without having to wait until the end of the tax year.

IRPR 20.1.92

3.4.2 Repayment supplement for income tax

When income tax is repaid more than 12 months after the end of the year of assessment, a tax-free repayment supplement is added to the amount repaid. This supplement is calculated (at rates which follow those for interest on overdue tax) from the 'relevant time' (defined below) until the end of the tax month in which the repayment order is issued. A tax month runs from the 6th of one calendar month to the 5th of the following month (eg. 6 April to 5 May).

s.824 ICTA 1988

If the repaid tax was originally paid within the 12 months after the end of the year of assessment, the relevant time begins immediately after the end of the 12-month period. For example, if tax for 1995/96 is paid by 5 April 1997, the relevant time begins on 6 April 1997.

If the tax was paid after the end of that 12-month period, the relevant time begins immediately after the end of the year of assessment in which payment was made. For example, if tax for 1995/96 is not paid until, say, July 1997 then the reckonable time begins 6 April 1998.

At the time of writing the rate for repayment supplement was 6.25%, this rate being effective from 6 February 1996. Previously the rate was 7%.

Example

Tax of £600 for 1994/95 is assessed for payment on 1 January 1995 and is paid on that date. As a result of the appeal being determined no tax is due and a repayable order for the £600 is issued on 1 May 1997.

Tax was originally paid before the expiry of 12 months after the year of assessment, ie. before 5 April 1996. The relevant time therefore begins on 6 April 1996. The repayment supplement is calculated from that date to 5 May 1997 since the cheque for repayment made on 1 May 1997 falls within the month ending 5 May 1997.

Assuming that the rate of 6.25% is still in force at 5 May 1997 the repayment supplement will be calculated as follows:

6 April 1996 to 5 May 1997: £600 x 6.25% x 13/12 = £40.62

The legislation at s.824 provides that repayment supplement is payable where the repayment is of tax paid for a year of assessment in which the individual was resident in the UK. However, under a concession, supplement is also paid where the individual was resident in an EC member state.

ESC A82

A taxpayer may have underpaid some tax but also be entitled to a repayment of overpaid tax. It is Revenue policy to allow a set-off in the most beneficial way for the taxpayer. Where a set-off is made repayment supplement stops running at that date and interest also stops running on the unpaid tax thereby settled.

ICAEW memo published June (1992) STI 659

3.4.3 Repayment supplement for CGT

When CGT repayments are delayed, a tax-free repayment supplement may be added to the amount repaid. A repayment of CGT to an individual made more than 12 months after the year of assessment to which the repayment relates, will attract repayment supplement. This will be calculated from the later of the:

s.283 TCGA 1992

(a)   end of the tax year in which the payment was made; and

(b)   end of the tax year following that for which the repayment is made;

to the end of the tax month in which the repayment order is issued.

Example

> CGT for 1993/94 is paid on 1 May 1995 and a repayment order is issued on 12 June 1997. Repayment supplement will be calculated (at the same rates ruling for interest on tax paid late) from 6 April 1996 to 5 July 1997.

3.4.3 Summary

The above rules relate to 1995/96 and earlier years (ie. before the introduction of self assessment).

Non-taxpayers can claim a repayment of tax of £50 or more before the end of the tax year.

A claim for repayment of tax must be submitted not later than six years after the end of the relevant year of assessment.

Where income tax or CGT is repaid to a taxpayer, a tax-free repayment supplement will be added to the repayment if the 'relevant time' has expired. The 'relevant time' expires at the end of the year of assessment in which the tax is originally paid or, if later, 12 months after the end of the year of assessment to which it relates. The supplement is calculated from that date to the end of the tax month in which repayment is made.

3.5   Re-opening assessments

3.5.1   Discovery

An Inspector or the Board may make an additional assessment for 1995/96 or an
earlier year on 'discovery' that:

s.29(3)

(a)   profits which ought to have been assessed to tax have not been assessed;

(b)   an assessment to tax already made is or has become insufficient; or

(c)   any relief given is or has become excessive.

In effect, within the time limits which apply (paragraph 3.2.2) the Revenue
may simply change its mind and demand more tax. For example, they may have
discovered that a company already assessed as an investment holding company
should properly be treated as an investment dealing company; or that their
previous view of the legal position was incorrect. However, if in the
determination of an appeal, including a determination by agreement, a specific
matter has been adjudicated or agreed, the Revenue cannot re-open the matter by
making a further assessment. Whether a specific matter has been agreed may be
difficult to decide if the Inspector agrees the complete set of computations
without reference to that specific matter. But if it is a matter which an
ordinarily competent Inspector would have considered, then a global agreement is
an agreement on that matter (see details of the *Cenlon* and *Olin* cases below).

Parkin v Cattell
(1971) 48 TC
462

Cenlon Finance
Co Ltd v
Ellwood (1962)
40 TC 176

Scorer v Olin
Energy Systems
Ltd (1985)

From 1996/97 new rules relate to the making of discovery assessments under the
new self assessment rules (see 2.6.2).

Cenlon Finance Company Limited v Ellwood (1962) 40 TC 176 (HL)

In this case, the main issue was whether a capital dividend received in full by a
share dealing company was a taxable receipt. Whilst this point was decided in
favour of the Crown, it is no longer significant following the introduction of
Schedule F by FA 1965.

Assessments were made for 1953/54 and 1954/55, and in support of its appeal
against these assessments, the company submitted computations excluding the
capital dividend from receipt. The accounts and computations were relevant for
the four years from 1953/54 to 1956/57. HMIT accepted the computations, settled
the two outstanding appeals, and raised a first assessment for 1955/56. The
company did not appeal against this assessment.

A different Inspector then raised additional assessments for 1953/54 to 1955/56
and a first assessment for 1956/57, including the dividend as a taxable receipt.

Held: there had been a 'discovery' by the Revenue, but whilst this upheld the
additional assessments for 1955/56 and 1956/57, additional assessments could not
be raised for 1953/54 and 1954/55 since the point in dispute had been agreed under
s.54 TMA 1970.

Scorer v Olin Energy Systems Ltd (1985) STC 218 (HL)

Olin Energy had two trades, shipping and manufacturing. It raised a loan to
purchase the ship and interest charges exceeded profits by a substantial amount.
In 1967 the company sold the ship and ceased the shipping trade. In its 1968
computations the excess interest brought forward was set against profits from the
manufacturing trade. The Inspector agreed the computations reducing an
estimated assessment to nil.

In 1969 the same off-set was claimed. A new Inspector refused the claim and
furthermore, decided to reopen the 1968 computations. The statutory provisions
are:

(a)   excess charges paid wholly and exclusively for the purpose of a trade may be added to trading losses and carried forward for offset against profits of the same trade s.393(1) and (9) ICTA 1988;

(b)   an agreement in writing between the Inspector and the taxpayer has the like consequences as if the Commissioners had decided to the same effect (s.54 TMA 1970).

The company argued that:

(a)   the loan benefited both trades in that it improved cash flow; and

(b)   the Inspector was precluded from reopening the 1968 computations in any event.

Held:

(a)   The excess charges could only be set against profits of the same trade. They could not be set against profits of the manufacturing trade.

(b)   The Inspector could not have allowed the appeal and varied the assessment to nil without deciding that the company's claim to have the interest charges treated as allowable losses was well founded. The accountants' tax computation had by implication directed the Inspector's attention to that particular claim. It was the kind of claim that an ordinarily competent Inspector must have appreciated being made. The Inspector had agreed to allow the set off of the interest charge and it was of no consequence why he had done so, provided that it was not due to misleading information. The new Inspector was therefore debarred from reopening the 1968 computation.

Note: a Statement of Practice sets out the Revenue's view of the principles established in *Cenlon Finance Co Ltd v Ellwood* and *Scorer v Olin Energy Systems Ltd.*   SP 8/91

Two more recent cases have thrown further light on this topic.

Richart v Bass Holdings Ltd (1993) STC 122

In this case there had been a determination under s.54 but the final assessment included a double deduction for the same amount of group relief. It was held that as this result was clearly not intended by either party to the contract (ie. agreement) under s.54, and until the figures had been corrected the assessment had not become final and conclusive and could therefore be amended.

Gray v Matheson (1993) STC 178

An Inspector of Taxes issued estimated assessments for three tax years in respect of the trade carried on by the taxpayer. The taxpayer appealed against the estimated assessments to the Inspector and submitted accounts showing the profit for the three relevant years. On the strength of the figures in the accounts, the assessments were determined by agreement under s.54 of the Taxes Management Act 1970.

The Inspector's successor reviewed the accounts of the previous four years and concluded that the profit rates for two of these years had been understated as the figures were disproportionately low. The Inspector raised further assessments for these years.

The taxpayer appealed to the Commissioners who held that the Inspector was precluded from making further assessments because the earlier assessments were determined by agreement under s.54. There was no evidence of any new factor being discovered over and above what was contained in the accounts for the relevant years. The Revenue appealed to the High Court.

Held: reversing the decision of the Commissioners, that the agreement under s.54 had been entered into on the assumption that the taxpayer's statement of his trading profits was correct. The Inspector was not precluded from raising further assessments relating to the same periods if he later discovered that the tax-payer's statements were incorrect. It did not matter that the understatement of the profits was innocent.

3.5.2 Error or mistake claims

A taxpayer who alleges that tax was paid under an excessive assessment by reason of an error or mistake in a return may at any time within six years of the end of the year of assessment make a claim to the Board for relief. The Board must consider the claim and the relevant circumstances and may give such relief by repayment as is reasonable and just. The taxpayer has a right of appeal against refusal to the Special Commissioners. No relief may be given where the return was made on the basis of the practice prevailing at the time when it was made.

s.33

A taxpayer may challenge an assessment on grounds of non-delivery: it should be sent to his usual or last known place of residence. But a mistake of form, eg. an error in spelling a name or in referring to property does not invalidate the assessment. The test for error is whether in *substance* the notice of assessment complies with the Acts.

ss.114 & 115

The above rules relate to 1995/96 and earlier years. Under the system of self assessment which applies for 1996/97 and later years (para 2.4.3) there are new procedures for claims.

3.5.3 Time limit for making claims

Except where provided to the contrary, a claim for relief under the Taxes Act must be made within six years of the end of the chargeable period to which it is to relate. For income tax (or CGT) on individuals, trusts or partnerships the 'chargeable period' is the fiscal (ie. tax) year. Thus a MCA for 1990/91 must be claimed by 5 April 1997 (as s.257 makes no contrary provision) but a claim for loss relief under s.380(1) ICTA 1988 under the pre self-assessment rules must be made within two years of the year to which it is to apply since s.380(1) so provides. A claim for capital allowances on plant used in a trade must be made before the relevant assessment to Schedule D Case I becomes final and conclusive.

s.43

If a 'discovery' assessment is made in circumstances which do not involve fraudulent or negligent conduct of the taxpayer or his agent, the taxpayer may claim or elect for reliefs which would otherwise be out of time. This time limit extension runs for a period of 12 months from the end of the year of assessment in which the new assessment is made. Within the same time limit, the taxpayer can revoke or vary any claim or election made earlier unless it is irrevocable by law. This does not alter the other requirements of a revocation such as the consent of other parties where necessary. However, the consent of a deceased person is satisfied by the consent of his personal representative.

s.43A

There is a similar provision where a year is opened up by an investigation.

s.36(3)

The claims or elections that can be made or revoked can only extinguish the further tax assessed by the 'discovery' assessment. They cannot give rise to repayment of tax paid earlier.

There will be occasions when such late claims etc., could alter the tax liability of another person. The power to make a late claim cannot be exercised without the written consent of that other person (or his personal representative if he has died). Note that the extended time limit for claims does not apply to that 'other person' even if his liability is increased as a result of the late claim, etc.

s.43B

The above rules relate to 1995/96 and earlier years. Under the system of self assessment which applies for 1996/97 and later years (para 2.4.3) there are new procedures for claims, elections and notices required.

3.5.4 Summary

The rules described above relate to 1995/96 and earlier years (ie. before the introduction of self assessment).

An Inspector or the Board may make additional assessments if they discover an earlier assessment was incorrect or inadequate.

This rule does not allow the Revenue to re-open assessments where a specific matter has been adjudicated or agreed in the determination of the appeal. The decision in *Olin* provides useful guidance on this point.

A taxpayer may make an error or mistake claim under s.33 if it comes to his attention that an earlier assessment was excessive, due to some inaccuracy in a return. The claim must be submitted within six years of the end of the relevant year of assessment.

Time limits for claims etc. are a crucial part of tax administration and tax accountants need efficient working practices to ensure they are not overlooked.

Time limits for claims etc. are extended when the Inspector makes a 'discovery' assessment to reduce or extinguish the extra tax liability arising. There must be absence of fraud or negligent conduct.

3.6 Penalty interest

3.6.1 Penalty interest under s.88

S.88 interest can be charged from *the normal due date* where an income tax or CGT assessment for 1995/96 or an earlier year is made to recover tax lost by a failure to give notice or make a return or an error made in a return. Failing to make a return on time is sufficient for a s.88 interest charge to apply. Note that there is no need for the taxpayer's conduct to be fraudulent or negligent; if additional tax becomes payable even as a result of innocent error on the part of the taxpayer, s.88 can apply. s.88

S.88 interest can be charged where a further assessment has to be raised following the taxpayer's acceptance and payment of an inadequate assessment. In a recent case a taxpayer disposed of a property and marked his tax return showing the existence of the disposal with the gain 'to be agreed'. He supplied no disposal details so the Inspector raised an estimated CGT assessment which proved to be inadequate. The court held that the Revenue were correct to charge s.88 interest when they raised a further assessment after the true position became known as the taxpayer had been neglectful in not appealing against the original assessment. Nuttall v Barrett
(1992) STC 112

S.88 interest can apply to late paid Class 4 NIC.

The Board have discretion to mitigate the amount of any interest chargeable under this provision, but this power is not delegated to individual Inspectors, and in practice mitigation of s.88 interest is rare. s.88(4)

Consideration will be given to charging interest under s.88 unless sufficient information to enable the Inspector to issue an estimated assessment is provided by the later of: SP 6/89

(a)   30 days after the issue of the tax return; or

(b)   31 October following the end of the relevant tax year.

This approach applies to new sources of income and to gains. It also applies to continuing sources where inadequate assessments are not appealed against and to Schedule E where information concerning emoluments, benefits and expenses is not submitted by 31 October.

S.88 interest is determined by an Inspector in the same way as tax is assessed with the taxpayer having a right of appeal. The appeal Commissioners may set aside, confirm or revise the determination. s.88A

If it is uncertain whether interest should be charged under s.86 (late paid tax) or under s.88 (penalty interest), any interest paid under s.86 is to be set against amounts finally determined under s.88. s.88(3)

S.88 has been abolished for 1996/97 onwards but will still apply to assessments made before 6 April 1998 where the assessment relates to income tax or capital gains tax for 1995/96 or an earlier year. para 17(3)
Sch.18 and para
8 Part V Sch.41
FA 1996

3.6.2 Specimen question

UNPAID TAX

Your client, a small trader, unexpectedly made a chargeable gain of £100,000 on 1 May 1994 on an asset which had been in his attic since 1940. He has only given you the vaguest information with no indication of the size of the gain, and you therefore enter 'to be agreed' in the appropriate section of the return which the

Inspector issued on 5 May 1995 and which you returned, signed by your client, on 20 May 1995.

Compute the sums which may be payable under current law by your client to the Revenue in the following circumstances:

(a) Your client tells you all on 1 December 1995, you tell the Inspector on 2 December 1995, the Inspector assesses the gain on 3 December 1995 and your client pays the tax on 4 December 1995.

(b) Your client tells you all on 1 April 1996, you tell the Inspector on 1 May 1996, the Inspector assesses the gain on 1 June 1996 and your client pays the tax on 1 August 1996.

(c) Your client tells you all on 1 April 1997, you tell the Inspector on 1 May 1997, the Inspector assesses the gain on 1 June 1997 and your client pays the tax on 1 August 1997.

Assume for convenience that interest on overdue tax is charged at 6.25% throughout any period concerned. Also assume that the trader has already fully utilised his CGT annual exemption for 1994/95 and that he is a higher rate tax payer.

3.6.3 Solution

UNPAID TAX

In each of (a) to (c) below there will be a CGT assessment for 1994/95. Interest on unpaid tax and penalties are discussed below.

(a) The due, payable and reckonable date is 2 January 1996. Tax was paid on 4 December 1995 so no s.86 interest would be payable. However, 'to be agreed' is not a valid return, and the Inspector may argue that s.88 interest, which will run from 1 December 1995, is in fact due. As this is very close to the date payment was made, the Inspector may not take the point. A penalty of £300 may have arisen under s.93(1) TMA 1970 (failure to make a return), but s.93(5) operates (the failure has been remedied) so that the client is not liable.

(b) The due, payable and reckonable date is 1 July 1996. Tax was paid on 1 August 1996 so that s.86 interest amounting to $31/365 \times 6.25\% \times £40,000 = £212.33$ would be payable. However, the Inspector would apply s.88 interest from 1 December 1995 to 1 July 1996 ie. $£40,000 \times 6.25\% \times \frac{213}{365} = £1,458.90$. This is because the assessment is made to recover tax lost because of a failure to make a return. Note that the Inspector may charge s.88 interest from 1 December 1995 to 1 August 1996. However the s.86 interest for August 1996 would be deducted, leading to the same net result. No penalty arises, see (a) above.

(c) The due, payable and reckonable date is 1 July 1997. The tax was paid on 1 August 1997. S.86 interest of £212.33 calculated as in (b) above, would be payable. However, on the same grounds as in (b) the Inspector would make a determination of s.88 interest at $£40,000 \times 6.25\% \times \frac{578}{365} = £3,958.90$.

A penalty of £40,000 arises under s.93(2) TMA 1970 because the Inspector was notified after 5 April 1997. The Board have power under s.102 to mitigate any penalty, and this is likely in this case.

3.7   Appeals procedure

3.7.1   Introduction

We have already noted that a taxpayer may appeal against a notice of
assessment within 30 days of issue of that notice (paragraph 3.2.3). The relevant
assessment is then described as 'under appeal'. In most cases, the Inspector and
the taxpayer are able to come to an agreement as to whether the assessment
should be varied, and, if so, by how much. The Taxes Management Act states that
such an agreement shall be treated in the same way as a determination of the
appeal by the Commissioners.

s.54

3.7.2   Hearings before the Commissioners

The most common reason for cases being listed (by the Inspector) for hearing before
the General Commissioners is that the taxpayer has been late in providing
accounts, tax returns, etc. Such hearings are referred to as 'delay hearings' and the
vast majority of these are settled by producing the required details prior to the
date of the hearing. In practice, the Revenue defer listing certain appeals where
the assessment:

(a)   is in respect of income tax (Schedule A or D or taxed income); and

(b)   charges tax of £10,000 or less and the payment on account was reasonable,

provided that, in the case of a business, it continues.

Such appeals will not be listed until two years' accounts are outstanding. These
will be listed together after June following the second year.

Otherwise the appeals system explained in section 1.6 above applies for the
determination of appeals for 1995/96 and earlier years.

QUESTIONS

1.   Who is normally required to make a return of partnership income?

2.   Under what circumstances can a notice be issued by the Commissioners for the production of documents?

3.   An assessment for 1989/90 is entered in the Revenue's assessment book on 1 April 1996 and received by the taxpayer on 8 April 1996. Is the assessment valid?

4.   In the situation referred to in 3. above, assuming the assessment is itself dated 1 April 1996, by what date must any appeal be made?

5.   Helen receives a Schedule D Case VI assessment for 1995/96 dated 15 December 1995. She appeals and applies for postponement of tax of £2,000, out of total tax assessed of £4,500, on 12 January 1996. The postponement application is agreed on 28 January 1996. When does the tax not postponed of £2,500 become due for payment?

6.   Prior to the introduction of self assessment, when does any higher rate tax liability in respect of dividends from UK companies fall due for payment?

7.   Ronald pays tax under Schedule D Case III in respect of 1995/96 on 3 March 1996. The tax is subsequently repaid on 1 July 1997. During what period does repayment supplement accrue?

8.   Michael, a sole trader, discovers that his 1990/91 Schedule D Case I assessment was excessive, due to the omission of £1,500 of allowable expenses from his accounts. What action (if any) can he take and by when?

9.   When is CGT assessed for 1995/96 normally due for payment?

10.   What is the Table date for 1995/96 for CGT?

11.   To avoid penalty interest details of asset disposals in 1995/96 must be provided by when?

12.   Sam's chargeable gains for 1995/96 amount to £4,400 with aggregate disposal proceeds of £14,000. Is Sam required to submit a detailed return of the gains arising?

SOLUTIONS

1.   The 'precedent', ie. senior, partner of the firm.   (3.1.2)

2.   Where there is an assessment under appeal.   (3.1.4)

3.   Yes, following Honig v Sarsfield.   (3.2.2)

4.   By 1 May 1996, ie. 30 days from 1 April 1996.   (3.2.3)

5.   On 27 February 1996.   (3.2.4 and 3.3.1)

6.   On 1 December following the end of the year in which
      the dividends are received (or 30 days from the date
      of assessment if later).   (3.3.1)

7.   From 6 April 1997 to 5 July 1997.   (3.4.2)

8.   He is entitled to make an 'error or mistake' claim under s.33 TMA 1970,
      but must do so by 5 April 1997.   (3.5.2)

9.   1 December 1996 or, if later, 30 days after a notice of assessment is
      issued.   (3.3.4)

10.   1 June 1997.   (3.3.5)

11.   31 October 1996.   (3.6.1)

12.   Yes.   (3.1.3)

SESSION 4

THE ADMINISTRATION OF CORPORATION TAX

By the end of this session you will be able to:

- understand the rules under pay and file regarding a 'section 11 notice' requiring a return, and the circumstances when notice of chargeability must be given to the Inspector where such a notice is not received

- identify when a company is required to pay corporation tax under pay and file

- explain the rules under pay and file relating to group relief and capital allowances

- understand the interest and penalty provisions under pay and file

References: TMA 1970 unless otherwise stated

4.1 Scope of legislation

Pay and File is the title of the administration system under which companies have to pay tax and file tax returns. 'Company' is defined as 'any body corporate or unincorporated association but does not include a partnership, a local authority or a local authority association'. This definition is extended to include authorised unit trusts.

s.832(1) ICTA 1988

s.468 and s.832(2) ICTA 1988

4.2   Pay and File in practice

4.2.1   Notice of chargeability

Every company which is chargeable to corporation tax for any accounting period   s.10
and has neither made a return of its profits for that period, nor received a notice
requiring a return to be made, must, within 12 months from the end of that period,
give notice to the Inspector that it is so chargeable.

In most cases a notice requiring a return ('the section 11 notice') will have been
issued by the Inspector of Taxes. However, that will not always be the case.

Example

> A subsidiary company within a group makes up its statutory accounts for the year
> ended 31 December 1996. On 29 February 1996 it transferred its trade, intra group.
> There is, therefore, a two month accounting period ended on that date because of the
> cessation of the company's trade.
>
> The company is required to give notice of chargeability to the Inspector of Taxes no
> later than 28 February 1997 with respect to the two month accounting period, unless
> on or before that date the company has *received* a section 11 notice.
>
> If a company fails to notify a chargeability to corporation tax then it may be liable
> to a penalty (see section 4.5).

Pitfalls and Planning

The position in the example above is not necessarily uncommon. Companies in
large groups that have short tax accounting periods could find themselves
overlooking the fact that notice of chargeability must be given. In this example
the group is probably heavily involved in its end of year audit and the fact that
there is a short tax accounting period could easily be overlooked. In practice, it
would be advisable, therefore, to review as part of the audit planning process all
group companies and identify those with potential short tax accounting periods.

Details of penalties (and planning opportunities) for failure to notify
chargeability are given in section 4.5).

4.2.2   Section 11 notice

Under Pay and File a notice is issued to companies requiring tax returns. This is   s.11
commonly referred to as the 'section 11 notice'.

No obligation to make a corporation tax return exists until the company has been
given notice to make such a return. Section 11 notices are issued approximately
three months after the end of the accounting period.

The Inspector of Taxes will require a tax return for a period specified in the   s.11(2)
section 11 notice. This is known as the *'specified period'* .

In most cases the 'specified period' will coincide with a tax accounting period of
the company, but in some instances it will not. A company is required to make a
return:

(a)   for each accounting period that ended in or at the end of the 'specified   s.11(2)(a)
        period' (it follows that if the 'specified period' equates to a tax
        accounting period then a return is required for that period); or

(b)   if no accounting period ended in or at the end of the 'specified period', a   s.11(2)(b)
        return is required for that part of the 'specified period' which does not
        fall within an accounting period; or

(c) if no part of the 'specified period' overlaps with an accounting period, a
     return is required for the whole of the 'specified period'.

s.11(2)(c)

If none of the above scenarios apply (ie. the 'specified period' falls wholly
within an accounting period) then no return is required to be made by the
company.

Tax returns are therefore made for each accounting period of a company, although
it may have to make returns for periods which are not accounting periods (eg.
when the company is dormant). A period for which a return has to be made
(whether it is an accounting period or otherwise) is referred to as the *return
period*.

In the following four examples the 'return period' is determined by s.11(2)(a)
TMA 1970.

Example

A company has a tax accounting period ended on 31 December 1996. The 'specified
period' in the section 11 notice is for the period 1 January 1996 to 31 December
1996.

The 'return period' is the year ended 31 December 1996.

Example

The company makes up accounts annually to 30 June. The 'specified period' in the
section 11 notice is 1 January 1996 to 31 December 1996.

The return period is the year ended 30 June 1996.

Example

A company makes up its statutory accounts for the eighteen months to 30 June 1997,
and annually thereafter. Its tax accounting periods are therefore the year ended 31
December 1996, the six month period to 30 June 1997, and twelve months to 30 June
1998. The 'specified period' in the section 11 notice is 1 August 1996 to 31 July 1997.

There are two 'return periods'. The first is the year ended 31 December 1996 and the
second is the six months to 30 June 1997.

Example

A company within a group makes up accounts to 31 December each year. It is
dormant until 1 July 1996 when it commences to trade. Its tax accounting periods are
therefore the six months to 31 December 1996 and 12 months to 31 December 1997.
The 'specified period' in the section 11 notice is 1 January 1996 to 31 December
1996.

The 'return period' is the six months to 31 December 1996.

In the next two examples the 'return period' is determined by s.11(2)(b) TMA 1970.

Example

A company is dormant until 1 July 1996 when it commences to trade making up its
first annual accounts to 30 June 1997. The 'specified period' in the section 11 notice
is 1 January 1996 to 31 December 1996.

The 'return period' is the period 1 January 1996 to 30 June 1996, ie. when the
company was dormant.

Example

A company is dormant. The 'specified period' in the section 11 notice is that for 1
January 1996 to 31 December 1996.

Although the company is dormant, a return is required for the 'return period' ie. the year ended 31 December 1996.

The following example illustrates section 11(2)(c).

Example

The company has a tax accounting period covering the year ended 31 December 1996. The 'specified period' in the section 11 notice is for the period 1 January 1996 to 31 October 1996.

In this example no return is required and the notice may be ignored.

Attached to the section 11 notice is a payslip. This should be retained as it will be required in the next step of the process, the payment of the tax liability.

4.2.3 Payment of tax

Each company is expected to pay its estimated corporation tax liability within nine months and one day of the end of the tax accounting period.

s.10(1)(a) ICTA 1988

No assessment to tax is issued in the first instance. A company will be 'expected' to pay tax by the due date. Any payment of tax after the due and payable date will attract heavy interest charges (see section 4.4).

When making payment of tax the company should use the payslip that is attached to the section 11 notice. If, as in one of the examples above, there is more than one tax accounting period, then a covering letter should be sent to the Collector of Taxes (copy to the Inspector) detailing how the payment should be split between the two tax accounting periods.

If, having made a corporation tax return, a company believes that it may have overpaid tax the company may by giving notice make a claim for the overpaid tax to be repaid. Any dispute as to the amount of the claim will be dealt with under the claims provisions of s. 42 TMA 1970. However, provided the company has grounds for believing that the amount paid exceeds the company's *probable* liability for corporation tax, then repayment should be automatic.

s.10(3) ICTA 1988

Exceptionally, an assessment to corporation tax may have been made against which an appeal and postponement application has been lodged. The normal postponement application provisions of s.55 TMA 1970 will apply to the assessment. In either case, whether the amount payable on account is to be determined under s.42 or s.55 of TMA 1970, the company has the right of representation before the Appeal Commissioners.

s.10(5) ICTA 1988

Pitfalls and planning

Companies that make up accounts annually to the same date will become accustomed to having to pay tax nine months and one day after the end of the accounting period. Where, however, there is a short accounting period then tax payments will be accelerated. The resultant cash flow disadvantages must be taken into account.

Example

A subsidiary company within a group makes up its statutory accounts for the year ended 31 December 1996. On 29 February 1996 it transferred its trade intra group. There is, therefore, a two month accounting period ended on that date.

The due and payable date for the two month accounting period to 29 February 1996 is 1 December 1996, one month before the company's year end. If tax is not paid on that date then interest will accrue.

4.2.4 Filing of tax returns

A company must file its corporation tax return on or before the 'filing date' if it is to avoid penalties for late filing. Normally the 'filing date' will be twelve months from the end of the statutory period of account.

The 'filing date' is the later of:

s.11(4)

(a) the first anniversary of the last day of the period to which the return relates;

(b) the first anniversary of the last day of that period of account of the company in which falls the last day of the accounting period (if any) to which the return relates; and

(c) the end of the period of three months beginning on the day following that on which the section 11 notice was served.

In most cases, where companies make annual accounts the dates in the first two instances above will be the same. Where the tax accounting period ends before the accounting reference date (eg. where companies prepare accounts for longer than twelve months) the second date above will always be later than the first.

Example

> A company makes up its accounts for the eighteen month period to 30 June 1997. Its tax accounting periods are therefore the twelve months to 31 December 1996, and the six months to 30 June 1997. The 'specified period' in the section 11 notice issued on 1 February 1997 covers the period 1 July 1996 to 30 June 1997.
>
> The 'return periods' covered by the notice are for the two accounting periods in question. In each case the 'filing date' is twelve months from the end of the statutory period of account, ie. 30 June 1998. Note, however, that although the filing date is longer than twelve months for the tax accounting period to 31 December 1996 there is no extension to the due and payable date of 1 October 1997.

Example

> The facts are the same as in the previous example, except that the section 11 notice is issued on 1 May 1998.
>
> In this case the 'filing date' is extended because of the late issue of the section 11 notice. The 'filing date' cannot be before the expiry of three months following the date of the issue of the notice. The 'filing date' therefore becomes 2 August 1998 with respect to both tax accounting periods.

Where the company makes up a set of accounts which extend beyond eighteen months then those accounts are deemed to be no longer than eighteen months for the purposes of calculating the 'filing date'.

s.11(5)

Example

> An unincorporated association makes up accounts for the two years ended 31 December 1997. The tax accounting periods are therefore the year to 31 December 1996 and the year to 31 December 1997. The 'specified period' in the section 11 notice issued on 1 February 1998 is for the period 1 January 1996 to 31 December 1997.
>
> The 'return periods' are therefore for the two accounting periods in question. The filing date for the accounting period to 31 December 1997 is twelve months thereafter, ie. 31 December 1998. The 'filing date' for the accounting period 31 December 1996 is not, however, extended to the same date. The extended 'filing date' is restricted to 30 June 1998 as if the period of account ended on 30 June 1997.

The tax return form CT200 is a nine page document and must be completed in all cases. There are three specific requirements that must be met:

(a)   the return must be signed by the company secretary or, except where a liquidator had been appointed, any other person with the express, implied or apparent authority of the company;   s.108(1)

(b)   the form must be accompanied by the corporation tax computations; and   s.11(1)

(c)   the form must be accompanied by the accounts.   s.11(1)

In relation to a company which is UK resident throughout the period to which the return relates and is required under Companies Act to prepare accounts for a period consisting of or including the 'return period', then the reference to 'accounts' in s.11(1) TMA 1970 is a reference only to such accounts, containing such particulars and having annexed to them such documents, as are required under the Companies Act to be so prepared. It is considered that this requirement includes group consolidated accounts required under s.227 Companies Act 1985 and also the unaudited profit and loss account of the parent company under s.230 Companies Act 1985.

The Inland Revenue has indicated that as regards non-resident companies 'accounts' means copies of the company's profit and loss account and balance sheet as well as the UK branch or agency profit and loss accounts together with, if prepared, the UK balance sheet. In other cases (such as unincorporated associations) the Revenue requires copies of any accounts and balance sheets required by statute or by the company's constitution to be prepared.

Substitute and computer generated returns are permitted provided that they have been approved by the Inland Revenue in advance.

Companies are also required to make the following returns under the quarterly accounting system described in your Paper IIIb: Corporation Tax study text:

(a)   return of franked payments giving rise to a charge to ACT;   Sch 13 ICTA 1988

(b)   return of relevant payments giving rise to a liability to income tax;   Sch 16 ICTA 1988

(c)   return of distributions which do not give rise to a liability to account for ACT.   s.234(5)-(9) ICTA 1988

Pitfalls and planning

Some companies might find it difficult to complete a tax return form within the stated time. Companies should not delay sending in their tax returns simply because information is not available. Estimated figures should be entered on the tax return form and a full explanation should be given in the covering letter. It is possible that the Revenue will accept such returns as having been validly made within the time limit, but companies should not rely upon this approach. It should also be borne in mind that if estimates are unreasonable then it will be open to the Inspector of Taxes to consider a penalty for an incorrect return.   s.96

4.2.5   Assessments

Having filed the corporation tax return form the Inspector will make any enquiries that are considered necessary (see also section 4.6). The Revenue will follow the same examination procedure that they had previously. Generally this means that returns will be placed into one of three categories:

(a)   Cases accepted without further enquiry.

(b)   Cases where a number of technical issues are raised.

(c)   Cases where it is considered necessary to make an in depth investigation into the company's affairs, and probably also into the affairs of the directors.

The Inspector of Taxes will only issue an assessment at this stage if it is clear that a contentious point is to be heard by the Appeal Commissioners, or where there is a delay in the company responding to the Inspector's enquiries, or where the normal six year time limit is about to expire. In all cases the existing appeals machinery is open to the taxpaying company. Notice of appeal must be made within thirty days of the issue of the assessment, and it may be accompanied by an application to postpone payment of tax.

In most cases, however, the amount of tax liability will be agreed. The Inspector will be under an obligation to issue an assessment where there is a tax liability. If no liability to corporation tax exists then no tax assessment will be issued (see also para 4.3.1).

s.8(3) ICTA 1988

Upon receipt of the agreed tax assessment the company must settle up any balance of liabilities with the Revenue. If insufficient tax has been paid, further monies must be remitted immediately to the Revenue. Conversely, if too much tax has been paid then the Revenue will make a refund. Either way an interest adjustment will be appropriate (see section 4.4).

4.3   Loss reliefs and capital allowances

4.3.1   Loss determinations

ss.41A-C

Broadly the rules permit an Inspector to make a determination of the amount of loss and to give notice of his decision in writing to the company. The normal appeals procedures will apply so that any dispute may be heard by the General or Special Commissioners. Normally loss determinations are not issued until the tax position of the company has been agreed with the Inspector so appeals are not generally necessary.

Once a determination is made it is final and conclusive for all corporation tax purposes. There are, however, 'discovery' provisions similar to those found in s.29(1) TMA 1970 as they relate to self assessments (and as they will relate to corporation tax self assessment, see section 4.6). Under the loss determination procedures should an Inspector 'discover' that a determination is excessive then he may make a direction to reduce the amount previously determined. Directions made under these provisions, like determinations, are subject to the normal appeals machinery.

Also like the assessing procedure the normal time limit for making determinations and directions is six years from the end of the accounting period, except that a direction to reduce an existing loss etc. may be made within twenty years in the case of fraudulent or negligent conduct.

These procedures apply only to trading losses under s.393 (ie. those activities where profits are assessable under Schedule D Cases I or V). The rules do not apply to Schedule D Case VI losses. However, the previous requirement in s.396 ICTA 1988 to make a claim with regard to Case VI losses has also been removed. This means that Case VI losses are dealt with in the same way as capital gains tax losses. There is no machinery within which to settle any dispute as regards the amount of such losses until such time as the loss is utilised against future Schedule D Case VI income.

4.3.2   Group relief

Claims to group relief must be made within two years of the end of the *claimant's* accounting period or, if later, until such time that the claimant company's liabilities to tax have been agreed. This is subject to a long stop rule of six years from the end of the accounting period. If the liabilities remain unsettled at this time the company has a further three months to make a 'conditional claim' to relief. 'Conditional claims' can only be made where:

(a)   an assessment has been made before the expiry of six years;

(b)   an appeal has been lodged against the assessment; and

(c)   the assessment has not become final and conclusive for tax purposes.

A *'conditional claim'* is only admissible if it is expressed to be conditional as to the amount claimed, on, and only on, the outcome of one or more relevant matters specified in the claim. A matter is relevant if it is relevant to the determination of the assessment of the claimant company to corporation tax for the period for which the claim is made.

Example

This example is new.

A Ltd has a wholly owned subsidiary B Ltd. Both companies prepare accounts annually to 31 December. What is the time limit for A Ltd to surrender a loss for its year ended 31 December 1996 by way of group relief to B Ltd?

Solution

A claim should be made by 31 December 1998, two years from the end of the claimant's accounting period.

If B Ltd's liabilities for the year to 31 December 1996 are still unagreed by 31 December 1998 the time limit is extended to the date of the agreement.

However if B Ltd's liabilities are still unagreed at 31 December 2002, the group has until 31 March 2003 to make a conditional claim to group relief.

Claims to group relief (including 'conditional claims') must be made in the corporation tax return of the company. If the tax return has already been submitted then the making of further claims, or withdrawal or variance of existing claims, is made by submitting an amended corporation tax return. This return form is an abbreviated version of the full corporation tax return.

In addition to the requirement that a claim is made in the tax return, the claim will not be valid unless it is:

(a)   in a quantified amount (except 'conditional claims'); and

(b)   accompanied by a copy of the letter of consent to surrender.

The surrendering company must send the original letter of consent to surrender to its Inspector on or before the date that the claim is made. Additionally the surrendering company must show details of the surrender in its corporation tax return. If that return has already been submitted the surrendering company must submit an amended tax return on or before the date of the claim.

Where the surrendering company's losses are the subject of more than one 'conditional claim' then an order of priority must be set out in the letter of consent to surrender.

One important aspect of group relief claims is that the claimant company will be given the relief claimed (provided all of the relevant documentation is submitted) notwithstanding that the surrendering company's losses may not have been agreed. If, at some later time, the amount of loss available from the surrendering company is reduced then a clawback assessment is made on the claimant company. Where the surrendering company has consented to surrender losses to more than one company then it may decide on the revised allocation. If it fails to do so the Inspector will make the appropriate adjustment considered necessary.

If the clawback assessment is made beyond two years from the end of the accounting period of the claimant company then that company could be time-barred from making further claims to group relief to set against the clawback assessment. This could operate harshly, particularly where a group has made losses overall. For this reason, FA 1993 extended the provisions of s.43A TMA 1970 to lengthen the time limit for making group relief claims when a clawback assessment has been made.

Provided the clawback assessment had not been made to correct a loss of tax arising from fraudulent or negligent conduct, the time limit for a further group relief claim is extended to one year after the accounting period in which the clawback assessment is made. `s.43A(1) & (2)`

Where the amount available for surrender as group relief consists of management expenses, capital allowances, debits on non trading 'loan relationships' or charges on income, the amount of loss available for surrender will be determined under the same provisions referred to in the section on Loss Determinations (4.3.1 above). Technically, the law does not provide for a formal determination of a trading loss available for surrender under s.393A ICTA 1988. However, the amount will be determined for the purposes of s.393 and since the wording in ss.393(7) and 393A(9) is almost identical, the effective result will be the same.

A group of companies whose affairs are mainly dealt with by one tax district and who have a common accounting date may be able to make special arrangements which

SP 10/93

(a)   simplify the making and revision of group relief claims, and

(b)   simplify the procedure for giving and revising notices of consent to surrender.

These arrangements enable the group to submit a joint amended return for group relief purposes (only) and to dispense with the need to provide individual notices of consent to surrender.

Detailed conditions for eligibility and the manner in which these special arrangements operate are given in Statement of Practice 10/93.

4.3.3   Capital allowances

Capital allowance claims are made in the same way as group relief claims. Claims must therefore:

Sch A1 CAA
1990

(a)   be made in a corporation tax return or an amended corporation tax return; and

(b)   be quantified in amount.

Similar time limits to group relief claims also apply. There is a general limit for claims to be made within two years of the end of the accounting period or, if later, until such time as the liabilities of the claimant company are agreed. There are similar six year long stop rules that apply to group relief whereby claims that are only 'conditional' will be permitted.

4.4   Interest on late paid and overpaid tax

4.4.1   Introduction

If a company pays tax late interest will run from the due and payable date. If too much tax is paid, interest on overpaid tax will be paid to the company. Interest on overpaid tax will run from the later of the date the tax was paid and the due and payable date.

There is, however, a sting in the tail. There is an interest rate differential in favour of the Revenue. At the time of going to print, the rate of interest on overdue tax was 6.25% and on overpaid tax, 3.25% (from 6 February 1996). Interest is neither taxable nor tax deductible.

s.90 & s.826(5)
ICTA 1988

4.4.2   Late payment of tax

Interest is calculated by reference to the nine month due and payable date. There is no difference between non-culpable and culpable interest previously chargeable under the provisions of s.86 and s.88 (now repealed) TMA 1970 respectively. These provisions do not and did not apply under Pay and File.

s.87A

4.4.3   Tax refunds

If a company pays too much tax, or is entitled to a repayment of income tax in respect of payments received by the company, or is entitled to a payment of a tax credit comprised in any franked investment income, then the refund of tax will carry interest with effect from the later of:

s.826 ICTA 1988

(a)   the due and payable date of nine months and one day after the end of the accounting period; and

(b)   in the case of corporation tax paid late , the date the tax was actually paid to the Collector of Taxes.

The refund is presumed to be of tax paid later rather than tax paid earlier, as illustrated in the example below.

Example

A company has an accounting period ended on 31 December 1995. The due and payable date is, therefore, 1 October 1996. On 1 September 1996 it pays £10,000 on account of its corporation tax liability. On 1 November 1996 it pays a further £5,000. Following submission of the corporation tax return the liability is eventually agreed in a sum of £7,000.

Interest will be paid to the company on the refund of £8,000 calculated at the prescribed rate to the repayment date on £5,000 from 1 November 1996, and £3,000 from 1 October 1996.

4.4.4 Carry back of trading losses and ACT

If trading losses are carried back to an earlier period the calculation of interest on unpaid or overpaid tax is affected as follows.

s.87A(4) & (6),
s.826(7), (7A) &
(7B) ICTA 1988

If the carry back claim results in a repayment, interest is calculated from the due and payable date of the accounting period of the loss unless the repayment is for an accounting period falling wholly within the twelve months immediately prior to the loss making period. In that case interest is paid as if the repayment was an overpayment of the period using the loss.

Similarly, if the carry back results in a reduction in an amount of unpaid tax, in calculating the interest on unpaid tax the reduction is ignored for all the carry back periods except any accounting period wholly within the twelve months immediately prior to the loss making period.

However, interest payable to the Revenue will cease to run on that part of the tax comprised in any such carry back claim from the due and payable date of the accounting period in which the loss was incurred.

Example

A company has an accounting period ended 31 December 1996. It pays its agreed tax liability on the due and payable date 1 October 1997. The company makes trading losses in each of the following two years ended 31 December 1997 and 31 December 1998. The company makes claims under s.393A ICTA 1988 to have the losses set against the profit for the year to 31 December 1996. The claims are agreed and tax is repaid to the company on 1 November 1999.

The repayment relating to the 1998 loss cannot carry interest except to the extent that the repayment is made after the due and payable date of the 1998 accounting period. The due and payable date is 1 October 1999, and since the repayment was made on 1 November 1999 then interest will be paid for one month.

Since the accounting period to 31 December 1996 (the period to which the repayment relates) is wholly within 12 months of the accounting period to which the 1997 loss relates, the restriction on the interest calculation does not apply with respect to that year's loss. Consequently the repayment relating to 1997 will be repaid with interest with effect from 1 October 1997.

Where surplus ACT is carried back this has no affect on the calculation of interest either on overpaid or underpaid corporation tax for an earlier period. Any repayment is treated as though it was a repayment of corporation tax for the accounting period in which the surplus ACT acrose. However, just as for losses, interest payable to the Revenue on the related tax unpaid for an earlier period ceases to run from the due and payable date of the surplus ACT accounting period.

When a carry back of a loss results in the creation of surplus ACT, which is in turn carried back to even earlier years, the reference period for the commencement of repayment interest (or the cessation of interest on an outstanding liability) will be the period in which the loss occurred, not the period in which the surplus ACT is deemed to have arisen.

Example

This example is new.

A company makes up accounts to 31 December each year and makes a loss in its year to 31 December 1996. It claims under s.393A to carry the loss back where it is fully used in the year to 31 December 1995. This in turn generates a surplus of ACT for the year to 31 December 1995 which, on a claim, is carried back and produces repayments for earlier years.

The corporation tax repayments are treated as a repayment of corporation tax for the year to 31 December 1996 (the loss making year) so that interest only runs from 1 October 1997, the due and payable date for the loss making period.

4.4.5 Group tax surrenders

The Inland Revenue have recognised that the differential in interest rates could operate unfairly where tax is unpaid by some companies in the group, but overpaid by others. Although the group may have made an overall payment sufficient to cover the group's tax liabilities there would, in these circumstances, be net interest charged.

Provisions have been introduced enabling one company to surrender a tax repayment to another which is a member of the same group.   s.102 FA 1989

For a tax surrender to be effective a number of conditions must be satisfied:

(a)   both companies must be members of the same group as defined for group relief purposes;

(b)   both the surrendering company and the recipient company must be members of the same group throughout the period beginning with the accounting period to which the refund relates and ending on the date of the surrender notice. A joint surrender notice must be given to the Inspector before the refund is made to the surrendering company; and

(c)   the accounting period of the surrendering company and the recipient company must be the same.

The effect of a surrender is that the recipient company is treated as having paid corporation tax on the later of:

(a)   the due and payable date of the accounting period to which it relates; and

(b)   the date the tax was paid by the surrendering company.

The surrendering company is treated as having received a refund on the same day.

Any interest paid by the surrendering company is treated as if it were paid by the recipient company.

Like payments for group relief, payments made under these arrangements are not to be taken into account in computing profits or losses of either company for corporation tax purposes, and are not regarded as distributions.

Example

This example is new.

Thread Ltd has two wholly owned subsidiaries, Cotton Ltd and Wool Ltd. The group has a 30 June year. Before any group relief claims, Cotton Ltd has a corporation tax liability of £100,000 for the year to 30 June 1995 but, anticipating a group relief claim, only paid £60,000 on 1 April 1996, the due and payable date. For the year to 30 June 1995, Thread Ltd had a trading loss and Wool Ltd had substantial profits and had paid its correct tax liability on the due date, 1 April 1996.

It was subsequently decided that a group relief claim by Wool Ltd would be more tax efficient than a group relief claim by Cotton Ltd. Accordingly, Wool Ltd had overpaid its tax liability by £45,000 on 1 April 1996 but Cotton Ltd had made an underpayment of £40,000.

Wool Ltd will therefore surrender £40,000 of its repayment to Cotton Ltd resulting in no underpayment and hence no interest charge on Cotton Ltd. Wool Ltd receives £5,000 of overpayment and interest thereon from 1 April 1996.

Without this provision and assuming that overpayments and underpayments are settled on 31 March 1997, there would be an interest charge on Cotton Ltd of £2,500 (£40,000 x 6.25%) and an interest payment to Wool Ltd of £1,462 (£45,000 x 3.25%), ie. a net payment by the group of £1,038 interest when the group was in a net tax overpaid position.

4.5   Penalties

4.5.1   Failure to notify chargeability

As set out in section 4.2, a company is liable to give notice of chargeability to tax within twelve months of the end of the accounting period unless it has made a tax return or received a section 11 notice.

If a company fails to give the appropriate notice then it is liable to a penalty not exceeding the amount by which the corporation tax chargeable on its profits for that period remaining unpaid twelve months after the end of that period exceeds any income tax available for deduction from gross corporation tax under s.7 ICTA 1988. For the purposes of determining the amount of tax unpaid no account may be taken of any claim to carry back surplus ACT from subsequent accounting periods.

s.10(3)

s.10(3) and (4)

Example

> A subsidiary company within a group makes up its statutory accounts for the year ended 31 December 1996. On 29 February 1996 it transferred its trade intra group. There is, therefore, a two month accounting period ended on that date. The company did not receive a section 11 notice, nor did it give notice of chargeability, nor had it paid any corporation tax by 28 February 1997.
>
> The tax computation is agreed as follows:
>
> | | | £ |
> |---|---|---:|
> | Schedule D | Case I | 100,000 |
> | | Case III | 20,000 |
> | | | £120,000 |
>
> | | £ |
> |---|---:|
> | Tax @ 33% | 39,600 |
> | Less IT @ source | (5,000) |
> | Net tax due | £34,600 |
>
> The maximum penalty under section 10 TMA 1970 is therefore £34,600. This penalty is mitigable.

Since the amount of penalty is tax geared (ie. it relates to the amount of unpaid tax twelve months after the end of the accounting period) then opportunities may exist to reduce 'tax unpaid'. This is examined in para 4.5.3.

4.5.2   Late tax returns

The main penalties under Pay and File are the fixed rate and tax geared penalties for late filing of tax returns. The provisions relating to these two types of penalty are independent of each other and companies could become liable to a fixed rate penalty, or a tax geared penalty, or both.

Fixed rate penalties

These provisions impose a penalty of £200 for the late filing of any tax returns. This penalty is reduced to £100 provided the tax return is filed within three months of the filing date.

s.94(1)-(5)

It should be noted that a tax return will not be regarded as properly filed unless it is signed by the proper officer of the company, and accompanied by the accounts and tax computations.

By concession, the Revenue will not impose a penalty provided the return is in their hands on or before the last business day within seven days following the filing date.

IRPR 14.9.95

In any case where:

(a)   the company is within the charge to corporation tax for three consecutive accounting periods, each of which is a 'return period', and

(b)   at no time between the beginning of the first of those periods and the end of the last is the company outside the charge to corporation tax, and

(c)   the company fails to make proper delivery of the return for the third of those periods, and

(d)   the company was liable to a penalty under this section in respect of each of the first two of those periods,

then the fixed rate penalty of £200 is increased to £1,000; and the fixed rate penalty of £100 is increased to £500.

Tax geared penalties

There is a tax geared penalty where there has been a failure to make a tax return within eighteen months of the end of the 'return period'. The amount of penalty is 20% of the 'tax unpaid'. The penalty is reduced to 10% of the 'tax unpaid' provided the tax return is filed within 24 months following the 'return period'. The amount of 'tax unpaid' is defined in para 4.5.3.

s.94(6)-(8)

Note that the trigger date is determined by reference to the 'return period', whereas the trigger date for fixed rate penalties is the 'filing date'. In a straightforward case where a section 11 notice is issued in time and in respect of a twelve month accounting period matching the company's period of account, the penalty provisions may be illustrated by the table set out below. Where, however, the 'filing date' is not twelve months following the accounting period, then the table does not apply (see the example below).

TABLE

Penalties for late returns:

Up to 3 months late	£100	(£ 500)	
3 to 6 months late	£200	(£1,000)	
6 to 12 months late	£200	(£1,000)	plus 10% 'tax unpaid'
Over 12 months late	£200	(£1,000)	plus 20% 'tax unpaid'

Figures in brackets may be substituted for the third successive offence. 'Tax unpaid' means tax unpaid 18 months after the end of the 'return period'.

Example

A company makes up its statutory accounts for the eighteen month period to 31 December 1996. Its tax accounting periods are, therefore, the year to 30 June 1996 and the period to 31 December 1996. The section 11 notice covering both periods is issued on 28 February 1997. The company files both tax returns on 12 January 1998.

The 'filing date' for both periods is 31 December 1997. Since both returns are late by more than 7 days, fixed rate penalties of £100 (filed within three months) will apply in respect of each return. In addition, a tax based penalty of 10% will apply with respect to the accounting period ended 30 June 1996. The amount of penalty will be based on tax unpaid' as at 31 December 1997.

It is possible for the 'filing date' to fall more than 18 months after the end of the 'return period'. This might happen, for example, where the section 11 notice is issued late. Suppose a company prepares its statutory accounts for the year to 31 December 1996 but transferred its trade, intra group, on 29 February 1996 thereby bringing a two month accounting period to an end. The filing date will be 31 December 1997, but the 18 month period will expire on 1 September 1997. It is therefore provided that the trigger date for a tax geared penalty is the *later* of 18 months from the return period and the filing date (ie. 31 December 1997).

4.5.3   The measure of 'tax unpaid'

Tax geared penalties are chargeable by reference to the amount of 'tax unpaid' at a specific point in time. For failure to notify chargeability the measure of 'tax unpaid' is that unpaid twelve months after the accounting period to which it relates. For late tax returns, the trigger date is eighteen months after the 'return period' (or accounting period) to which it relates. Both s.10(3) and s.94(7) TMA 1970 measure the amount of 'tax unpaid' as the amount by which the corporation tax chargeable on the profits of the company for the period remain unpaid at the trigger date reduced by any amount of income tax available for set off under s.7 ICTA 1988. S94(8) TMA 1970 also permits the deduction of surplus ACT carried back from an accounting period ending not more than 2 years after the end of the return period. Surplus ACT carried back cannot be deducted under s.10(4) TMA 1970.

A company which finds itself liable to a tax geared penalty under these provisions might, therefore, be able to manipulate the amount of 'tax unpaid' by a combination of planning techniques. These might include:

(a)   withdrawing claims for capital allowances in earlier periods thereby increasing the pool of expenditure in the accounting period of default;

(b)   carry back of losses of future periods claimed under s.393A ICTA 1988;

(c)   re-organisation of group relief plans so as to utilise losses/group relief/ACT within the defaulting company.

4.5.4   Incorrect tax returns

The penalty for an incorrect return or accounts is an amount equal to the tax that would have been lost as a result of the error. This maximum amount of penalty can be mitigated by the Revenue to take account of circumstances; for example, the degree of co-operation with Revenue enquiries.

s.96

4.6 Self assessment for companies

4.6.1 Introduction

The pay and file rules are to be amended to incorporate a self assessment. The changes are less radical than those under the income tax regime, as pay and file already incorporates a number of the relevant features.

Self assessment will be adopted from a day as yet to be appointed, but which is not expected to be before 1 April 1996.

The main features of self assessment will follow those for income tax, but a brief summary is given here as a reminder.

4.6.2 Self assessment

A company's corporation tax return will include a self assessment of the company's corporate tax liability.

s.182 FA 1994

new s.11AA TMA 1970

The Revenue have 9 months from receipt of the self assessment, and the company have 12 months from the filing date, to correct any errors in the self assessment.

4.6.3 Enquiries

The Revenue have 12 months from the filing date within which to notify the company that they intend to make enquiries into the return. If the return was not submitted by the filing date the period is extended to the quarter day (31 January, 30 April, 31 July or 31 October) following the anniversary of the date the return was filed.

s.183 FA 1994

new s.11AB TMA 1970

The company may amend the self assessment within 30 days of the end of the enquiry, failing which (or if he is not satisfied with the amendment) the officer of the board has a further 30 days to make amendments.

4.6.4 Determinations and discoveries

When no self assessment is made by the company, an officer of the board may make a determination, which is treated as if it were a self assessment.

s.190 FA 1994

new s.28C TMA 1970

If the officer discovers that tax has been lost, he may, in certain circumstances, make a discovery assessment to recover lost tax. He will be prevented from making a discovery assessment where he has failed to make timely use of into information available to him.

s.191 FA 1994

new s.29 TMA 1970

4.6.5 Claims

Claims, so far as possible, are to be made in the corporation tax return.

Sch.19 para 13 FA 1994

new s.42 TMA 1970

Capital losses will only be allowed if notified to an officer of the board, and the notification is dealt with as if it were a claim. Losses carried forward which were notified under these rules will be set off against capital gains in priority from losses brought forward from before the appointed day.

s.113 FA 1995

new s.16(2A) TCGA 1992

4.7 Summary

4.7.1 The 'Pay' element

Under the 'Pay' element:

(a) a company is required to pay corporation tax on a fixed date (nine months and one day after the end of its accounting period), whether or not an assessment has been made by then;

(b) interest runs from the same fixed payment date on any tax paid late by the company or tax repaid by the Revenue. There is, however, a lower rate of interest in respect of repayments than the rate charged on tax paid late.

There is no difference between culpable and non-culpable interest payable: s.86 and s.88 (now repealed) TMA 1970 are replaced by s.87A TMA 1970.

(c) interest receivable by companies on overpaid tax is governed by provisions in s.826 ICTA 1988. Interest will run from the normal due date (or the date on which the tax was paid if later).

4.7.2 The 'File' element

Under the 'File' element:

(a) a company is allowed twelve months from the end of its period of account (in this context referred to as the 'return period') to supply its return (form CT200) and accounts to the Revenue. This period is extended, if the company receives a late notice from the Inspector requiring the submission of a return, to three months from the date on which the notice requiring the submission of a return was served;

(b) unless reasonable excuse can be shown, failure to submit the return and accounts in the required time will incur an automatic flat rate penalty of £100 if the company is up to three months late or £200 for a longer delay;

(c) if the return and accounts are not submitted on time for three consecutive accounting periods these penalties are increased to £500 and £1,000;

(d) if the return and accounts are submitted more than six months late, a further tax-geared penalty is due in addition to the flat rate penalty of £200 or £1,000. This further penalty is 10% of the tax unpaid six months after the due date for the return if the return is between six and twelve months late and 20% of the tax unpaid at the same date if the return is more than a year late.

(e) if a company fails to give notice of a liability to corporation tax for any accounting period a maximum penalty can be charged equal to 100% of the corporation tax (net of recoverable income tax) remaining unpaid 12 months after the end of the accounting period.

(f) the above penalties will be charged by assessment, with the company having the right to appeal.

4.7.3 The CT 'Pay and File' tax return

The corporation tax return for Pay and File purposes comprises:

(a) form CT200, a nine-page return which must be completed in all cases;

(b) corporation tax computations; and

(c) the company's statutory accounts.

The form CT200 must be signed by an authorised officer of the company or by the liquidator if the company is in liquidation.

4.7.4   General

Under Pay and File, the corporation tax due is payable without the need to issue an assessment and so assessments which do not agree with the corporation tax return are rare, generally being raised only if there is a contentious point which it is expected will be resolved by the Commissioners, or to force an appeal in delay cases so that proceedings may be brought before the Commissioners, or to protect the Revenue if the normal six year time limit for making assessments is about to expire.

In other situations, a corporation tax assessment is issued only when the computations are agreed and there is a resulting tax liability. On receipt of the agreed assessment, the company must remit any outstanding tax due or the Revenue will refund any overpayment of tax.

If the company does not have any taxable profits (ie. it has made losses) the Revenue does not issue a corporation tax assessment when the computations are agreed. Instead, a loss determination is made, setting out in writing the amount of the company's loss. The company is not required to claim loss relief under s.393(1) ICTA 1988 (see section 5.3 in Paper IIIb: Corporation Tax study text) as, under Pay and File, the loss is specified in the CT200 return.

An appeal may be lodged against a loss determination in the same way as a corporation tax assessment.

4.7.5   Self assessment

A self assessment regime similar to that applying for individuals from 1996/97 will apply for companies from a day yet to be appointed (the statutory earliest deadline of 1 April 1996 has been missed).

QUESTIONS

1. Y Ltd estimated its corporation tax liability for its year ended 17 July 1995 as £20,000. This tax was paid:

   (a)   on 18 April 1996; or

   (b)   on 17 July 1997.

   The estimate is subsequently found to be excessive. From what date will interest on overpaid tax run?

2. Why is it important under Pay and File for a company to pay its best estimate of its corporation tax liability by the due date?

3. W Ltd submits a Pay and File return for the year ended 31 December 1996 on 16 July 1998. What are the consequences of this?

4. V Ltd submits a Pay and File return for the year ended 30 June 1998 on 17 November 2000. Its two previous returns were also late. What penalties may be charged?

5. (a)   George plc has a tax accounting period to 31 March 1996. Draft accounts indicate a profit chargeable to corporation tax of £320,000. What is the amount of the payment to be made by the company and on what date should it be paid, at latest to avoid interest charges?

   (b)   As a result of a cash flow crisis, payment of the sum you recommended was actually made on 28 February 1997. A this time, it is believed, on the basis of accounts submitted to the registrar of companies, that the profit chargeable to corporation tax may be as large as £400,000. should any further payment be made by the company and, if so, how much and by which date?

   (c)   Subsequently the company submits computations and accounts to the Revenue on 30 June 1997, having paid the additional sum that you recommended on 30 April 1997. The Revenue determined the final profit chargeable to corporation tax to be £380,000 on 31 December 1997, and issue a determination to that effect. What is the amount of the tax refund that will be made?

   (d)   For what periods will interest be payable or allowable in respect of this company and what will be the tax on which the interest paid or refunded is calculated?

6. Key Ltd prepares accounts to 31 December. It estimates its liability for the AP end 31 December 1995 to be £500,000, and pays this amount on 1 December 1996.

   The inspector agrees the company's figures and in due course makes an assessment.

   Subsequently, on 31 March 1997, the company submits an amended return claiming group relief, reducing the tax liability to £400,000.

   The inspector agrees the amended return and repays £100,000 on 1 May 1997.

   Assuming a rate of interest of 6.25% on underpaid tax and 3.25% on overpaid tax, what interest consequences flow from the above facts?

7. Why is there no distinction under Pay and File between culpable and non culpable interest?

8. What is the time limit for a claim to group relief?

9. What are the necessary conditions for a claim to surrender a tax refund?

10. What is the maximum penalty for incorrect returns under Pay and File?

SOLUTIONS

1.   (a)   Tax paid on due date. Interest runs from 18 April 1996.

      (b)   Tax paid after due date. Interest runs from 17 July 1997.   (4.4.1)

2.   Under Pay and File, interest on overpaid tax is calculated at 3.25% but interest on underpaid tax is charged at 6.25%. Generally neither position is commercially attractive.   (4.4.1)

3.   The return is due on 31 December 1997 and is therefore six and a half months late. A penalty will be charged of £200 plus 10% of any tax unpaid as at 30 June 1998.   (4.5.2)

4.   The return is a third consecutive late return and over 12 months late. The penalty is £1,000 plus 20% of any unpaid tax as at 31 December 1999. (4.5.2)

5.   (a)   Liability: £82,000   33% x £320,000 - 1/50 x (£1,500,000 - 320,000)

                            Due 1 January 1997   (4.2.3)

      (b)   Additional liability: 35% (marginal rate) x £80,000

          £28,000   Due 1 January 1997 or as soon as possible to avoid interest   (4.2.3)

      (c)   Refund: £7,000   35% (marginal rate) x £20,000   (4.2.3)

      (d)   On £82,000 from 1 January 1997 to 28 February 1997.

          On £21,000 from 1 January 1997 to 30 April 1997 (resulting in a repayment of interest charged).

          Interest on refund of £7,000 from 30 April 1997 to the repayment date - refund matched with last tax payment made.   (4.4.3)

6.   Initial payment:

      The payment of £500,000 is after the due and payable date:

      Due and payable date 1 October 1996

      Payment date   1 December 1996

      Interval   61 days

      Interest arising: £500,000 x 6.25% x $\frac{61}{365}$ =   £5,222.60

      Repayment

      Interest paid above must be reworked, ignoring the amount due to be repaid:

	£
(500,000 - 100,000) x 6.25% x $\frac{61}{365}$ =	4,178.08
Interest paid	5,222.60
Repay	£(1,044.52)

Interest is also due on the amount repaid from 1 December 1996 to 1 May 1997:

$$\frac{152}{365} \text{ days} \times 100,000 \times 3.25\% = £1,353.42$$

Total repayment	£
Tax	100,000.00
Interest repaid	1,044.52
Interest on repaid tax	1,353.42
	£102,397.94

(4.4)

7. Because interest will run from the due date whether the tax is culpable tax or not. (4.4.2)

8. Two years from the end of the claimant company' accounting period, with a possible extension to the time when the claimant company's affairs are determined for the accounting period. This last is subject to a 'backstop' limit of six year. However, if the six year limit is reached, the company has three months to make a 'conditional claim'.

    The Inland Revenue will consider late claims provided the delay results from circumstances beyond the company's control. (4.3.2)

9. (a) Joint surrender notice must be made before the refund is received.

    (b) Companies involved must have been members of the same group throughout the period beginning with the AP to which the refund relates, and ending with the date of the surrender notice.

    (c) The companies must have the same accounting periods. (4.4.5)

10. 100% of the tax that would have been lost. (4.5.4)

By the end of this session you will be able to:

- explain the s.348 rules that apply when an annuity or annual payment is paid out of profits brought into charge to income tax, and the s.349 rules when the payment is not made or only partly made out of profits chargeable to income tax

- describe how Schedule D Case III (or IV or V) applies to deduct tax at source from public revenue dividends, the distinction between 'short' and 'annual' interest and which of them is paid net, and how the MIRAS rules operate

- outline the interaction between Schedule F income tax and advance corporation tax on qualifying distributions, and how the tax credit is not available to non-residents

- describe the workings of the PAYE system

- explain how deduction of tax at source applies in the construction industry, entertainment and sporting world and to payments to non-residents

References: ICTA 1988 unless otherwise stated

5.1 Annuities and other payments

5.1.1 Payment out of chargeable profits (s.348)

When the payer makes a payment of an annuity or other annual payment (eg. royalties, easements and wayleaves) but not interest, wholly out of profits or gains brought into charge to income tax:

s.348

(a) the payer is entitled on making the payment to deduct and retain an amount equal to basic rate tax on the gross amount of the payment; and

(b) he is taxed (for basic rate purposes) on the whole of his income without regard to the payment; ie. the payment is ignored (see below). In this way he is made accountable to the Revenue for the payee's tax which he has deducted under (a) above.

Example

P, who has been carrying on a trade for some years, makes up his accounts to 31 December each year. On 1 January 1995 P covenants to pay £200 per annum to charity on 30 April of each year. The profits of P's business for the year ended 31 December 1995 and the year ended 31 December 1996 are £15,000 and £17,000 respectively.

Solution

For the tax year 1996/97 P's trading profits are assessed at £16,000 ie. 12 months average of the 24 months period ending in 1996/97 under the transitional rules. The tax charged on P for 1996/97 includes basic rate tax of £48 (24% on £200) due to charity during the year ie. on 30 April 1996. But P will only pay the charity £152

(£200 less 24%) and P will retain the £48 to relieve him of the basic rate tax on the £200 which is still included in his income.

In practice the method of assessment is different though the result is the same. Taking the facts of the example above, £200 would be deducted from P's income before computing his tax on the remainder. When that amount of tax has been computed, £48 ie. the sum deducted from the payment to the charity, is added to P's tax assessment. This method is convenient for two reasons:

(a)   in some circumstances P is entitled to deduct the payment (£200) from his taxable income for the purposes of higher rate tax. This applies here as the recipient is a charity, and would apply if P and the recipient had formerly been partners in the business;

s.683

(b)   although P is liable for basic rate tax on the £200 payment, it has ceased to be his income for the purpose of deducting personal allowances.

For both rules it is necessary to know the amount of P's income after deducting the gross payment.

The payer can only claim to retain tax deducted if he has in fact made the payment eg. by cheque or by crediting the payee with interest in his books. Unpaid income which is merely added to capital (ie. capitalised) is not 'paid' at all.

Paton v CIR (1938) 21 TC 626

The payee is obliged to accept the net payment as discharge of the payer's liability to pay the gross amount. The payee is entitled to receive from the payer a *certificate of deduction of tax*. The payee must include the gross amount of the payment in his total income and may then be liable for higher rate tax on it. If however he is not liable to basic rate tax up to the full amount deducted or is only liable at the lower rate, he may recover the excess from the Revenue.

s.352

5.1.2   Payment not (wholly) out of chargeable profits (s.349)

When a payment of an annuity or other annual payment is not made out of profits brought into charge to basic rate income tax (or not wholly out of such profits) the person by (or through) whom the payment is made must deduct an amount equal to basic rate tax on the gross amount of the payment. Insofar as the payment is not made out of profits brought into charge to income tax the payer must then deliver to the Inspector an account of the payment. He will be assessed on the payment so that the tax may be recovered from him. This rule requires the comparison of the gross annuity with gross income.

s.350

Example

Facts as in the previous example, except that P's income for 1996/97 after the personal allowance is £150 only.

Solution

P again pays £152 to the charity ie. £200 less basic rate tax at 24%. Of that payment £150 (gross) is paid out of P's income for 1996/97, and £36 basic rate tax (not lower rate) is paid by P to correspond with that part of the deduction from the payment to the charity. But £50 (gross) of the payment to the charity is not made out of P's chargeable profits, ie. it exceeds the amount of which P can be assessed by reference to P's income. P must deliver a return of the payment of £50 and will be assessed to pay £12 tax on it under s.350.

5.1.3   Which section, s.348 or s.349?

The main differences between s.348 and s.349 are:

(a)   in the case of a s.348 payment, the payer *may* (he has no legal duty but has a right) deduct tax and if he does so he retains it. Whether or not he makes the deduction his own tax assessment includes the amount of the payment (for basic rate tax). In the case of a s.349 payment, the payer *must* deduct basic rate tax and will usually be assessed for basic rate tax regardless of his personal tax position;

(b)   in the hands of the payee, a s.348 payment is income of the year in which it is *due* (even if paid later) and bears basic rate tax at the rate in force in that year. A s.349 payment is income of the year of *actual receipt* and is taxed at the rate in force in that year.

The example in paragraph 5.1.1 illustrates that the availability of income (to determine the choice between s.348 and s.349) is generally computed under normal rules. A taxpayer's Schedule D Case I income for example, is computed on a current year basis (for new businesses or from 1997/98 for old businesses) and all reliefs (personal allowance and losses brought forward) must be deducted. If what remains equals or exceeds the gross amount of the payment it is then normally a payment within the scope of s.348.

If the payer has available both capital and income (computed as just described) he is normally treated as having made the payment out of income. This would be the position if an annuity is paid out of a trust fund which includes both original capital and accumulated income. But if the taxpayer chooses to treat the payment in his accounts as made out of capital, he cannot then claim the benefit of s.348 since by his own choice he has not made the payment out of available income. This was the result where (to conserve a balance on profit and loss account to cover dividends) a company treated interest on a loan as a capital item.

Postlethwaite v CIR (1963) 41 TC 224

Chancery Lane Safe Deposit and Offices Co Ltd v CIR (1965) 43 TC 83

If there are no profits available to cover the payment in the year when it falls due, the payer (if a trader) cannot claim to make the payment out of accumulated profits of earlier years so as to secure the benefit of s.348. If the payer had profits available in the year when payment fell due but delays making payment until a later year, he is in principle liable to assessment under s.349 but is by concession given credit for the tax which he might have deducted if the payment had been made when due. He will of course have been assessed in that earlier year on an income which included the amount of the payment.

ESC A16

Interaction of tax retained with 'tax reducers'

The amount of tax reduction available (see your Paper IIa: Personal Tax Study Text) for the married couple's allowance, for example, is the lower of:

(a)   15% of the amount of the allowance; and

(b)   the amount which reduces the tax liability to nil.

To ensure that tax deducted from the charges is collected, tax at the basic rate which the claimant is entitled to deduct or retain is excluded in determining his tax liability, for the purposes of the above.

s.256(3)

Example

This example is new.

Bill is a 50 year old married man with Schedule E income of £8,000 for 1996/97. He pays a covenanted amount of £2,000 (gross) each year to a charity.

Income liability for 1996/97	£
Schedule E	8,000
Less: Charge	2,000
Statutory total income	6,000
Less: personal allowance	3,765
Taxable income	£2,235
	£
Income tax payable @ 20%	447

Less: tax reduction for MCA £1,790 x 15%	269
	178
Add: basic rate tax retained on covenant 2,000 x 24%	480
Income tax liability	£658

5.1.4 Failure to deduct tax

If in a s.348 case the payer fails to deduct tax when making the payment, the Revenue will (just as if he had done so) assess him on the basis that his income includes the amount paid. Therefore the Revenue still effectively collect the basic rate tax and are not concerned with the payer's failure to exercise his rights. But if the Revenue are unable to obtain the tax in this way from the payer, they are free to assess the payee under Schedule D Case III: it is the payee's taxable income and he will not be able to produce a certificate to show that tax has been deducted.

It may sometimes be assumed in favour of the payee that tax has been deducted. This was the position where the payer was abroad and the payments had been made under a court order which required payments to be made net of tax.

Stokes v Bennett (1953) 34 TC 337

If in a s.349 case the payer fails to deduct tax, the Revenue may still assess him on the payment to obtain the tax from him. Alternatively the payee may be assessed under Schedule D Case III on income which has been paid without deduction.

As between payer and payee, failure to deduct tax in making payment gives no right to the payer to recover it from a later payment nor to claim repayment. He is treated as having made a gift of the amount of tax under a mistake of law. There are three exceptions to this general rule:

(a)   when failure to deduct was due to a mistake of fact;

(b)   when a total annual sum is payable by instalments over the year it is treated as a single payment over the year. Hence the payer may deduct from a later instalment tax which he failed to deduct from an earlier one in the same year;

(c)   when the basic rate of tax is increased by the Finance Act and tax has been deducted at the old rate from a payment already made, the payer can recover the amount of the under-deduction from the next payment following the passing of the Act. If there is no next payment he may recover the amount as if it were a debt.

5.1.5 Tax free payments

An agreement for the payment of a sum 'free of tax' is construed to mean whatever gross amount less basic rate tax (but no other tax) is required to produce the agreed net payment.

An agreement is void insofar as it prohibits the deduction of tax.

Where it is intended that the payee shall be entitled to a net annual sum it is usual to provide for the payment of 'such sum as after deduction of income tax at the basic rate for the time being in force will leave £x per annum'. In any such case:

(a)   any higher rate tax for which the payee may be liable is calculated on the gross amount of the payment; and

(b)   the payee can obtain repayment of the basic rate tax deducted if his tax position so allows.

This rule does not apply to wills. If the testator gives a tax free annuity the executors must pay *all* tax (including higher rate tax) on that gross amount which (net of that tax) leaves the specified annuity. On the other hand if the annuitant recovers any basic rate tax he must account to the executors for that fraction of it which corresponds to the proportion of his total income represented by the gross amount of the annuity (see Paper IIc, Inheritance Tax and Trusts study text).

Re Pettit (1922)
2 Ch 765

5.1.6 Purchased life annuities

When a life annuity has been purchased, part of the annuity payments when received are treated as a return of capital and that part is free of income tax. The fraction is found by dividing the *purchase price* of the annuity by the annuitant's *normal expectation of life* at the date of purchase. If, for example, the purchase price is £7,000 and the annuitant's expectation of life is 20 years, then £350 of the annuity paid each year is treated as capital. The position is unaltered even though the annuitant in fact lives to receive the annuity for a longer or a shorter period than his expected life span.

s.656

Up to 5 April 1996, the income element of a purchased life annuity is paid net of basic rate tax. For 1996/97 onwards it is paid net of lower rate tax and is taxed as 'savings' income.

There are some annuities to which this does not apply. In particular it does not apply to a retirement annuity obtained in return for premium payments; an annuity which is purchased under the directions given in a will; an annuity purchased for an employee at retirement; nor an annuity payable under an approved personal pension plan. These annuities are treated wholly as income and are not taxed as 'savings' income.

5.1.7 Summary

Where an annuity or other annual payment is made entirely out of profits brought into charge to income tax, s.348 applies so that the payer is *entitled* to deduct and retain an amount equal to basic rate income tax thereon. He is effectively made accountable to the Revenue for that tax by including the amount of the gross payment in his own income.

If an annuity or other annual payment is not made or is only partly made out of profits chargeable to income tax, s.349 applies. The payer *must* deduct an amount equal to basic rate income tax thereon. He must also deliver an account to the Revenue, so that he may be assessed and the tax recovered from him.

These rules do not apply to interest payments, which are subject to special rules (paragraph 5.2.2 and 5.2.3).

If the payer fails to deduct tax when he is either entitled (under s.348) or required (s.349) to do so, the Revenue will continue to act as if he had deducted tax. Therefore, in the first case, his taxable income will still include the amount of the payment and, in the second, the Revenue may still assess the payer in order to collect the tax from him. Generally, the payer has no right to recover from the payee the amount of any tax which he failed to deduct in making a payment.

Where a taxpayer receives amounts from a purchased life annuity, part of the payments received will be treated as a return of capital. The capital portion will be received without deduction of income tax.

5.2 Interest

5.2.1 Schedule D Cases III, IV and V

Cases III, IV and V of Schedule D provide charging provisions and a mechanism enabling tax to be collected by deduction from 'public revenue dividends'. The appropriate Case applies to those public revenue dividends of both the UK and elsewhere which are paid to the recipient via a UK paying agent, eg. the Bank of England or a banker. In such circumstances, the paying agent must deduct lower rate (basic rate prior to 6 April 1996) income tax from the payment and account for the tax to the Inland Revenue.

s.17

A paying or collecting agent is generally only required to deduct tax on foreign dividends and interest if he acts as a custodian of the shares or securities for the UK investor. There is no requirement for deduction if the agent merely arranges for the cheque paying the dividend or interest to be cleared.

Example

> M is a UK resident who owns U$100,000 8% loan stock issued by the government of Utopia. The gross half-yearly dividend amounts to a sterling equivalent of £1,200. The coupon is paid via a UK paying agent who also holds the stock certificates for M.
>
> The agent deducts lower rate income tax of £288 (£1,200 x 24%) and pays the net amount (£912) to M. The agent accounts to the Revenue under Schedule D Case IV for tax of £288.

The term 'public revenue' encompasses the public revenue of *any* government and also the revenue of any public authority or institution in a country other than the UK. Income derived from a UK public authority is chargeable to tax under Schedule D Case III.

s.45
s.582

'Dividends' subject to the charge under Schedule D Cases III, IV and V include any interest, public annuities, dividends or shares of annuities. By and large, the income concerned is interest, the other categories being of historic significance only.

s.45

Tax is charged on an 'actual' basis, ie. the paying agent is liable to pay over tax on the basis of the income arising in the chargeable period. If the dividend is received by the paying agent net of overseas withholding tax, UK income tax is deducted only to the extent that the foreign withholding tax rate falls short of the lower rate of income tax.

Example

> If the interest received on M's behalf (see previous example) by the UK paying agent has suffered 12% Utopian withholding tax, UK tax is deducted as follows

	£	£
Gross interest		1,200
Less: withholding tax @ 12%		(144)
		1,056
UK income tax @ 24%	288	
Less: Utopian tax	(144)	
		(144)
Net interest		£912

> M is treated as receiving gross income of £1,200, with the following tax credits:

Foreign tax	144
UK tax	144
	£288

Finally, note that income derived by individuals not ordinarily resident in the UK from certain UK government securities is exempt from UK income tax (FOTRA securities), eg. 3$^{1}/_{2}$% War Loan, certain issues of Funding Loan, Treasury and Exchequer Stock. You will find a full list of FOTRA securities in your Hardman's or Whillans's Tax Tables although copies of Tax Tables are not allowed in the exam room.

s.47

5.2.2 Yearly interest

The system of deduction of tax described in section 5.1 for annuities and other annual payments does not apply to interest, which is subject to special rules.

s.350(4)

The rules only apply to 'annual' (or 'yearly') interest. Tax can never be deducted from payment of 'short' interest. The distinction between 'annual' and 'short' interest depends mainly on the expected duration of the relevant loan. If it is *likely* to last for a year or more the interest is 'annual' even though (as with a conventional mortgage of house property) it is repayable on six months' notice. If the loan is expressed to be for a briefer period than a year the interest is 'short'. No significance attaches to:

Corinthian Securities Ltd v Cato (1969) 46 TC 93

(a) interest on a short-term loan being expressed at an annual rate; nor

(b) interest on a long-term loan being made payable at shorter intervals than a year eg. monthly.

There is an anomalous early decision that if completion of the sale of property is delayed beyond the contractual date the interest payable on the purchase money is 'yearly'.

Bebb v Bunny (1854) 1 K&J 216

Lower rate tax (basic rate prior to 6 April 1996) is to be deducted in the following cases (but subject to exceptions concerning banks):

(a) when annual interest is paid by a company or local authority (otherwise than as trustee) or by or on behalf of a partnership of which a company is a member; or

(b) when annual interest is paid to a person whose usual place of abode is outside the UK.

It is under the rule in (a) that a company deducts lower rate tax in paying interest to its debenture holders.

The provision for deduction of tax from annual interest does not however apply:

(a) to interest payable in the UK on an advance from a bank which carries on a bona fide banking business in the UK; or

(b) to interest paid by such a bank in the ordinary course of that business (other than to individuals).

Bank overdraft and deposit interest is usually short interest. But the above exceptions put bank interest transactions beyond doubt, ie. the interest is to be paid to the customer (other than an individual) or charged against him as a gross amount.

A person who is assessed under Schedule D Case I or II may not deduct (as an allowable expense) interest paid to a person who is not UK resident unless he has complied with s.349(2) by deducting tax from any annual interest (although there are exceptions eg. for companies).

s.82

Building societies can pay interest gross on general undesignated client accounts (eg. held by solicitors) and on time deposits with a duration of between one and five years.

SI 1986/482 Reg 6(1)(hh)

Interest is paid net by building societies to discretionary and accumulation trusts. With effect from 6 April 1996 such trusts which have no connection with the UK will be able to receive their interest gross if they produce a signed declaration to that effect.

From 6 April 1996 discretionary and accumulation trusts will receive bank interest under deduction of tax.

5.2.3   MIRAS

ss.369-379

Relief for mortgage interest is generally given by the borrower paying the interest to the lender net of tax relief. The rate of tax relief for 1995/96 and 1996/97 is normally 15% (20% for 1994/95). For 1993/94 and earlier years, relief was given at 25%. For 1996/97, the main exception to the 15% tax relief rule is where the interest is paid on a loan used by a person aged 65 or more to purchase an annuity. Relief on such loans continues to be at the basic rate (currently 24%).

s.365

Tax relief at source is given under the MIRAS (Mortgage Interest Relief at Source) scheme where a 'qualifying borrower' pays 'relevant loan interest' to a 'qualifying lender'. Interest not coming within the scheme but otherwise qualifying for relief will be paid gross but will attract relief as a tax reduction (see your Paper IIa: Personal Tax Study Text).

Under the MIRAS scheme relevant loan interest is not a charge on income but will qualify for 15% relief regardless of the level of the borrower's income. Therefore it plays no part in the computation of taxable income or income tax liability.

A 'qualifying borrower' is any individual paying interest on a loan. However, where a borrower or his spouse receive emoluments which are exempt from tax under Schedule E, eg. a foreign diplomat, he is not a 'qualifying borrower'. Joint borrowers, who are not married couples, must all be 'qualifying borrowers' to come within the scheme. Only interest on the first £30,000 attributable to each 'qualifying borrower' will qualify for relief under MIRAS.

'Relevant loan interest' comprises interest on a loan:

(a)   used for the purchase or improvement of the borrower's only or main residence, or that of a dependent relative or former or separated spouse of the borrower where relief continues to be available; or

(b)   secured on land and used to purchase a life annuity by a borrower aged 65 or over.

In each case, the property in question must be located in the UK. The scheme does not extend to property located in Eire. Also, the property must be used wholly or to a substantial extent (at least two-thirds) as a main residence. Interest on loans in respect of rented property is outside the scheme.

For MIRAS to apply the borrower has to notify the lender on the appropriate form that all the conditions have been met, or the Revenue must notify the lender and borrower that the interest can be brought under MIRAS. If interest ceases to be relevant loan interest or if the borrower ceases to qualify the borrower must notify the lender.

The Revenue will allow capitalised interest to be part of a relevant loan provided it does not exceed the greater of £1,000 or 12 months arrears.

The list of 'qualifying lenders' includes building societies, local authorities and friendly societies. The Treasury may authorise banks and certain insurance companies as 'qualifying lenders' by statutory instrument.

Qualifying lenders are required to bring into MIRAS new loans made in excess of the £30,000 limit from 6 April 1987 onwards. Where the limit is exceeded because there is more than one loan, both must be from the same lender in order for the later loan which exceeds the limit to qualify.

s.373

A loan taken out partly to buy a main residence and partly for another purpose cannot be dealt with under MIRAS even where the qualifying part is in excess of £30,000 so that only £30,000 of the total loan would qualify for relief in any case. In a tax case it was pointed out that the borrower could have relief under MIRAS in those circumstances if he required the lender to split the loan into two separate loans - one of which was only applied for the house purchase.

s. 370(2)(b)
R v H M
Inspector of
Taxes, ex parte
Kelly (1991)
STC 566

Where the property is used partly as a main residence and partly for business purposes or for letting, the Revenue will allow the loan to be split and the appropriate proportion of the interest will be allowed under MIRAS. The balance will be deductible from the business profits or rental income. Apportionment is also possible where the property is only sometimes used for business purposes. Relief is also given during periods of temporary absence.

ESC

ESC A27

5.2.4 Summary

Tax is collected by deduction at source from public revenue dividends under Schedule D Cases III, IV or V, as appropriate, ie. interest on securities issued by any government or by a public authority of an overseas country. Account is taken of any foreign withholding tax already deducted in computing the amount of the deduction in the UK.

Interest paid on a loan likely to be outstanding for more than a year is termed 'yearly' or 'annual interest'. Annual interest paid by a company or local authority is required to be paid net, as is annual interest paid to a person who resides outside the UK.

Despite this rule, interest payable in the UK on an advance from a bank carrying on business in the UK is paid gross. Interest paid to investors by such a bank in the ordinary course of its business is also paid gross, except where the lower rate scheme applies.

With the exception of loans to purchase an annuity, tax relief under the MIRAS scheme is given at 15%.

Loans to purchase an annuity qualify for 24% (ie. basic rate) tax relief under the MIRAS scheme.

5.3   Dividends and other distributions

5.3.1   Schedule F

Income tax under Schedule F is chargeable in respect of all dividends and other distributions received by an individual from a UK company. The liability to tax is computed on the basis of the amount received in the year of assessment.

s.20

Schedule F income tax is payable regardless of whether the distribution is qualifying or non-qualifying for the purposes of ACT (paragraph 5.3.2). If, however, the distribution is non-qualifying, eg. bonus redeemable shares, no lower rate assessment is made. The *net* amount received is treated as the taxpayer's income for higher rate purposes only with a lower rate tax credit. In effect a higher rate tax payer is charged to tax at 20% (40-20)% on the net amount of the distribution.

s.233

Similarly, where no tax credit is available to the taxpayer (eg. because he is not resident in the UK), only a higher rate tax assessment may be made. The liability to higher rate tax is computed on the basis of the amount received with credit for the lower rate.

Example

> Fritz is not resident in the UK. On 21 August 1996 he receives a dividend from a UK company of £1,500.
>
> Since Fritz is not entitled to a tax credit, he is treated as having Schedule F income of £1,500, for the purposes of computing any liability to higher rate tax only. If he is liable at the higher rate tax will be charged of £300 (£1,500 x (40-20)%).

In all other cases, ie. where the taxpayer is entitled to a tax credit (paragraph 5.3.2), the liability to tax under Schedule F is calculated by including the aggregate of the amount received and the related tax credit in the taxpayer's statutory total income.

5.3.2   Interaction between Schedule F and ACT

The UK operates an 'imputation system' which means that, when a company pays a dividend, it makes an advance payment of its own liability to corporation tax ('advance corporation tax' or ACT). Hence, dividends are not paid under deduction of income tax, but do have a tax credit attached to them. Because the rate of ACT is linked to the lower rate of income tax, it appears to the shareholder as if he is receiving his dividend net of income tax at the lower rate.

For 1994/95 onwards, both the ACT and the tax credit available to the individual are at the rate of 20%.

The imputation system is dealt with fully in your Paper IIIb: Corporation Tax study text. However, distributions (which include not only dividends but also certain other payments out of the assets of a company to a shareholder, eg. a gift of an asset) may be either qualifying or non-qualifying. ACT is paid on a qualifying distribution but not on a non-qualifying distribution.

Most distributions are qualifying, but a bonus issue of redeemable shares or securities is non-qualifying.

With the exception of Foreign Income Dividends (FIDs), if ACT has been paid on a distribution and the shareholder is UK resident, he is entitled to a tax credit equal to the ACT paid by the company thereon. As the individual's Schedule F income is the aggregate of the amount received by him and the tax credit attaching thereto, the tax credit satisfies his lower rate income tax liability. If the shareholder's income tax liability is less than the tax credit or is nil, the excess or unutilised tax credit will be paid to him by the Revenue. If the individual is a basic rate tax payer he has no further tax to pay because the dividends are taxed only at the lower rate. If he is a higher rate taxpayer he pays a further 20% (40-20)% on the gross value of the dividends. This is quite a complicated topic and is discussed fully in your Paper IIa: Personal Taxation study text.

Foreign Income Dividends (FIDs)

With effect from 1 July 1994, a company may opt for a dividend paid to be a FID (see your Paper IIIb: Corporation Tax study text). A FID does not carry a tax credit as such. However, the recipient is treated as receiving income net of lower rate tax and is taxed on the grossed up ($\frac{100}{80}$) equivalent. The lower rate tax is available as a notional tax credit and the FID is taxed as any other UK dividend with the exception that the notional tax credit can never be refunded.

5.3.3 Summary

Distributions from UK companies are chargeable to income tax under Schedule F. Where a tax credit is available to the taxpayer, the aggregate of the amount received and the tax credit is included in the taxpayer's total income. Where no tax credit is available, eg. in the case of a non-qualifying distribution, there is no lower rate assessment. The net receipt is included in the taxpayer's total income for higher rate only.

Strictly, UK dividends are not received under deduction of income tax. However, they do have a tax credit attached which can be used by a UK resident taxpayer in satisfaction of his liability to lower rate tax. This is known as the 'imputation system', under which the payment of a qualifying distribution by a UK company triggers an advance payment of corporation tax.

5.4   PAYE

5.4.1   The PAYE system: introduction

The legislation covering the PAYE (Pay As You Earn) system appears in ss.203-203L ICTA 1988. This is continually amended and added to by means of various statutory instruments. A large number of the PAYE regulations are incorporated in the Revenue Pamphlet P7 (Employer's Guide to PAYE); however, this has no statutory force. The relevant statutory instrument giving effect to ss.203-203L is the Income Tax (Employments) Regulations 1993.

SI 1993/744

The PAYE method of deducting income tax from salaries and wages applies to all income from offices or employments. Thus PAYE applies not only to weekly wages but also to monthly salaries, annual salaries, bonuses, commissions, directors fees, pensions and to any other income from an office or employment. PAYE also applies to certain payments not made in a cash form (para 5.4.2).

s.203

It is the employer's duty to deduct income tax from the pay of his employees, whether or not he has been directed to do so by the Revenue. If he fails to do this he may be required to pay over the tax which he should have deducted (para 5.4.7) and, in addition, may be subject to penalties (para 5.4.9). In certain instances a person other than the employer is made responsible for operating PAYE (para 5.4.3).

Employers are required to pay PAYE and NIC deductions made on paydays falling between 5th of a calendar month and the 6th of the next calendar month to the Collector within 14 days of the end of the tax month. For example, PAYE deducted on 26 September 1996 payday for monthly salaries must be paid over to the Collector by 19 October 1996.

However, for employers whose monthly payments of PAYE and NIC are less than £600 on average, payments can be made quarterly. Payments for quarters ending 5 July, 5 October, 5 January, and 5 April will be due on the 19th day of those months.

Officers of the Inland Revenue are empowered by law to make inspections of employers' records from time to time in order to satisfy themselves that the correct amounts of tax are being deducted and paid over to the Revenue.

5.4.2   Emoluments liable to PAYE

The objective of PAYE is to deduct the correct amount of tax over the year, so the scope of PAYE is very wide. It applies to most cash payments, other than reimbursement of business expenses incurred by the employee, and certain non cash payments.

In addition to wages, salaries etc. PAYE applies to lump sum payments on leaving (unless and to the extent that, they are exempt), most lump sum payments on joining, round sum expense allowances, payments instead of benefits in kind. PAYE also applies to statutory sick pay and statutory maternity pay.

Tips paid direct to an employee are outside the PAYE system (although still assessable under Schedule E). An exception to this can apply in the catering trades where tips are often pooled. Here the PAYE position depends then on whether a 'tronc' administered other than by the employer exists. If the employer, and not a representative of the staff, effectively shares out the pool of tips, the employer is liable to account for PAYE (and NIC) on the tips. On the other hand, if a representative of the staff shares out the tips, there is no PAYE liability (nor NIC) for the employer even though the tips are nevertheless taxable. Where there is a 'troncmaster' the troncmaster must operate PAYE (independently of PAYE operated by the employer on the staff wages). In a recent case the absence of a 'troncmaster' other than the company's directors left the company responsible for the PAYE.

Figael Ltd v Fox (1992) STC 83

Whilst benefits in kind are liable to Schedule E, PAYE is not normally operated on them; instead the employee's PAYE code is restricted (para 5.4.5).

s.206 (A)

An employer may enter into a PAYE settlement agreement whereby the employer meets the employee's tax liability on certain minor benefits-in-kind or expenses for the employee and then no information need be provided about these benefits or expenses at the year end.

Various schemes were devised, primarily for the avoidance of NIC (see session 7) which involved payments in the form of assets which the employee could realise for cash.

Anti-avoidance legislation was subsequently enacted to counteract the avoidance of NIC on certain payments to employees in forms such as gold bars and coffee beans and also the avoidance of PAYE on the same (but note that tax had still been due under Schedule E).

Tradeable assets

Any provision of assessable income to a director/employee in the form of a tradeable asset is to be treated as a payment by the employer for PAYE purposes.

s.203F

A tradeable asset is:

(a)   any asset capable of being sold/realised on a recognised investment exchange (eg. the Stock Exchange and London Commodity Exchange) or the London Bullion Market;

(b)   any asset capable of being sold/realised on any market specified in the PAYE regulations; and

(c)   any other assets for which, at the time when the asset is provided, trading arrangements exist.

203F(2)

Trading arrangements for an asset are arrangements for the purpose of enabling the person to whom the asset is provided to obtain an amount similar to the expense incurred in the provision of the asset. In other words, PAYE will be due if the employer provides an asset and has already arranged for the employee to sell it.

s.203K

The amount of the payment which is to be subject to PAYE in the above circumstances is the amount for which the asset is capable of being sold/realised/traded. Thus, the tax collected through PAYE should be equal to the employee's tax liability on the asset.

s.203F(3)

The regulations exclude shares, or rights over shares (eg. options), in the employing company (or in a company controlling that company) from the above provisions.

Non-cash vouchers

The PAYE provisions have been extended to remuneration in the form of non-cash vouchers chargeable to income tax under s.141 ICTA 1988 where at the time it is provided:

(a)   the voucher is capable of being exchanged for tradeable assets; or   s.203G

(b)   the voucher can itself be sold, realised or traded.

Credit-tokens

s.203H

PAYE is to be operated on each occasion on which a director/employee uses a credit-token (eg. a credit card) to obtain money or goods which are tradeable assets. However, the regulations state that the use of a credit-token to defray expenses is not subject to PAYE.

Cash vouchers

s.203I

The former requirement to operate PAYE when a cash voucher was provided for a director/employee (s.143(1) ICTA 1988) has been repealed and replaced by a similar requirement under new s.203I ICTA 1988. The regulations provide that a cash voucher which is used to defray expenses is not subject to PAYE.

Administration: operation of PAYE

Where PAYE is to be operated under any of the above provisions the procedure will be:

(a)   The amount of the payment treated as made in the form of tradeable assets, or by way of a voucher or credit-token (the notional payment) is to be entered on the PAYE deduction card at the time of payment and the PAYE due calculated in the normal manner.

(b)   The PAYE due in respect of the notional payment is then to be recovered from any payments of remuneration actually made by the employer to the employee during the tax month in which the notional payment is made. (NB: for this purpose the whole of any actual remuneration (net of PAYE due on the actual payment(s)) for the tax month can be withheld as PAYE on the notional payment; ie. there is no 50% overriding limit as there is for K codes (see para 5.4.5.)

(c)   Any PAYE not so recovered by the employer by the end of the tax month   s.203J
must be paid by the employer to the Inland Revenue within 14 days after the end of that month. The employer will then seek to recover this tax from the employee.

s.144A

If within 30 days of making the notional payment the employer fails to recover the PAYE which he has been required to pay without deduction from the employee, the amount of that tax is treated as income of the employee assessable to tax under Schedule E and as having been received by the employee at the date the notional payment was made.

Example

On 1 April 1997 a company pays a bonus of £100,000 to a director in the form of gold bullion. The director's previous remuneration for 1996/97 was £50,000. The PAYE due for month 12 in respect of the notional payment in the form of a tradeable asset is £40,000 (£100,000 @ 40%). There is no further payment to the director in 1996/97 and the company is required to account to the Inland Revenue for the PAYE by 19 April 1997.

If the director fails to pay the company the amount of £40,000 before 1 May 1997, he will be treated as receiving further 1996/97 remuneration of £40,000 in addition to the £100,000 of gold bullion and £50,000 ordinary remuneration. In such circumstances, ignoring the ordinary remuneration and related PAYE, the director is treated as having paid £40,000 income tax on the income of £140,000 and the employer will have to include the £40,000 on form P11D (the £100,000 gold bullion payment having already been entered on the tax deduction card).

5.4.3 Persons liable to operate PAYE

The normal rule is that an individual's employer is responsible for operating PAYE on that individual's earnings. Special rules apply in certain situations to impose the responsibility for operating PAYE on a third party where PAYE might otherwise be avoided.

Agency Workers

Where an individual, including a partner, has a contract or arrangement with another person (usually an agency) whereby he renders services to a client which are subject to that client's supervision, direction or control, he is chargeable under Schedule E on the remuneration received for those services. The agency is normally responsible for operating PAYE. These regulations do not apply to entertainers, fashion models, home workers, or workers who are construction industry sub-contractors (section 5.5).

s.134

The client will however, be responsible for operating PAYE if:

(a)   the client pays the agency worker direct, or pays a third party at the agency workers direction;

(b)   the agency worker is engaged through a foreign agency; or

(c)   the client pays a third party who is outside the UK and who is not the agency.

Payment by intermediary

Prior to 1994/95 some employers made payments of remuneration to directors/employees through a third party outside the UK, thus avoiding the need to operate PAYE. From 3 May 1994 s.203B ICTA 1988 treats any payment of assessable income to a director/employee which is made by an intermediary of the employer as a payment made by the employer for the purpose of the PAYE regulations. Therefore, if the intermediary fails to operate PAYE, the responsibility for deducting and accounting for income tax in accordance with the PAYE regulations falls on the employer. Any person acting on behalf of and at the expense of the employer (or a person connected with the employer) is an intermediary for this purpose, whether in or outside the UK. Payments by trustees holding property for any persons (or class of persons) which includes the director/employee are also within the scope of the new legislation.

s.203B

Employees of overseas employers working in the UK

The scope of the PAYE regulations was extended from 3 May 1994 to cover situations where a director/employee who is employed by an overseas employer works for a person based in the UK. In such circumstances, assuming the overseas employer does not operate PAYE and the director/employee is assessable to income tax in the UK, the person for whom the director/employee is working in the UK is treated for the purposes of the PAYE regulations as making payments of assessable income to the director/employee and is required to operate PAYE. In other words, the person in the UK for whom the director/employee works has to account for the tax under PAYE which would have been deducted from the payments to the director/employee had the PAYE regulations applied to the overseas employer.

s.203C

This applies even if the overseas employer pays the employee's salary. It is necessary for the person based in the UK to ascertain the remuneration paid by the overseas employer and calculate the PAYE to be deducted. (If the salary is paid without deduction, it will need to be grossed up.) The overseas employer may either reimburse the person based in the UK directly, or allow a deduction from any charges made for the employee's services.

Non-resident employees working in the UK

A director/employee who is non-resident in the UK is taxed only on remuneration for UK duties. Directors/employees who are resident but not ordinarily resident in the UK are taxed on payments for UK duties and on payments for overseas duties to the extent that they are received in the UK.

From 3 May 1995 employers paying remuneration to directors/employees who are not resident or not ordinarily resident and who work in the UK and also work (or are likely to work) outside the UK may apply to an officer of the Board to make a direction that PAYE need only be operated on a certain proportion of payments made to such individuals. This proportion will usually be a best estimate of how much of the remuneration will be taxable in the UK. Where no direction is made by the Revenue, the employer is required to operate PAYE on the whole of the remuneration paid.

s.203D

Mobile UK workforces

Where a person enters into an agreement that the employees of another person (the contractor) will work for him for a period, the responsibility for operating PAYE normally remains with the contractor. From 3 May 1994 where it appears likely to the Inland Revenue that PAYE will not be deducted or accounted for in accordance with the regulations, the Board may issue a direction requiring the person for whom the contractor's employees are to work to deduct PAYE tax from the payments he makes to the contractor in respect of the work done by each of those employees. Where reasonably practicable, the Board is to supply the contractor with a copy of the direction.

s.203E

As the payments to the contractor will usually be considerably greater than his employee's remuneration, the above provisions should ensure that too much tax is deducted under PAYE. Any subsequent repayments of tax would appear to belong to the employees.

5.4.4 How PAYE works

In the following sections 'employer' includes any person required to operate PAYE.

To operate PAYE the employer needs:

(a) deductions working sheets;

(b) codes for employees which reflect the tax allowances to which the employees are entitled; and

(c) tax tables.

The amount of tax an employer has to deduct on any pay day is calculated as follows:

(a) the pay due to the employee is determined and added to the total of all previous payments made to the employee from 6 April to date;

(b) using the employee's code and Tables A (the 'Pay Adjustment Tables'):

(i) if the employee has a suffix code (eg. 376L) the tables will show the total pay to date that the employee may have free of tax (the 'Free Pay'); or

(ii)   if the employee has a K code, the tables will show the pay to be added (the 'Additional Pay') to the employees total pay to date.

(c)   the tax due to date is then determined by looking up the taxable pay to date in the taxable pay tables (Tables LR and B to D);

(d)   from the figure of tax due to date, the total tax already paid is deducted, leaving the tax due to be deducted from the employee's pay on the payday in question.

Although PAYE is normally operated on a cumulative basis, an employee may have a 'week 1/month 1' code (para 5.4.5). In this case the figures for pay and tax deducted are not cumulated, and the tax on each pay day is worked out on the pay on that pay day as if it were the first pay day in the tax year (using week 1 or month 1 tables).

Where a K code (see para 5.4.5) is in operation, there is a restriction on the amount of tax that may be deducted (para 5.4.5). On a cumulative basis, this restriction will be recouped on a later pay day (subject to the overriding limit on the later pay day). On a week 1/month 1 basis the restriction cannot be recouped, and will be dealt with by the Revenue after the end of the tax year.

The employer must keep records of each employee's pay and tax and of the total of the employee's and employer's National Insurance contributions, and separately, of the employee's National Insurance contributions at each pay day. He must also make a return at the end of the tax year (para 5.4.6). The employer has a choice of three ways of recording and returning these figures:

(a)   he may use the official deductions working sheet (P11) which is supplied by the Revenue;

(b)   he may incorporate the figures in his own pay records each pay day using a substitute document;

(c)   he may retain the figures on a computer.

5.4.5   Code numbers

An employee is normally entitled to various personal tax allowances. Under the PAYE system a proportion of these allowances is set against his pay each normal pay day. In order to determine the amount to be set against his pay the allowances are expressed in the form of a code which is used in conjunction with the Pay Adjustment Tables (Table A). Generally, a tax code number is arrived at by deleting the last digit in the sum representing the employee's tax free allowances (eg. the personal allowance of £3,765 becomes 376L).

The code number may also reflect other items. For example, it will be restricted to reflect benefits in kind, and small amounts of untaxed income. It may be restricted to recover unpaid Schedule E tax from earlier years. The married couple's allowance is also given through the code. In these two last instances an amount of tax is in point, so it is necessary to gross up the tax using the taxpayers estimated marginal rate of income tax.

Example

Adrian is a married man who earns £15,000 pa. He has benefits in kind of £560 and receives interest on War Loan of £175 each year. His unpaid Schedule E tax for 1995/96 was £57.50.

What is Adrian's PAYE code for 1996/97?

Adrian's PAYE code is 393H:

	£
Personal allowance	3,765
Benefit in kind	(560)
Standard interest £175 x $^{20}/_{24}$	(145)
Unpaid tax £57.50 x $^{100}/_{24}$	(239)
MCA 1,790 x 15% x $^{100}/_{24}$	1,118
Available allowances	£3,939

Each employee's code is determined by the Revenue and is amended by the Revenue as the employee's circumstances change. The code is normally notified to the employer on a code list or Form P6. The employer is obliged to act on the code notified to him until amended instructions are received from the Revenue, even though the employee may have appealed against the code.

To prevent unnecessary paperwork, the employee's code is carried forward from one tax year to the next. Where there is a change in the rate of personal allowance the Revenue may issue blanket instructions on form P9X instructing the employer to adjust all codes with a particular suffix from 6 April. For example form P9X(1996) instructed all suffix L codes to be increased by 24, to reflect the increase in the personal allowance by £240 from £3,525 to £3,765. Codes for specific employees may be changed by a list on form P9T from 6 April, in which case the instructions on form P9X are not also applied to these employees.

By using the code number in conjunction with the tax tables, an employee is generally given 1/52nd or 1/12th of his tax free allowances against each week's/month's pay. However because of the cumulative nature of PAYE, if an employee is first paid in, say, September, that month he will receive six months' allowances against his gross pay. In cases where the employee's previous PAYE history is not known (eg. he cannot produce form P45 from his previous employment), this could lead to under-deduction of tax. To avoid this, codes for the employees concerned are operated on a 'week 1/month 1' basis, so that only 1/52nd or 1/12th of the employee's allowances are available each week/month.

An employee's code may be any one of the following:

(a)   a code of one, two or three numbers followed by the suffix L, H, P T or V (a suffix code): for example 376L; Code L refers to the normal personal allowance (ie. without the MCA), Code H to the normal personal allowance where MCA is also due and Codes P, T or V apply where an age related allowance is due (eg. P for normal personal allowance in the 65 - 74 age range); or

(b)   the prefix D usually followed by the number 0; these codes apply on a one-off basis and require the use of higher rate tax tables D.

(c)   code BR, which means that tax will be deducted at the basic rate with no tax free allowances.

(d)   code NT, which means that no tax is to be deducted.

(e)   a code with a K prefix, followed by one to four numbers

'K' codes are in effect negative codes which increase taxable pay instead of reducing it. This has become more desirable administratively as benefits such as cars exceed the allowances due and lead to the need to issue Schedule E assessments to collect tax on the excess. The PAYE deducted under a K code could remove all of an employee's actual remuneration for a pay period. As this could cause hardship, the PAYE deducted on any pay day is not to exceed 50% of the amount of actual remuneration on that pay day.

Example

This example is new.

> Under Darren's K code for month 8 in 1996/97, he has a gross salary of £1,234 and tax to deduct of £738. The tax deduction for month 8 cannot exceed £617, 50% of his actual remuneration.

5.4.6 Other formalities: year end returns and employees leaving or joining

After the end of each tax year, the employer must provide each employee with a form P60. This shows total taxable emoluments for the year, tax deducted, code number, NI number and the employer's name and address. From 1996/97 the P60 must be provided by 31 May following the year of assessment (so that the employee can complete his self assessment tax return).

Also following the end of each tax year, the employer must send to the Inspector of Taxes the following items in respect of each employee:

(a)   within 44 days (ie. by 19 May):

   (i)   End of Year Return P14 (showing the same details as the P60);

   (ii)   Form P35 (summary of tax and NI deducted).

(b)   within 91 days (ie. by 6 July):

   (i)   Forms P11D (benefits in kind etc., for directors and employees paid £8,500+ p.a.);

   (ii)   Forms P9D (benefits in kind etc. for other employees).

From 1996/97 a copy of the form P11D must also be provided to the employee by 6 July. To ensure that the employee can complete their self assessment, the details to be shown on the P11D are to be extended, particularly with regard to entertainment expenses, payments from third parties, business mileage and mileage allowances and beneficial loans.

When an employee leaves (or dies), a certificate on form P45 (Particulars of Employee Leaving) must be prepared. This form shows the employee's code and details of his income and tax paid to date and is a four part form. One part is sent to the Revenue, and three parts handed to the employee. One of the parts (part 1A) is the employee's personal copy. If the employee takes up a new employment, he must hand the other two parts of the form P45 to the new employer. The new employer will fill in details of the new employment and send one part to the Revenue, retaining the other. The details of tax code, pay and tax deducted are then used by the new employer to calculate the PAYE due on the next payday.

If an employee joins with a form P45, the new employer can operate PAYE. If there is no P45 the employer still needs to operate PAYE. The employee is required to complete a form P46. If he declares that the employment is his first job since leaving education, or his only or main job, the emergency code (376L for 1996/97) applies, on a cumulative basis or week 1/month 1 basis respectively. Otherwise the employer must use code BR. The P46 is sent to the Revenue, unless the pay is below the PAYE and NIC thresholds, and the emergency code applies. In this case no PAYE is deductible until the pay exceeds the threshold.

5.4.7 Failure to deduct correct amount of PAYE

The Inspector has two courses of action available to him where the employer fails to deduct the correct amount of PAYE, or any PAYE at all. He can take steps to recover the tax from the employer, or he may, in certain circumstances, seek to recover the tax from the employee.

The more usual course of action is for the Inspector to issue a notice of determination on the employer (a 'Regulation 49 determination'). The Inspector will determine the amount of tax under-deducted to the best of his judgement and will issue a notice of determination. Unless the employer submits an appeal, the determination becomes final and conclusive 30 days after the date of issue.

Reg 49 SI
1993/744

Under a Regulation 49 determination, interest is payable under the IT (Employments) Regulations, and interest is charged from the 'reckonable date' (the 14th day after the end of the tax year concerned) and runs until payment. The rate of interest charged is the same as the rate applying for s.86 TMA 1970 purposes.

Regs 50 & 51 SI
1993/744

Where the Collector is satisfied that the employer took reasonable care to comply with his PAYE obligations and that any under-deduction of PAYE was due to an error made in good faith, the Collector can direct that the under-deduction should be recovered from the employee instead of the employer.

Reg 42(2) SI
1993/744

In addition, if the Board of Inland Revenue consider that the employee had received his emoluments knowing that the employer had wilfully under-deducted tax, the Board can direct that the under-deducted tax be recovered from the employee rather than the employer. Again, interest can be charged on the under-deducted tax.

Reg 42(3) SI
1993/744

Reg 42(4) SI
1993/744

5.4.8 Interest

Late paid PAYE/ NIC attracts interest (at the rate applying to late paid income tax) from 19 April following the end of the year of assessment in which the deduction was made.

There are provisions for paying repayment supplement on the same basis as applies for overpaid income tax if PAYE/NIC has been overpaid.

From 14 July 1995 the Revenue charge interest on tax recovered from employers in respect of amounts incorrectly paid tax free from PRP schemes.

Reg 7 SI
1995/917

5.4.9 Penalties

Late returns

A form P35 is due on 19 May after the end of the year of assessment. Under s.98A TMA 1970 a two tier penalty structure applies in respect of late forms P35.

s.98A TMA
1970

Where a form P35 is late, a penalty of £100 per month per 50 employees may be imposed. This penalty cannot be mitigated. This penalty ceases 12 months after the due date and a further penalty of up to 100% of the tax (and NIC) for the year which remains unpaid at 19 April may be imposed. This penalty can be mitigated.

For 1995/96 onwards, a 7 day extension to the due date of 19 May is allowed. Only returns not received on or before the last business day in the 7 day period following 19 May will incur penalties.

IRPR 14.9.95

Incorrect returns

Where a person has fraudulently or negligently submitted an incorrect form P35 the penalty is 100% of the tax (and NIC) attributable to the error. This penalty can be mitigated.

5.4.10 Summary

PAYE operates to deduct at source income tax due in respect of income from an office or employment. The employer has a duty to operate PAYE. Failure to comply could lead to a determination to recover the tax and penalties may be levied. Interest applies if the amount due has been formally determined. However, interest is charged automatically if any PAYE/NIC due for a year is unpaid on 19 April the following year. Penalties apply for late and incorrect end of year returns.

Each employee has a code number which reflects his personal circumstances, eg. reliefs available to him. This code number, together with deductions working sheets and tax tables, enables the employer to compute the amount of tax due in respect of each pay day. This computation is on a cumulative basis.

Form P45 is required to be prepared when an employee leaves the particular employment. At the end of each fiscal year, each employee should be provided with Form P60. This will enable the employee to complete his income tax return in so far as income from his employment is concerned. From 1996/97 the employee is also provided with a copy of form P11D or P9D, with details of assessable benefit, to enable his self assessment to be completed.

5.5   Tax deducted in the construction industry

5.5.1   Introduction

Subcontractors in the construction industry (that is casual workers operating what is known as the 'lump') have been a headache to the Revenue for many years. Evasion of tax, particularly by labour only subcontractors, is all too easy when remuneration is paid gross.

The Finance Act 1971 introduced a system of providing for deduction of tax at source on payments within the industry unless the contractor held an exemption certificate. Even this system proved inadequate and a brisk trade in exemption certificates followed! The Finance (No.2) Act 1975 substantially redrafted the provisions. The rules are contained in the Income Tax (sub-contractors in the construction industry) Regulations 1993. The current scheme is described below.

SI 1993/ 743

5.5.2   What the scheme applies to

The scheme applies to payments made by 'contractors' to 'subcontractors' for work involving construction, and also work involving installation, repairs, fitting, decorating and demolition.

ss.559-567

The terms 'contractor' and 'subcontractor' go very much wider than the meanings they normally have in the industry. The term 'contractor' includes:

(a)   persons whose trading activities include construction operations

(b)   property developers

(c)   local authorities and housing corporations

(d)   and even non-construction businesses (eg. a Bank or department store) if the business spends on average more than £250,000 a year on construction operations

Private householders having work done on their own premises are *not* contractors.

A 'sub contractor' is any business which has agreed to carry out construction operations for another business (the contractor).

5.5.3   How the scheme works

The scheme requires action to be taken whenever a contractor pays a subcontractor. Briefly, if the subcontractor holds a subcontractor's tax certificate (714) issued by the Inland Revenue, the contractor pays the subcontractor in full. A certificated sub-contractor is required to issue a voucher to a contractor who pays him without deduction of tax. If, on the other hand, the subcontractor does not hold a certificate the contractor makes a deduction of basic rate tax from the labour element of the payment and passes it over to the Inland Revenue. The sub contractor will be provided with form SC60 as evidence of the payment and the tax deduction. For payments made before 1 July 1996 the rate of deduction is 25%; thereafter the actual 1996/97 basic rate of 24% applies.

s.559

Where a subcontractor does not have a certificate, there are restrictions on the repayment of the tax deducted at source. It is treated as a credit against the income tax and NIC Class 4 contributions payable in respect of the profits of the building trade, and tax will only be repaid when there is no outstanding liability in respect of that trade for current or past years.

The same payment arrangements, including those where payments average less than £600 per month apply to the contractor as apply for PAYE collection.

Similarly, deductions for a year of assessment, whether monthly or quarterly, attract interest from 19 April following the year end if they remain unpaid. They also qualify for repayment supplement under the usual rules if overpayments of subcontractor deductions are made.

A return of payments to sub-contractors during the tax year must be made by 19 May following the tax year. If the return is late penalties, as for PAYE, are automatically imposed, at the rate of £100 per 50 persons, per month. This penalty ceases after 12 months, and a further (mitigable) penalty, of up to 100% of the tax not paid by 19 April following the year of assessment to which the return related, may be imposed. For 1995/96 a 7 day extension to the 19 May into deadline is permitted.

s.98A TMA 1970

5.5.4 Obtaining a sub contractor's exemption certificate

Certificates are issued to bona fide businesses in the industry which have a clean tax history going back at least three years. Further conditions include a business bank account, business premises and business accounts.

Individuals must show employment or self-employment for a continuous period of three years out of the last six years, and have a clean tax history from the start of that three year period to the date of application for a certificate. The Inland Revenue have discretion to ignore gaps of up to six months in the three year period.

School and college leavers can obtain a new certificate (714S) provided that they qualify by substituting their time at school or college for the continuous period of employment and self-employment as referred to above. Persons still not qualifying may obtain a certificate provided they can offer a bank guarantee.

The Inland Revenue will issue registration cards to persons who are or are likely to become sub contractors who do not qualify for 714 certificates. Any person intending to make payment to such a sub contractor without deduction of tax must inspect and record details of the registration card of that subcontractor or will be liable to a penalty of £3,000.

ss.566 (2A) & (2B)

5.5.5 Proposed changes

Various changes are to be made to the construction industry tax scheme. These changes will take place from a date to be appointed by the Treasury which will probably be 1 August 1998.

s.139 FA 1995 & Sch.27

In outline, the main changes will be:

IR Press Release 1 March 1995

(a) the rate of tax deduction from payments to sub-contractors who do not have an exemption certificate will be determined by the Treasury but will not exceed the basic rate for each year of assessment.

(b) all new sub-contractor exemption certificates issued or renewed from January 1995 until the early part of 1998 will show an expiry date of 31 July 1998. This is intended to allow a clean break between the old and new certificates.

(c) the present limited exemption certificates for school leavers and persons in respect of whom a bank guarantee has been given will be abolished.

(d)   the definition of a contractor will be extended to include government departments, certain other public bodies, and bodies designated by the Board of Inland Revenue which are carrying out statutory functions. A business outside the construction industry will not have to operate the scheme so long as its average expenditure on construction work does not exceed £1m (previously £250,000).

(e)   the present criminal sanction of a maximum £5,000 fine where a person gives false information etc. to obtain an exemption certificate, or disposes of or illegally possesses such a certificate, will be replaced by a tax penalty of up to £3,000.

(f)   exemption certificates will only be issued passing an annual business turnover test.

(g)   an individual applying for an exemption certificate will no longer have to have worked in the UK for a period of three years. However, in such cases applicants will have to show that they have not been working or have been out of the UK. Where an applicant has been abroad, he will have to satisfy the Inland Revenue that he has complied with the tax laws of the country in which he was resident. (NB: there is no change to the previous requirement for an applicant to have complied with all his UK tax obligations throughout the period of three years ending with the date of his application.)

5.5.6   Summary

Special provisions apply to payments made by 'contractors' to 'sub-contractors' (as defined in the legislation) in the construction industry. If the sub-contractor holds the appropriate Revenue certificate, payments may be made gross. Otherwise, the payment should be made under the deduction of tax. Fairly stringent conditions must be met before a certificate will be issued. Any tax withheld will be repaid in limited circumstances only.

The impact of the forthcoming changes to the sub-contractors scheme should not be under-estimated. At present some 80% of sub-contractors can obtain a tax exemption certificate. From August 1998 this figure is likely to fall to 20%.

5.6   Other payments made net

5.6.1   Fees paid to international entertainers and sportsmen

In order to counter the non-payment of tax by visiting non-resident entertainers and sportsmen, rules levying withholding tax on the UK income of such non-residents apply.

ss.555-558

Where a person makes a payment of £1,000 or more to a non-resident entertainer or sportsman in connection with a 'relevant activity' ('connected payment'), the payer must account to the Revenue for basic rate income tax thereon.

SI 1987/530

The term 'entertainer' is widely defined in the Regulations. It includes individuals who give performances in their character as entertainers or sportsmen in any kind of entertainment or sport. 'Entertainment or sport' includes any activity of a physical kind, performed by such an individual, which is or may be made available to the public. The Regulations therefore cover payments made to tennis players, golfers, racing drivers, pop and film stars, actors and musicians.

SI 1987/530
Reg 2(1)

The rules apply not only to payments in cash, eg. fees, prize money, etc., but also to transfers of assets, eg. a car or sports equipment. 'Relevant activities' include both actual performances, eg. the giving of a concert, and appearances designed to promote the forthcoming event. Participation by the entertainer, etc. in or for any film or video or for radio or television is also a relevant activity.

s.555(2)&(3)
SI 1987/530
Reg 6

The payer is required to account for tax regardless of whether the payment is made to the entertainer himself or, for example, to his personal holding company or a settlement created by him.

SI 1987/530
Reg 7

If the connected payment is in cash, the tax payment is simply calculated at the basic rate (or such lower rate as may be agreed with the Revenue - see below).

Example

> Oscar, a Hungarian pianist, comes to London to play in a concert. He is paid £5,000 by the concert promoter. The promoter must deduct basic rate tax of £1,200 (ie. £5,000 x 24%) from the payment so that Oscar receives the balance of £3,800. £1,200 is paid by the promoter to the Revenue.

If there is a transfer of *assets* to the entertainer, the value of the asset, is treated as an amount from which basic rate tax has been withheld. The value of the asset is defined as the net cost to the provider. The payer's liability to tax is therefore computed by grossing up the value of the non-cash payment and applying the basic rate of tax to the gross equivalent (or such lower rate as may be agreed - see below).

Example

> Paul is an Australian tennis player. As part of his prize for winning a tournament in the UK, he receives a car which cost the tournament organisers £9,000.
>
> The organisers must account for UK income tax as follows:
>
> | | |
> |---|---|
> | Cost of car | £9,000 |
> | Grossed up @ 100/76 = | £11,842 |
> | UK income tax: £11,842 x 24% = | £2,842 |

In so far as accounting for the tax withheld is concerned, the Regulations provide for a return system, similar to the quarterly accounting system for companies (see your Paper IIIb: Corporation Tax study text). A person who makes a connected payment is required to make a return for the period in which the payment is made. The return periods end on 30 June, 30 September, 31 December and 5 April in each tax year. The return, together with the amount of tax due, must be submitted to the Revenue within 14 days after the end of the return period. There is also provision for the Revenue to raise assessments for the tax.

SI 1987/530
Regs 9 & 10

As we have seen, the withholding tax is normally equal to 24% of the cash payment or grossed-up equivalent of the non-cash payment. If, however, it can be shown to the Revenue's satisfaction that the ultimate UK tax liability will be less than 24% of the gross payments to the entertainer, etc. it may be possible to arrange for a lower rate of withholding to apply (or nil). The arrangement will be between the payer, the entertainer or the person receiving the payment (eg. the entertainer's holding company) and the Revenue, and is dependent upon the production of forecasts of income, expenses, etc. Obviously, there could be a distinct cash flow advantage in seeking such an arrangement.

SI 1987/530
Reg 4

Example

Robert, an American actor, brings his 'one man show' to the UK. The show is to run for two months, during which period Robert expects to receive gross income of £250,000. The budget for the show incorporates estimated expenses of £215,000.

If no arrangement is made with the Revenue, the cash position at the end of the two-month run is as follows:

	£
Gross receipts	250,000
Less: 24% withholding tax	(60,000)
	190,000
Less: expenses	(215,000)
Cash shortfall	£(25,000)

If, however, Robert arranges for tax to be withheld in accordance with the estimated net profit from the venture, the cash position is as follows:

	£
Gross receipts	250,000
Less: expenses	(215,000)
	35,000
Less: 24% withholding tax on £35,000	(8,400)
Cash surplus	£26,600

Without the arrangement, Robert will have to submit a claim for repayment of the excess tax deducted of £51,600 (ie. £60,000 - 8,400).

5.6.2 Other situations in which tax must be deducted

Certain payments usually made gross must be paid net of basic rate tax where the *recipient* is *not resident* in the UK. The payer must account for the tax to the Revenue, under s.349(1).

Rents payable

Rents payable *directly* to non-residents prior to 6 April 1996 had to be paid net of basic rate tax. As the tax withheld related to gross income, the deduction usually lead to an overpayment of tax which the non-resident had to reclaim. Care had to be taken to make the correct deduction on each payment of rent made as any under deduction could not be adjusted for on a future rent instalment even if made in the same fiscal year (see case below).

s.43 (now repealed)

Rents paid *via UK agents* prior to 6 April 1996 were paid gross, the agents being assessable to tax on the net profit, at the higher rate as well as basic rate tax.

s.78 TMA 1970 (now repealed)

For rent paid on or after 6 April 1996 regulations enable the Revenue to authorise the payment of rent without deduction of tax if the non resident landlord comes within the self assessment regime. The regulations also govern the deduction of tax, the making of returns and the provision of tax deduction certificates. These rules apply for 1996/97 onwards in order to harmonise with the self assessment provisions.

SI 1995/2902

s.42A

Tenbry Investments Ltd v Peugeot Talbot Motor Co Ltd (1992) STC 791 (ChD)

Tenbry (the landlord) was resident in Jersey and let premises to Peugeot (the tenant). Peugeot made four payments under the lease to Tenbry but failed to deduct tax under s.349(1) ICTA 1988. Peugeot then discovered it ought to have deducted tax and so did not pay the next instalment to Tenbry, claiming it was entitled to set-off the payment against the tax it should have deducted. The landlord sued for unpaid rent.

Held: the right to deduct tax was in respect of each payment as it arose and was lost in respect of that payment if it was made gross. The landlord's action therefore succeeded.

Copyright royalties

Copyright royalties paid 'by or through any person' in the UK to a non-resident must be paid net of basic rate tax.

s.536

Patent rights

Where a non-resident sells UK patent rights, the purchaser must deduct basic rate tax from the purchase monies. A UK patent is a patent granted under UK laws.

s.524(2)

5.6.3 Summary

Persons making payments to visiting non-resident entertainers and sportsmen will be required to deduct and account for income tax thereon. Unless alternative arrangements are made with the Revenue, tax at the basic rate should be deducted from cash payments and, in the case of payments in kind, the cost to the provider should be grossed up and basic rate tax calculated on that gross value.

Certain payments which are usually made gross should have basic rate tax withheld at source if the recipient is non-UK resident, eg. rents paid direct to non-residents, copyright royalties. However, where a non-resident landlord elects to be taxed under self assessment rents may be paid gross.

5.7   Illustrative question

You are required to state:

(1)   the circumstances in which a trader should deduct tax at source under the construction industry tax deduction scheme; and   (9)

(2)   the matters with which the Inland Revenue must be satisfied before they will issue a sub-contractor's certificate.   (6)

Total (15)

Solution

(a)   There is a requirement to deduct tax under the construction industry tax deduction scheme where a contractor carrying on a business which includes construction work makes any payment to a sub-contractor in respect of construction operations in the UK unless the sub-contractor has a sub-contractor's certificate.

From 1 July 1996 onwards the deduction to be made is at the rate of 24%, being the basic rate of tax, and this should be deducted from all of the payment (excluding VAT) other than that which represents the cost of materials.

A contractor is any person who is carrying on a business which includes construction operations; any local authority; any development corporation or new town commission; the Housing Corporation; any housing association or trust; the Scottish Special Housing Association; and the Northern Ireland Housing Executive. It can include a person who is himself a sub-contractor.

A contractor is also any person in business if his annual expenditure on construction operations average in excess of £250,000 over a three year period ending with his last period of accounts. To cease to be a contractor once in the basis just described it is necessary to show that in each of the past three years such expenditure fell short of £250,000.

Construction operations are widely defined and include:

(i)   installing heating, lighting and drainage systems

(ii)   internal cleaning of buildings in the course of their construction, alteration or repair

(iii)   internal and external decorating

(iv)   constructing, altering, repairing or demolishing buildings, walls and roadworks

They exclude inter alia the following:

(i)   professional services of architects

(ii)   sign-writing and advertisements

(iii)   security and public address system

(iv)   fitting of carpets

(b) To receive payment for services without deduction of tax, a sub-contractor requires a Tax Certificate issued by the Inland Revenue. The Revenue will issue such a certificate if they are satisfied on a number of factors which include:

(i) the sub-contractor is carrying on a business in the UK

(ii) the business is a construction business

(iii) operated with proper premises, equipment, stock and other facilities

(iv) conducted through a bank account

(v) the sub-contractor must have a satisfactory record of compliance of all taxation, NIC and Company Act obligations in the three years prior to the application

(vi) an individual also has to meet an additional requirement that he must have been employed or traded in the UK for a continuous period of at least three of the previous six years

The Revenue may insist that the directors of a company applicant also satisfy the additional requirements imposed on individual applicants.

The Revenue recognise that the requirement regarding trading in the UK for three years cannot be met by people leaving full-time education. Special certificates can therefore be issued which permit payments in full by the contractor up to a specified weekly amount. A special certificate will be issued if the individual has left school or college and can show that in the previous six years he was in full-time education for a continuous period of three years up to the date of the application or if there was a gap after the three years up to the application a reasonable explanation for this is provided. Alternatively a special certificate will be provided if it can be arranged for a bank to guarantee payment of the tax on the amounts received in full by reason of the special certificate.

QUESTIONS

1. Henry owns £10,000 9% loan stock issued by the government of Ruritania. Ruritania levies an 18% withholding tax on interest payments which are made half-yearly on 31 March and 30 September. How much UK income tax would be deducted in respect of interest paid on 30 September 1996 if the payment is made through a paying agent who holds the stock certificates?

2. Robert has a long-term loan from his Aunt Matilda who is resident in Australia. The principal is £8,000 and Robert agrees to pay interest at a rate of 8% per annum. How much does Aunt Matilda receive each year? (Assume 1996/97 rates of tax continue to apply.)

3. James has an endowment mortgage of £45,000 to purchase his main residence, which was taken up on 6 May 1990. If the current rate of interest is 8%, what is his monthly interest payment during 1996/97?

4. Luke has taxable income in 1996/97, after the personal allowance, of £500. During the year he pays £600 net to charity under a four year deed of covenant. What is Luke's liability under s.349 ICTA 1988?

5. Melanie receives a tax-free annuity of £760 per annum under the terms of her late uncle's will. Her total income in 1996/97 amounts to £2,200, before the personal allowance of £3,765. What adjustment is required between Melanie and the executors?

6. Jane purchased a life annuity in 1980, when her expectation of life was 35 years. The purchase price was £14,000. How much of the annuity is treated as a return of capital?

7. Albert, who is 70, takes out a loan of £25,000, secured on his house, in order to purchase a life annuity. Is the loan eligible for inclusion in the MIRAS scheme?

8. Baggins Ltd a company with 75 employees, paid PAYE of £8,000 due for the tax month to 5 April 1997 on 1 June 1997. The end of year return was not submitted until 23 July 1997. What penalties and interest are due?

9. What would your answer be to question 8 if the end of year return was submitted on 20 May 1998?

10. On 13 October 1996, a contractor pays a sub-contractor, who does not hold a tax exemption certificate, £27,000. What action is the contractor obliged to take?

11. On 24 August 1996 Star Promotions Ltd gives a Japanese golf player equipment costing £3,750 as part of his prize for winning a competition in the UK. How much income tax must the company pay over to the Revenue, and on what date?

SOLUTIONS

1. £27.00 (ie. £450 x (24% - 18%)).   (5.2.1)

2. £486.40 (ie. £8,000 x 8% x 76%).   (5.2.2)

3. £270, ie.   £

    £30,000 x 8% x 85% x $^1/_{12}$ =   170
    £15,000 x 8% x $^1/_{12}$=   100
    ──────
                                                                                          £ 270
                                                                                         (5.2.3)

4. £69 ie. (£(600 x 100/76) - 500) x 24%.   (5.1.2)

5. She must repay to them the basic rate tax recovered of £240.00 (ie. £760 x
    24/76).   (5.1.5)

6. $\dfrac{£14,000}{35}$ ie. £400 per annum.   (5.1.6)

7. Yes (and relief of 24% will be allowed, not 15%).   (5.2.3)

8. Interest 20.4.97 - 1.6.97   £

    $^{42}/_{365}$ x £8,000 x 6.25%   57.53
    Penalties (3 months) 3 x £100 x 2   600.00
    ──────
                                                                                      £657.53
                                                                                (5.4.8 and 5.4.9)

9.   £

    Interest (as before)   57.53
    Penalties 12 x £100 x 2   2,400.00
    Tax based penalty (mitigable)   8,000.00
    ──────
                                                                                    £10,457.53
                                                                                         (5.4.9)

10. He must deduct tax of 24% from the payment, ie. £6,480, and pay it over
    to the Revenue.   (5.5.3)

11. £1,184 (ie. £3,750 x 24/76), payable on or before 14 October 1996.   (5.6.1)

SESSION 6

THE ADMINISTRATION OF INHERITANCE TAX

By the end of this session you will be able to:

*   identify the persons responsible for reporting chargeable transfers of value and the time limits for delivering an IHT 'account'

*   identify the normal due date for payment of IHT and explain the interest provisions where IHT is paid late

*   explain the instalment option available for payment of IHT

*   show the occasions on which penalties may be imposed

References: IHTA 1984 unless otherwise stated

6.1   Introduction

6.1.1   General

This session is concerned with the detailed rules for the administration of IHT. Those relating to payment of the tax, instalments and interest are of considerable practical importance.

6.1.2   Capital Taxes Office

IHT is under the care and management of the Inland Revenue. It is administered by the Capital Taxes Office (CTO). The Capital Taxes Offices are headed by a Controller (Registrar in Scotland).

s.215

6.2 Tax returns

6.2.1 Persons responsible

The persons required to report chargeable transfers of value (whether or not tax is due on them) are: s.216(1)

(a) in the case of death, the personal representatives;

(b) in the case of trusts, the trustees;

(c) in the case of a potentially exempt transfer that becomes chargeable because of the transferor's subsequent death within seven years, the transferee;

(d) in the case of a gift with reservation of benefit which is treated as a transfer on death, the transferee;

(e) in any other case (eg. a chargeable lifetime transfer), the transferor.

Note that the personal representatives are responsible for delivery of an account of all the property in the deceased's estate for IHT purposes, other than property deemed to be included in the estate as a gift with reservation of benefit. Thus the PRs must include in their account property in which the deceased had an interest in possession and jointly owned property which passes by survivorship.   s.216(3)

The persons responsible must render an 'account' for the transfer within the following time limits:

(a) personal representatives: within 12 months from the end of the month in which death occurs (or, if later, within 3 months of first acting as PRs). In practice, however, since an account must be submitted before an application for grant of probate/letters of administration can be made, the account is usually submitted within a few months of death;   s.216(6)(a)

(b) transferees of PETs: 12 months from the end of the month in which the transferor's death occurs. Again, in practice, details of these will be included by the personal representatives on their form and so a separate form is not required (s.216(5)).   s.216(6)(aa)

(c) donees of gifts with reservation: 12 months from the end of the month in which the death occurs (unless included by personal representatives).   s.216(6)(ab)

(d) any other persons: within 12 months from the end of the month in which the transfer is made (or, if later, within 3 months of the date on which they become liable):   s.216(6)(c)

The forms of account to complete for personal representatives applying for a grant of representation are as follows:

(a) account where deceased died UK domiciled: IHT 200.

(b) account where deceased died foreign domiciled: IHT 201.

(c) account where estate is 'small': IHT 202.

To use form IHT 202 (small estates) the following conditions must be satisfied: IR booklet IHT 210

(i) the total gross value of the estate before exemptions and reliefs does not exceed twice the nil band (ie. twice £200,000);

(ii) the deceased died UK domiciled;

(iii) the estate includes only property passing under the deceased's will or by intestacy or beneficially by survivorship;

(iv) all assets are UK situate;

    (v)   no lifetime transfers chargeable to IHT (including PETs) must have been made by the deceased in the previous seven years nor must the deceased have had any interest in settled property;

    (vi)   the net value of the estate must not exceed the nil rate band.

A form IHT 100 is required for transfers of value including:

(a)   PETs which become chargeable.

(b)   gifts of property other than PETs.

(c)   terminations of interests in possession.

(d)   other chargeable lifetime transfers.

A form IHT 101 is required for chargeable events involving settlements without an interest in possession.

6.2.2   Excepted transfers and excepted estates

There is no need to render an 'account' of a chargeable lifetime transfer which is treated as an 'excepted transfer', that is it falls below the reporting threshold. This applies where the total value of an individual's chargeable transfers in any one year does not exceed £10,000, and where his cumulative total of transfers in the last 10 years does not exceed £40,000.
    SI 1981 No 1440 and s.256(1)

An account need not be delivered in respect of a person's death if his estate is an 'excepted estate'. In order to be an excepted estate:
    SI 1995/1459, 1460, 1461 and s.256(1)

(a)   the total gross value of the estate must be no more than £145,000; and

(b)   the estate contains no settled property; and

(c)   not more than £15,000 (of the £145,000) may consist of property situated outside the UK; and

(d)   the deceased made no PETs or chargeable lifetime transfers in the seven years before his death; and

(e)   the deceased made no gifts with reservation of benefit where the reservation exists at death or ended in the seven years before death; and

(f)   the deceased died domiciled in the UK.

The £145,000 limit for excepted estates apply to deaths on or after 6 April 1995 where the account is delivered on or after 1 July 1995. The previous limit was £125,000.

6.3 Assessments, payment of tax and interest

6.3.1 Assessments

The form of assessment is produced in duplicate, the second part being a remittance document calling for payment to the Inland Revenue.

Where no IHT is payable no assessment is made but a simple letter is sent by the CTO confirming the figures and agreeing the cumulative total of chargeable transfers.

Note that the making of an assessment for IHT does not have the significance of an assessment for, say, income tax. The tax will be due on the normal due date (and interest will usually start to run from that date) regardless of whether an assessment is issued.

6.3.2 Normal due date

Tax must normally be paid within the following time limits:

(a)   The tax in respect of chargeable lifetime transfers is payable at the later of:

    (i)   six months from the end of the month in which the transfer is made; and   *s.226(1)*

    (ii)   30 April in the following tax year.

Example

Chargeable lifetime transfer made	Due date for IHT
1 - 5 April 1996	31.10.96
6 Apr - 31 Oct 1996	30.4.97
November 1996	31.5.97
December 1996	30.6.97
January 1997	31.7.97
February 1997	31.8.76
March 1997	30.9.97

(b)   By personal representatives - on delivery of their account to the Revenue (this is a prerequisite for the granting of probate or letters of administration, para 6.2.1). In practice, the Revenue only require that tax is paid at this time in respect of property where tax is not to be paid in instalments (see para 6.3.3). The first instalment of tax on instalment option property where the instalment option is claimed is due at the end of six months following the end of the month of death. If, of course, the grant of probate is obtained after the end of six months following the end of the month of death, the personal representatives must also pay any instalments which have already fallen due and are unpaid.   *s.226(2)*

The personal representatives are liable for tax on property which passes by will or intestacy and jointly owned property which passes by survivorship. They are not liable for tax on property in which the deceased had an interest in possession unless such property vests in them, which will not usually be the case.

(c)   The additional tax payable, due to the death of the transferor, on lifetime transfers within seven years of the death is due within six months from the end of the month in which death occurs.   *s.226(3), (3A) & (3B)*

6.3.3 Instalment option

On election, tax may be paid in respect of certain property by ten equal yearly instalments, starting on the normal due date for payment of the IHT as set out above or, if the chargeable transfer was made on death, six months after the end of the month of death. s.227(3)

The instalment option can only be claimed for:

(a) a death transfer; s.227(1)(a)

(b) a chargeable lifetime transfer where the donee has undertaken to pay the IHT liability on the transfer; s.227(1)(b)

(c) any lifetime transfer (PET or chargeable) where IHT or additional IHT is payable because of the donor's death within seven years. In this case the right to pay by instalments is only available if: s.227 (1A)

    (i) the donee has retained the original property transferred until the donor's (or the donee's earlier) death; or

    (ii) the original property has been replaced by property qualifying for business or agricultural property relief; and in addition s.227(1C)

    (iii) if the transfer is of unquoted shares they must remain unquoted until the donor's (or the donee's earlier) death. s.228(3A)
s272

(d) a charge on trustees of a discretionary trust provided the property continues to be settled property. s.227(1)(c)

Property to which the instalment option may apply is: s.227(2)

(a) land of any description, wherever situated; s.227(2)(a)

(b) shares or securities of a company which the transferor controlled immediately before the transfer; ss.227(2)(b) &
228(1)(a)

(c) shares or securities of an unquoted company: s.227(2)(b)

    (i) where on a death the IHT chargeable on their value and other instalment assets, excluding timber, is at least 20% of the IHT chargeable on the death; or s.228(1)(b) & (2)

    (ii) where IHT cannot be paid in one sum without undue hardship; s.228(1)(c)

(d) shares of an unquoted company where the value attributable to the shares is over £20,000 (before business property relief, if any) and the nominal value of the shares is not less than 10% of the nominal value of all the shares in issue at time of transfer; or, if the shares are ordinary shares their nominal value is not less than 10% of the nominal value of all ordinary shares in issue at the time of transfer (ordinary shares include participating preference and convertible shares); ss.227(2)(b) &
228(1)(d)& (3)

(e) a business or an interest in a business (such as a sole trader or partner) to the extent of the net value of the business assets; s.227(2)(c) & (7)

In determining whether a person has 'control' of a company, shares held as related property (eg. held by his spouse) must be included, as must shares in a trust in which he has an interest in possession. Control means sufficient voting power to control all the matters that affect the company. s.227(4)

In the context of instalment option assets, 'unquoted' means not quoted on a recognised Stock Exchange. 'Unquoted' therefore includes shares on the Unlisted Securities Market (USM) and on the Alternative Investment Market (AIM). s.227(1AA) and
s.228(5)

Since business property relief for a business or an interest in a business will be 100%, assets in categories (c), (d) and (e) above are only likely to bear IHT in any case where the two year minimum ownership requirement (for BPR) has not been satisfied. Where 100% BPR is available the instalment option is obviously irrelevant.

Any unpaid instalments become due for payment immediately the instalment property is sold or disposed of by a chargeable lifetime transfer. An apportionment is made where only part of the property is sold or disposed of, and the subsequent instalments are reduced accordingly.

Example

Miss Allen died on 8 May 1996 and bequeathed 50,000 shares in a controlled company to her nephew, and the IHT liability arising is £20,000. The executor elects to pay the tax by instalments, ie. by ten annual payments of £2,000, commencing 30 November 1996 (the date six months after the month of death).

The nephew sells 40,000 shares on 30 December 1998. IHT due for payment on 30 December 1998 is:

	£
Tax due on 50,000 shares	20,000
Deduct payments (3 x £2,000)	(6,000)
Tax outstanding at 30.12.98	£14,000
Due on 30.12.98: 4/5 x £14,000	£11,200

The balance of £2,800 continues to be paid by annual instalments on 30 November each year. Since seven anniversaries remain, each instalment is:

1/7 x £2,800 =	£400

6.3.4 Interest

In the event of IHT on any transfer not being settled on the due date simple interest on the overdue tax will currently be charged at 5% from (and including) the day after the normal due date to the day of payment. The exception to this rule is in respect of tax paid by personal representatives (see para 6.3.2). Interest will run from the day after the end of 6 months after the end of the month of death, not from the actual due date which is usually on delivery of the account. `s.233`

Interest rates from July 1991 have varied as follows:

6 July 1991 to 5 November 1992	8%
6 November 1992 to 5 December 1992	6%
6 December 1992 to 5 January 1994	5%
6 January 1994 to 5 October 1994	4%
6 October 1994 onwards	5%

Interest rates will be supplied in the exam where they are needed. `s.235`

An overpayment of IHT will attract repayment with interest from the date the Revenue receives the payment to the date of repayment at similar rates. Where interest was paid on late tax which is later repaid, the repayment will consist of overpaid tax plus the interest wrongly paid thereon, and both carry interest from payment to repayment.

Interest paid is non tax allowable while interest received is tax free. `ss.233(3) & 235(2)`

6.3.5 Interest on instalments

Where tax is payable by instalments there are two alternative rules relating to interest due. In the first case the instalments are 'interest bearing' so interest on the unpaid portion of the tax will be added to each instalment and paid accordingly. This interest runs from the day after the normal due date of payment applicable where payment is not made by instalments; ie. in the case of the first instalment interest is charged on that instalment only from the day after the due date to the day the Revenue receives the payment. In the case of each subsequent instalment interest is charged on the whole unpaid portion of the tax.

s.234(1)

This first rule applies to unpaid instalments of tax relating to land (except land which qualifies for agricultural property relief) and to shares in an investment or property dealing company (except where the business of the company is that of a market maker or discount house in the UK).

s.234(2),(3)

Where the second rule applies the instalments are 'interest free'. In this case if the instalments are paid on time no interest is charged. This second rule applies to instalments of tax due on shares and securities (other than those mentioned above), a business (or interest therein), woodlands or property attracting agricultural property relief ie. for the IHT due on these assets, interest is only charged if the instalment itself is late.

Example

Paul died on 8 August 1996 leaving assets as follows:

	£
Cash, life policies and bank accounts	30,000
Quoted securities	80,000
Freehold house	120,000
Business 'Paul's antiques'	180,000
	£410,000

He had made no lifetime transfers. The antiques business had been owned for less than two years so BPR is not available. The tax on the non-instalment option property was paid on 1 January 1997. The first instalment was paid on 12 March 1997 and the second on 11 March 1998.

IHT due is 40% (£410,000 - £200,000) = £84,000

This is allocated:

	£
Non-instalment property (cash etc and quoted securities)	
£84,000 x $\frac{110,000}{410,000}$	22,537
Interest bearing instalments (house)	
£84,000 x $\frac{120,000}{410,000}$	24,585
Interest free instalments (business)	
£84,000 x $\frac{180,000}{410,000}$	36,878
	£84,000

Payment on 1 January 1997

Non instalment option property	£22,537

Date after which interest runs is 28 February 1997 - no interest due

Payment on 12 March 1997 (due 28 February 1997)   £

1st instalment $\frac{1}{10}$ x (£24,585 + £36,878)   6,146.30

Interest on late instalment

$\frac{12}{365}$ x 5% x £6,146.30   10.10

Tax and interest due   £6,156.40

Payment on 11 March 1998 (due 28 February 1998)   £

Interest on outstanding amount of tax due by interest bearing instalments

$\frac{9}{10}$ x £24,585 x 5%   1,106.33

2nd instalment due   6,146.30

Interest on late instalment

$\frac{11}{365}$ x 5% x £6,146.30   9.26

Tax and interest due   £7,261.89

This assumes that the rate of interest on unpaid tax will remain at 5%.

6.3.6 Inland Revenue charge

Where there is unpaid IHT, including interest, a charge (ie. a security) on the property concerned is imposed in favour of the Board. Such a charge is restricted in certain circumstances, the most important of which covers moveable or personal property beneficially owned by the deceased where the transfer arises on death. Property which was the subject of a PET made in the seven years before death and which has been sold is not subject to the Inland Revenue charge, but if the property has been otherwise disposed of, then the charge switches from the property to the consideration.   s.237

6.3.7 Disclosure

The Revenue can, by notice in writing and with the consent of a Special Commissioner, require any person (with some exceptions for solicitors and barristers with respect to their clients) to give information in connection with a chargeable transfer for the purposes of IHT.   s.219

A person who in the course of his trade or profession (other than the profession of a barrister) has been concerned with the making of a non-UK resident settlement (other than a settlement made by will) by a UK domiciled settlor must make a return of the names and addresses of the settlor and the trustees within three months of the making of the settlement. This requirement should be pointed out to clients wishing to make such settlements.   s.218

A settlement is regarded as non-UK resident unless the general administration of the settlement is ordinarily carried on in the UK and a majority of the trustees are resident in the UK.   s.218(3)

The Revenue can disclose information to the revenue authorities of other EC member states regarding a taxpayer's tax liability to those states. However, until a day appointed by statutory instrument, notices under s.219 cannot be used to collect information which is not needed by the UK authorities themselves but is merely requested by the tax authorities of other EC member states.   s.77 FA 1978   s.125 FA 1990

6.3.8 Notice of determination

The CTO can issue a Notice of Determination (in effect a notice of assessment) where an individual fails to pay or make returns, or where the CTO needs more information before it can proceed. The problem for the CTO is that it cannot take legal proceedings for recovery of tax and interest unless the amount has been agreed in writing, or has been specified in a Notice.

s.221(1)

The CTO will issue a Notice where it thinks a transfer has occurred and this Notice may include details of:

s.221(2)

(a)   the date of the transfer in question;

(b)   the value transferred;

(c)   the donor;

(d)   the amount of the IHT;

(e)   details of any interest on tax paid late or on an overpayment;

(f)   any other relevant information;

(g)   the appeal procedure (30 days).

The Notice may be used to confirm an estimated account or return.

s.222(1)

6.3.9 Appeals

Appeals against a Notice of Determination are to be made within 30 days in writing to the Special Commissioners, except on the question of land in the UK when appeals are to be made to the Lands Tribunal. By agreement between the parties, or on application by the taxpayer to the High Court, appeal may be made direct to the High Court where a question of law is at issue.

s.222

If the question of the value of land arises in the course of an appeal hearing before the Special Commissioners or the High Court this may be referred to the Lands Tribunal without recourse to a separate appeal.

s.222(4A)

6.3.10 Certificate of discharge

Provided a person liable for any tax has supplied the necessary account and paid all tax due, a certificate of discharge *will* be given on application where the transfer was made on death, or the transferor has died, and a certificate *may* be given on application in any other case. Except in the case of fraud or a failure to disclose material facts, the certificate discharges all persons from any further claim for tax on the property transferred. It cannot be issued until the tax liability has been finally settled.

s.239

It is not normally possible to apply for a certificate of discharge until two years after the transfer, or, in the case of a PET, until two years after the transferor has died, but the Board may allow an application at an earlier time after the death if it is clear that all the tax in respect of the transfer has been paid.

6.3.11 PRs relationship to lifetime transfers

PRs should obtain details of any chargeable lifetime transfers or PETs made by the deceased in the seven years prior to his death. If there are such transfers, they will affect the liability of the PRs on the death estate. In addition, the PRs are jointly liable, with the donee of any lifetime transfer, to pay the tax due on that lifetime transfer. In practice, the Revenue will try to collect the tax from the donee, but if this fails, the Revenue will collect the tax from the PRs.

This could lead to unexpected liabilities on the PRs. Therefore the Revenue have stated that they will not normally pursue the PRs for inheritance tax if the PRs have made the fullest enquiries that are reasonably practicable in the circumstances to discover lifetime transfers, and having done all in their power to make a full disclosure of them to the Revenue, *and* obtained a certificate of discharge *and* distributed the estate before a lifetime transfer comes to light.

IR letter in Law Society's Gazette 13.3.91

6.3.12 Penalties

Penalties may be incurred for:

(a)	fraudulent delivery of an account - not exceeding £50 plus twice the tax;	s.247(1)(2)
(b)	negligent delivery of an account - not exceeding £50 plus the tax;	s.247(1)(2)
(c)	failure to deliver an account or to comply with a notice - not exceeding £50 plus £10 per day following the award of the penalty;	s.245
(d)	giving false information - not exceeding £500 (fraud), £250 (negligence);	s.247(3)
(e)	failing to appear as a witness - not exceeding £50.	s.246

6.4 Summary

Various persons can be required to report transfers (submit an account) including personal representatives, trustees, and transferees as well as transferors.

Small transfers need not be reported. Small simple 'excepted' estates also need not be reported if the total value is below £145,000, of which no more than £15,000 is foreign property, the estate contains no settled property and the deceased made no lifetime gifts in the last seven years.

The due dates for payment of IHT are the later of 30 April following the tax year or six months after the end of the month in which a lifetime chargeable transfer takes place. On death the IHT must be paid to obtain probate, and any additional liability arising on PETs or on lifetime chargeable transfers is payable six months after the end of the month in which death occurs. This liability falls on the transferee.

In certain situations the IHT in respect of transfers of some types of property may be paid by 10 equal annual instalments.

Interest on unpaid tax and on repayment of overpaid tax is at the rate of 5% pa. with effect from 6 October 1994.

Instalments may be interest free, so they carry interest only if late, or interest bearing, so that in addition to interest if late, the outstanding balance carries interest from the due date for the first instalment. The interest accrued each year is added to the instalment payable at the end of that year.

6.5   Example

(a)   On 1 June 1995 Alan gave to discretionary trustees a sum of money in respect of which £9,400 inheritance tax was payable. This tax was paid on 1 July 1996.

(b)   On 1 June 1996 Bethan died leaving property in respect of which £20,000 inheritance tax was paid on the extraction of probate on 1 March 1997.

(c)   It was subsequently discovered that in (b) above, a debt of £20,000 was due from Bethan which, with other amendments which also came to light, meant that £5,000 too much tax had been paid. The overpaid tax was repaid on 1 September 1997.

(d)   Tony died on 15 June 1996 leaving property which included land valued at £50,000 in respect of which inheritance tax of £12,000 was payable, and a 20% holding of shares in a trading company valued at £60,000 and in respect of which inheritance tax of £14,400 was payable. BPR was not available as the shares had not been held for 2 years. The executors decided to pay the tax on these two items by 10 yearly instalments and submitted the accounts in respect of the first and second instalments on 31 December 1997 together with the tax due.

Calculate the interest payable or repayable for each of the above, giving your reasons for the calculations.

Solution

(a)   The tax is due on 30 April 1996. The amount of interest due is therefore 62 days on £9,400 as follows:

1 May - 1 July 1996 $\frac{62}{365}$ x 5% x £9,400 =   £79.84

(b)   The tax is due after the end of the six month period beginning with the end of the month in which the chargeable transfer was made, that is six months after the end of June 1996, ie. 31 December 1996. Interest runs from 1 January 1997 to 1 March (60 days): ie. interest due is 60 days on £20,000 at 5% per annum, ie.   £164.38

(c)   The overpaid tax of £5,000 is repaid on 1 September 1997. It is therefore necessary to repay the interest which has been charged on this sum, ie. 60 days on £5,000 at 5% per annum, ie. £41.10. It is also necessary to pay interest on the overpaid tax and interest of £41.10 from the date of payment of the tax(1 March 1997) to the date of issue of the repayment order (1 September 1997) inclusive (ie. 185 days):

1 March 1997 - 1 September 1997 $\frac{185}{365}$ x 5% x £5,041.10 =   £127.75

(d)   The first instalment in both cases is due on 31 December 1996 and therefore both are exactly one year overdue. The instalments on the land are interest bearing, those on the shares non-interest bearing.

Land	£
1st instalment	
interest 5% x £1,200 =	60.00
2nd instalment	
paid on time	
interest on balance 5% x 9/10 x £12,000	540.00
Total interest in respect of IHT on land	£600.00
Shares	
1st instalment	
interest 5% x £1,440	£72.00
2nd instalment	
paid on time	

QUESTIONS

1.   What is an excepted transfer?

2.   Harry dies on 1 September 1996. In what circumstances do his executors
        not have to submit an account in relation to his death?

3.   Do instalments of IHT relating to unquoted shares carry interest if the
        instalments are paid on time?

4.   IHT on a chargeable lifetime transfer can only be paid by instalments if
        the .... pays the tax.

5.   Tom creates a discretionary trust on 20 May 1996. When is the IHT arising
        on the transfer due?

6.   If Tom (Q5) dies on 3 November 1998, when will the additional IHT, due
        to his death within seven years of creating the trust, be due?

7.   An estate includes the following assets. State whether IHT is payable:

        (a)   in a single payment

        (b)   by interest free instalments

        (c)   by interest bearing instalments.

                (i)   Freehold house

                (ii)   Life assurance policy

                (iii)   Quoted shares

                (iv)   Shares in an unquoted trading company representing 15% of
                        the share capital of the company and worth £50,000

                (v)   Farmland

                (vi)   Chattels

                (vii)   Cash

8.   IHT of £50,000 is due on 31 July 1996. It is paid on 1 October 1996. On
        1 February 1997 £20,000 is repaid.

        (a)   How much is the payment, including interest?

        (b)   How much is the repayment, including interest?

SOLUTIONS

1. Under a 1981 statutory instrument, no account need be sent to the CTO of an excepted transfer, that is a chargeable lifetime transfer where:

    (a) the total of such transfers in that tax year does not exceed £10,000; and

    (b) the total of such transfers in the previous ten years does not exceed £40,000

    (6.2.2)

2. If the gross value of his estate does not exceed £145,000, does not contain settled property and not more than £15,000 worth of foreign property, provided that Harry has made no lifetime transfers within seven years of his death or gifts with reservation, and has died domiciled in the UK.

    (6.2.2)

3. If the company is not an investment or property dealing company, the interest is only charged if the instalments are late. If the company is an investment or property dealing company, interest runs from the normal due date.

    (6.3.5)

4. Donee.

    (6.3.3)

5. 30 April 1997.

    (6.3.2)

6. 31 May 1999.

    (6.3.2)

7. (i)   Interest-bearing instalments

    (ii) Single payment

    (iii) Single payment

    (iv) Interest-free instalments

    (v)   Interest-free instalments

    (vi) Single payment

    (vii) Single payment

    (6.3.3) & (6.3.5)

8.

			£
(a)	IHT		50,000.00
	Interest: $5\% \times \frac{62}{365} \times £50,000$		424.66
	Paid 1 October 1996		£50,424.66
(b)	IHT repaid		20,000.00
	Interest paid, now repaid		169.86
			20,169.86
	Interest on repayment: $5\% \times \frac{124}{365} \times £20,170$		342.61
	Repaid 1 February 1997		£20,512.47

    (6.3.4)

SESSION 7

THE ADMINISTRATION OF NATIONAL INSURANCE CONTRIBUTIONS

By the end of this session you will be able to:

- explain how each class of NIC is collected
- describe the consequences of late payment of NIC
- describe the enforcement provisions
- understand the proceedings which can be taken in the event of a disagreement with the DSS

References: Social Security Administration Act (SSAA) 1992 unless otherwise stated

7.1 Introduction

7.1.1 The Contributions Agency

National Insurance Contributions are administered by the Contributions Agency, which is part of the Department of Social Security (DSS). The Secretary of State, who is a member of the Cabinet, is at the head of the DSS.

The Contributions Agency is divided into specialist groups, for example, the Class 1A group, the Class 2 group, the deferment group etc. These groups are based in Newcastle upon Tyne.

Although the Central Office at Newcastle upon Tyne holds all contribution records on computer, it is likely that contact with the DSS will be made via the local office. If a matter is technically difficult or of a contentious nature, the local office will contact Central Office in Newcastle upon Tyne or Friars House in London which deals with questions of policy, assessment and collection.

7.1.2 Power to make regulations

The Secretary of State is granted wide legislative powers by the Social Security Acts and these powers are exercised by statutory instrument.

Proposed regulations which are to be introduced by statutory instrument must generally be referred to the Social Security Advisory Committee (SSAC) who provide an external check. However, consultation with the SSAC is not required where: s.172(1)
s.173(1)

(a) the matter is particularly urgent; or

(b) the SSAC has agreed that the matter need not be referred; or

(c) the statutory instrument is being made within six months of the enactment under which the regulations are being made. s.173(5)

In addition, there are certain matters, such as regulations relating to earnings limits, which do not require consultation with the SSAC.

The SSAC must report on matters referred to it and may make recommendations. A copy of the SSAC report then has to be laid before Parliament by the Secretary of State. If the SSAC report contains recommendations, the Secretary of State must advise Parliament of the extent to which he intends giving effect to the recommendations (or, if he does not propose to give effect to them, his reasons why not).

s.173(4)

7.2 Collection machinery and related matters

7.2.1 Introduction

The collection machinery depends upon the class of NIC in question. Therefore, each class is considered separately below.

7.2.2 Class 1 contributions

There are no formal provisions for the assessment of Class 1 NIC in the social security legislation. It is the duty of the secondary contributor (normally the employer) to pay over both the primary and secondary Class 1 liability via the income tax PAYE system (primary contributions may then be recovered from the employee). The contributions therefore will be payable within fourteen days of the end of the tax month (or quarter, if appropriate) (see para 5.4.1).

If the Collector of Taxes believes that the employer has failed to pay part or all of the NIC within fourteen days of the end of the month (or quarter) the Collector of Taxes can give a notice requiring the employer to render a return within fourteen days informing the Collector of the Class 1 NIC payable. If the employer fails to comply with this, the Collector can require the employer to make available wages record sheets and other relevant documents. The Collector can then prepare a certificate showing the amount of NIC payable. Alternatively, the Collector can use his judgement based on the employer's past contributions record and can give notice to the employer of the amount that he considers the employer liable to pay.

As the entire payment of income tax and Class 1 NIC is paid to the Inland Revenue, the Revenue must account to the Secretary of State for the NIC element.

7.2.3 Class 1A contributions

Collection of Class 1A depends upon whether the employer is paying Class 1 on a monthly or quarterly basis. Where the Class 1 is paid along with the PAYE on a monthly basis, the Class 1A must be paid by 19 June immediately following the end of the tax year to which the contributions relate. If Class 1 is paid on a quarterly basis (see para 5.4.1), the Class 1A must be paid by 19 July immediately following the end of the tax year to which the contributions relate.

Alternatively, the employer may apply to use the 'alternative payment method'. Under this method the Class 1A contributions are payable direct to the DSS (rather than via the PAYE system) on 19 June immediately following the end of the tax year.

Where an employee with a company car leaves before the end of the tax year, by concession, the employer may pay the Class 1A NIC due at the time of departure. This does not apply if the employer is using the alternative payment method.

7.2.4 Class 2 contributions

Unless exception has been granted or liability has been deferred, Class 2 contributions are payable for each week in which the individual is ordinarily self employed.

Payment may be made by the following methods:

(a)   making a payment to the DSS after the end of each quarter; or

(b)   making monthly payments by direct debit; or

(c)   by deduction from a war disablement pension or certain other Social Security benefits.

7.2.5   Class 3 contributions

Class 3 contributions can be paid by the following methods:

(a)   making a payment to the DSS after the end of each quarter; or

(b)   making a payment by direct debit; or

(c)   making a payment to the DSS after the end of the year to which the contributions relate.

7.2.6   Class 4 contributions

Unless liability has been deferred, Class 4 NIC is paid to the Inland Revenue along with the related income tax on the source of profits or gains being assessed. For 1996/97 onwards the Class 4 NIC is therefore payable in two equal estimated instalments, on 31 January in the year of assessment and 31 July following. Any underpayment is paid on 31 January following (see session 2).

s.16(1)(b) SSC &
BA 1992

The Inland Revenue has to account to the Secretary of State for the Class 4 NIC collected.

Where liability to Class 4 NIC has been deferred, responsibility for the collection of the NIC passes back to the Secretary of State. The Secretary of State will calculate and inform the earner of the Class 4 NIC which has been deferred but which is now payable. The earner then has 28 days from receipt of the notice to pay the NIC.

7.2.7   Summary

Class 1 NIC is payable via the PAYE system. Class 1A NIC is also payable via the PAYE system unless the 'alternative payment method' applies, in which case the NIC is paid direct to the DSS.

Class 2 and Class 3 contributions can currently be paid direct to the DSS quarterly or by direct debit. Class 2 can also be paid by deduction from certain social security benefits. Class 3 may be paid after the end of the year to which it relates.

Class 4 NIC is paid to the Inland Revenue along with the tax on the related profits as two payments on account and a final payment.

7.3 Late and unpaid contributions

7.3.1 Introduction

The consequences of late or non-payment depend upon the Class of NIC concerned. Each class is therefore considered separately below.

7.3.2 Late and unpaid Class 1 contributions

The TMA 1970 penalties for late and incorrect PAYE returns (see paragraph 5.4.7) generally also apply to contribution returns for Class 1 NIC purposes. The income tax penalties, with appropriate comments for NIC purposes, are shown below.

para 7, Sch 1 SSC & BA 1992

(a)   *Late returns*

There is an automatic penalty of £100 per month per 50 employees. This penalty which can apply only for the first 12 months of failure, does *not* apply in relation to a late contribution return if it already applies to a late PAYE return (ie. the penalty cannot be levied twice).

para 7 (3), Sch 1 SSC & BA 1992

Where the return is more than 12 months late a single penalty equal to the tax *and NIC* remaining unpaid at 19 April after the end of the relevant tax year can be imposed by the Inland Revenue. This penalty can be mitigated to take account of circumstances.

para 7(4), Sch 1 SSC & BA 1992

(b)   *Incorrect returns*

A single penalty equal to the difference between the correct amount of tax *and NIC* payable and the amount that would have been payable according to the incorrect returns. This penalty can be mitigated to take account of circumstances.

para 7(4), Sch 1 SSC & BA 1992

Interest under s.86 TMA 1970 applies. Interest may be charged on late paid Class 1 contributions. The interest will run from 14 days after the end of the tax year concerned on contributions unpaid by that date. For example, if Class 1 contributions for 1996/97 are unpaid by 19 April 1997, interest will start running on the unpaid amount from 19 April 1997.

7.3.3 Late and unpaid Class 1A contributions

Interest is charged on late paid Class 1A contributions. The interest will run where the Class 1A contributions are unpaid by 19 April following the year in which payment is due. For example, a contribution due for 1996/97 is *due in* 1997/98. S.86 TMA 1970 interest will therefore run on unpaid contributions from 19 April 1998.

7.3.4 Late and unpaid Class 2 contributions

Where a Class 2 contribution is paid late but is nevertheless paid within the tax year for which it is due, the NIC should be paid at the same rate as if the NIC had been paid at the due date.

Where a Class 2 contribution is paid after the end of the year to which it relates, the rate at which the NIC is payable depends upon when the contributor entered into an undertaking to pay the arrears in question. The rules are as follows:

(a)   if the undertaking was entered into in the tax year in which the contribution was due or in the following year, the NIC is payable at the rate at which it would originally have been paid;

(b)   if the undertaking was entered into in a later tax year, the NIC is payable at the highest rate in the period from the due date to the date of the undertaking.

7.3.5   Late and unpaid Class 3 contributions

If a late paid Class 3 contribution is paid within two years of the end of the year to which it relates, the contribution is payable at the same rate as would have been paid originally. Where the Class 3 contribution is paid more than two years after the end of the year to which it relates, the contribution payable is the higher of the original rate and the rate for the tax year of payment.

7.3.6   Late and unpaid Class 4 contributions

Late paid Class 4 contributions will attract an interest charge under s.86 TMA 1970.

Where an assessment for a year prior to 1996/97 has been issued to make good to the Crown a loss of tax wholly or partly attributable to a failure or an error on the part of the taxpayer, the Class 4 NIC will carry s.88 (now repealed) TMA 1970 interest in the same way as the related tax.

The penalties in Part X of TMA 1970 apply to Class 4 NIC in the same way as they apply to Schedule D Case I or II income tax (see 1.5.5).

s.16(1) SSC & BA 1992

7.3.7   Summary

The TMA 1970 interest and penalty provisions apply to Class 1 NIC generally in the same way that they apply to PAYE.

Interest on Class 1A contributions will run where the NIC is unpaid by 19 April following the year in which the payment of Class 1A was *due*.

Arrears of Class 2 NIC may need to be paid at the rate applying in the year of payment, rather than the originating year, if paid more than one year late.

Arrears of Class 3 NIC paid more than two years after the end of the year to which they relate will be paid at the higher rate applying in the year of payment.

Late paid Class 4 NIC attracts interest under s.86 TMA 1970 .

7.4 Enforcement

7.4.1 Introduction

DSS Inspectors have wide enforcement powers, including the power of entry, enquiry and examination.

7.4.2 Rights of the DSS Inspectors

The DSS Inspector has the right of entry to premises (excluding a private dwelling house) where he believes that persons are employed there or that an employment agency or similar business is carried on there.

s.110(2)

Entry cannot be forced by the Inspector; however, the obstruction of an officer can carry a penalty.

The Inspector has the right of examination and inquiry to enable him to ascertain whether or not the social security legislation has been complied with.

s.110(2)

If the Inspector reasonably requires information or documents to enable him to establish whether or not contributions are payable there is a duty to provide them to him. The duty to provide the information extends to the occupier of business premises, an employer, a person carrying on an employment agency, a servant or agent of the aforementioned and anyone who is, or has been liable to pay contributions.

s.110(6)

7.4.3 Penalties

(a)   *Delay or obstruction of an officer*

Where a person:

(i)   intentionally delays or obstructs an officer; or

(ii)   refuses or neglects to answer any question or furnish any information

on summary conviction, a fine of up to £1,000 can be imposed.

s.111

(b)   *False statements or documents*

Where a person:

(i)   knowingly makes a false statement or representation; or

(ii)   knowingly produces a document which is false

on summary conviction, a fine of up to £5,000 can be imposed.

s.112

(c)   *Contravention of regulations*

Where a person contravenes regulations, if there is no specific penalty imposed, on summary conviction he can be liable to penalty of up to £1,000. If the offence continues after conviction a further penalty of up to £40 per day can be imposed.

s.113

(d)   *Non payment of contributions*

Penalties for non payment of contributions are covered in section 7.3

7.4.4 Prosecution

If there is an offence under contribution law, proceedings may be conducted in a magistrates court.

s.116

Information must be laid before the court within either 12 months of the offence or within 3 months of the date on which evidence of the offence became available. A summons will then be issued to the defendant showing the place and time to appear and the general matter.

An Inspector or other officer is allowed to prosecute, even where he is not a barrister or solicitor. Both the defendant and the prosecution are entitled to be represented by a barrister or solicitor and both are entitled to call witnesses.

s.116(1)

7.4.5 Summary

DSS Inspectors have the right of entry to premises and the right of examination and inquiry.

Penalties can be imposed for the delay or obstruction of an officer (up to £1,000); for making false statements or documents (up to £5,000); for contravening the regulations (up to £1,000 plus £40 per day) and for non-payment of contributions (various).

7.5 Appeal procedure and adjudication

7.5.1 Introduction

The Social Security Acts do not have the equivalent of the TMA 1970 formal appeals procedure.

If there is a disagreement, this will initially be dealt with through negotiations with the local office, who may in turn obtain advice or a ruling from Head Office. If agreement is not reached, the case may be referred to the Solicitors Department of the DSS to enforce the payment considered due. At this point the disputed matter may be set before the Secretary of State for determination.

However, any disagreement which relates to a topic not specifically reserved as a Secretary of State 'Question' is initially referred to an Adjudication officer, thence to a Social Security Appeal tribunal, then to a Social Security Commissioner and finally to the Courts.

Appeals against Class 4 contributions however, may effectively be dealt with by the Inland Revenue (para 7.5.6).

7.5.2 Questions which may be set before the Secretary of State

The Secretary of State can determine questions on matters such as the following: s.17

(a) whether or not a person is an earner and if so, which category of earner does he belong in;

(b) whether the contribution conditions for a benefit are satisfied;

(c) whether or not a Class 1A contribution is payable

(d) whether a person is excepted from Class 4 liability, or whether that liability can be deferred

Only the Secretary of State can determine questions on the above matters. s.117(2)
Therefore, if a case is being heard in the magistrates court (see paragraph 7.4.4 above), the magistrate will have to adjourn the case and refer any relevant questions to the Secretary of State.

7.5.3 The application for a determination by the Secretary of State

The courts, adjudication officers, local tribunals, the Social Security Commissioners and 'a person interested' may apply for a determination. 'A person interested' is a person whose own liability is affected by the question.

It should be noted that the DSS themselves are not entitled to apply to the Secretary of State for a determination. Therefore if the DSS and a contributor are unable to reach agreement and the contributor does not wish to apply for a determination then the DSS will have to issue proceedings. When the matter is then heard in court, the court will be able to refer the question to the Secretary of State.

Any application to the Secretary of State must be made in writing on form CF90 or CF93 which may be obtained by the DSS. There is no time limit imposed for the filing of an application and the application may be withdrawn at any time before the matter is determined by the Secretary of State.

When the Secretary of State receives the application he must bring the application to the attention of other persons interested in it.

7.5.4 The determination by the Secretary of State

Before determination the Secretary of State can appoint someone, usually a lawyer from his own office, the Solicitors Department or a non-DSS lawyer, to hold an inquiry into the question referred to him. A report will then be prepared for the Secretary of State.

If the report shows that a question of law has arisen the Secretary of State may refer the case to the High Court for a decision. Otherwise, the Secretary of State will make the decision himself. Written notice of the decision is given to the applicant and other interested persons.

7.5.5 Dissatisfaction with the Secretary of State's decision

If the applicant is dissatisfied with the decision of the Secretary of State he may take the appropriate action, as outlined below.

(a)   *Apply for the decision to be set aside*

The original decision will either be confirmed or set aside. There is no appeal against this.

(b)   *Apply for the decision to be reviewed on factual or legal grounds*

The Secretary of State can review his original decision where new facts have come to light or where he is satisfied that he was originally mistaken over a fact or point of law. If the original determination is revised, this is usually with retrospective effect, back dated to the date of the original determination.

(c)   *Appeal to the High Court on a point of law*

If the applicant is dissatisfied with the Secretary of State's decision he may request a formal statement of the grounds for that decision. An applicant can then, within twenty-eight days of receipt of the statement, appeal to the High Court on a point of law. The Court will never determine questions of fact.

The High Court decision is final and will be back-dated to the date the question for determination first arose.

(d)   *Apply to the court for a judicial review*

A judicial review may be sought by a person with 'sufficient interest' where it is considered that the Secretary of State or the DSS have:

(i)   failed to perform an administrative duty; or

(ii)   exceeded their powers; or

(iii) acted contrary to natural justice.

The review may only be requested where no other course of redress is available.

(e)   *Complain through his MP to the Parliamentary Commissioner*

7.5.6 Class 4 NIC

Class 4 NIC is payable in accordance with the TMA 1970 and therefore an appeal against an assessment on Class 4 liability must be made in the same way as an appeal against the income tax charged on the same assessment.

The Secretary of State will only become involved with the following questions concerning Class 4 NIC:

(a)   whether a person is excepted from Class 4 liability or whether a liability is deferred; and / or

(b)   whether a person is liable to Class 4 NIC which may be collected direct from the DSS.

ss.17(3)-(6) & 18
SSC & BA 1992

7.6   Disclosure of information by the Inland Revenue

Information obtained by the Inland Revenue in connection with taxation matters can be disclosed to the DSS in connection with the calculation and collection of NIC.

s.122 (1)

Disclosure relating to a Schedule D Case I or II trade, profession or vocation is confined to:

s.122(2)

(a)   sufficient information so that the trader etc. and any employed earners in the trade may be identified; and

(b)   information regarding the commencement or cessation of the trade; and

(c)   the profits to be assessed if, in the case of a deferment, the responsibility for the collection of the Class 4 NIC has passed from the Revenue to the DSS.

The Inland Revenue and Customs and Excise are allowed to disclose information to each other and therefore it is possible that information passed to the DSS from the Inland Revenue may have originated from Customs and Excise.

s.127 FA 1972

QUESTIONS

1.   Does the Secretary of State always have to consult with the SSAC before introducing a statutory instrument?

2.   Are Class 1A NIC contributions always paid to the Collector of Taxes?

3.   The Inland Revenue is always responsible for collecting Class 4 NIC. True/False?

4.   Interest will start to run on 1996/97 Class 1 NIC which is unpaid on ......?

5.   Interest will start to run on 1996/97 Class 1A NIC which is unpaid on ......?

6.   What is the maximum penalty for refusing to answer the questions of a DSS Inspector?

7.   What action can be taken if there is dissatisfaction with a determination by the Secretary of State?

SOLUTIONS

1.   No. The SSAC need not be consulted where:

  (a)   the matter is urgent; or

  (b)   the SSAC has agreed that the matter need not be referred; or

  (c)   the statutory instrument is being made within 6 months of the original enactment.   (7.1.2)

2.   No. Class 1A contributions may be paid direct to the DSS under the alternative payment method.   (7.2.3)

3.   False. Responsibility passes back to the Secretary of State where liability has been deferred.   (7.2.6)

4.   19 April 1997.   (7.3.2)

5.   19 April 1998.   (7.3.3)

6.   £1,000 on conviction.   (7.4.3)

7.   (a)   Apply for the decision to be set aside.

  (b)   Apply for the decision to be reviewed.

  (c)   Appeal to the High Court (on a point of law only).

  (d)   Apply for a judicial review.

  (e)   Complain to the Parliamentary Commissioner.   (7.5.5)

Part 2
Indirect tax administration

Contents

RECORDS, RETURNS AND PAYMENT OF VAT

By the end of this session you will be able to:

- explain how Customs and Excise administer VAT

- describe the documents and records to be provided and retained

- define a prescribed accounting period

- describe the contents of a tax return and the records required to support it

- set out when tax must be paid

- describe the annual accounting system

- describe the circumstances in which monthly payments of VAT 'on account' are required

- explain how VAT due on imports is paid

- outline the additional reporting requirement for intra-EC trade

References: VATA 1994 unless otherwise stated

1.1   H M Customs and Excise

VAT is administered by the Commissioners of Customs and Excise ('the Commissioners') partly through a network of local offices situated in major towns and partly through specialist headquarters divisions. The most important division is VAT Central Unit in Southend which issues and receives tax returns, collects tax, makes repayments and maintains a central register of taxable persons. Local VAT offices deal with registration and deregistration applications, collect outstanding tax, carry out tax audits known as 'control visits' and deal with routine enquiries.

The Commissioners have wide powers to make decisions in a variety of matters. Some of these decisions give rise to a right of appeal to a VAT and duties Tribunal (an independent tax tribunal similar in many ways to the Special Commissioners). In other cases, taxpayers must involve the supervisory jurisdiction of the courts by way of judicial review, and a decision may be set aside if it has been made unreasonably or improperly. Judicial review is only available where there is no right of appeal under s.83 VATA 1994. The appeal procedure is covered in detail in section 3.2.

s.83

R v VAT Tribunal (ex parte Cohen & Ors.) (1984) STC 361

Local VAT offices frequently make rulings in individual cases, eg. that a specific supply of goods or services is taxable at the standard rate. Problems arise if an incorrect ruling is given: the doctrine of estoppel does not operate and the Commissioners are not, therefore, prevented from changing their minds and claiming back tax on the basis of their new ruling. However, the Commissioners have indicated that they will not seek to backdate a revised ruling provided the original ruling was given in writing on the basis of a full disclosure of the facts by the trader concerned.

Hansard 21.7.78

With effect from 1 April 1995, an external adjudicator has been appointed to deal with complaints against Customs, other than matters which are appealable to the Tribunal or are the subject of a criminal prosecution. The Adjudicator's role encompasses a supervisory function similar to judicial review as well as dealing with complaints about attitude, incompetence, errors and delays.

1.2 Tax returns, payment and repayment

1.2.1 Prescribed accounting periods

Input tax and output tax are accounted for by reference to 'prescribed accounting periods'.

A *prescribed accounting period* is usually three months, but 'repayment traders' (ie. taxable persons who habitually receive refunds of tax) are allowed to have a monthly prescribed accounting period. Prescribed accounting periods are staggered to prevent administrative bottlenecks, ie. a trader's VAT year can end on 31 March, 30 April or 31 May. The accounting dates are notified to taxable persons in their registration certificates and are allocated according to business classification. Traders can request certain accounting dates for their convenience but allocation is at the Commissioners discretion and is not a point on which the VAT tribunal can hear an appeal. SI 1995/2518
reg 25

The details of the annual accounting scheme are set out in 1.2.5 below.

1.2.2 Tax returns

A taxable person must furnish a tax return (form VAT 100) in respect of each prescribed accounting period. SI 1995/2518
reg 39

In addition to dealing with UK transactions, the VAT return must include entries for intra EC trade, for tax on imported goods dealt with under the postponed accounting system (see para 1.3.3) and for input tax on imported goods.

The tax return is completed by showing total figures for:

Box 1   output tax on supplies and deemed supplies made by the taxable person, and tax due on goods imported under the postponed accounting procedure;

Box 2   VAT due on acquisitions from other EC countries;

Box 3   total VAT due on sales and on EC acquisitions (ie. Box 1 plus Box 2);

Box 4   input tax available for credit on purchases (including imports and acquisitions from the EC);

Box 5   tax payable to or by the Commissioners (ie. Box 3 minus Box 4).

Customs also require statistical information partly for checking the reasonableness of the declared input tax and output tax figures. This now extends to information on trade with other EC member states. Boxes 6 to 9 of the VAT return therefore require:

Box 6   total value of sales and all other outputs (excluding VAT) made during the period and including the amount shown in Box 8;

Box 7   total value of purchases and all other inputs (excluding VAT) received during the period (including the amount shown in Box 9);

Box 8   total value of all supplies of goods and related services (excluding any VAT) to other EC member states;

Box 9   total value of all acquisitions of goods and related services (excluding any VAT) from other EC member states.

Boxes 1 and 4 are also used, as appropriate, to pay or recover tax in respect of partial exemption annual adjustments; adjustments made as a result of recalculation of retail schemes or the use of an approved estimation procedure; and for claims for bad debt relief.

Although all nine boxes must be completed ('if none write none'), clearly a trader who does not have transactions with other EC countries will only enter figures in boxes 1, 3, 4, 5, 6 & 7.

1.2.3 Accounting records

Every trader must keep a value added tax account in which only entries prescribed by regulations may be made. It is the totals of those entries for each prescribed accounting period which are used to complete the tax return. The value added tax account is divided into two parts: the tax payable portion and the tax allowable portion.

SI 1995/2518 reg 32

To support these entries the following records must be kept:

SI 1995/2518 reg 31

(a)   business and accounting records;

(b)   the value added tax account;

(c)   copies of all tax invoices issued;

(d)   all tax invoices received;

(e)   documentation on imports, acquisitions, despatches and exports;

(f)   all credit notes, debit notes or other documents which evidence changes in consideration received or given.

The Commissioners can add to this list for specific purposes provided they do it by publishing a notice.

The required records must be retained for six years unless Customs allow a shorter period of retention.

Sch 11 para 6

1.2.4 Payment and repayment of tax

Tax returns must be furnished and any tax due thereon paid not later than one calendar month after the end of the prescribed accounting period concerned. A return is 'furnished' when it is put into the possession of Customs, ie. when it is received, not when it is despatched. Thus returns and remittances in respect of the period ended 30 June, for example, must be furnished not later than 31 July which means that it should be posted in time for it to be reasonable to expect it to arrive by that date. Returns and remittances are sent to VAT Central Unit at Southend. The rules are varied for traders using annual accounting (see paragraph 1.2.5 later) and for very large traders (see paragraph 1.2.6 later).

SI 1995/2518 regs 25 and 40

Where a tax return shows a *repayment* of tax due to a taxable person, the amount concerned will be repaid by VAT Central Unit. Repayment supplement is dealt with in paragraph 2.4.1. Where possible Customs make repayments through the Bankers Automated Clearing Service (BACS).

s.25(3)

1.2.5 Annual accounting

A taxable person with modest turnover may apply to be authorised to account for and pay tax on an annual basis.

Under annual accounting, the VAT liability for the current accounting year is estimated by Customs. 90% of this estimated liability must be paid by direct debit in nine equal instalments beginning on the last day of the fourth month of the current accounting year. The actual VAT due for the year is established by means of a single annual return submitted by the last day of the second month following the end of that accounting year, accompanied by any balancing payment due. Alternatively, a repayment will be made where appropriate.

SI 1995/2518 regs 49-55

From 1 April 1996 businesses in the annual accounting scheme can choose to align their VAT accounting period with their financial year end, if necessary.

Example

Zach pays VAT for year to 31 March 1997 using annual accounting. Customs estimate his VAT liability for that year, based on the previous year's figures, to be £20,000. His actual liability turns out to be £21,500. What payments does Zach make?

Solution

Zach will pay by direct debit from 31.7.96 to 31.3.97:   £

9 months x £2,000	18,000
Zach should furnish his annual return by 31.5.97 together with balance of liability	3,500
	£21,500

A trader may apply to use the annual accounting scheme if:

(a)   he has been registered for one year; and

(b)   he believes that his taxable supplies will not exceed £300,000 (excluding VAT) in the coming year; and

(c)   he has made all returns due to date; and

(d)   he is not a repayment trader, and

(e)   he is not a member of a group registration.

A trader may be obliged to leave the scheme if his taxable turnover exceeds the relevant threshold on either of two tests:

(a)   if at the end of the year the value of his taxable supplies has exceeded £375,000 in that year, in which case his authorisation to use the scheme ceases forthwith; or

(b)   if at any time there is reason to believe that the value of his taxable supplies in the current year will exceed £375,000. In that case, the trader must notify Customs of that fact within 30 days. Customs may then terminate the trader's authorisation to operate the scheme.

In addition, Customs are entitled to withdraw a trader's authorisation in certain circumstances:

(a)   if a false statement has been made in the application for authorisation;

(b)   if an authorised trader fails to furnish his annual return on time;

(c)   if the trader fails to make any payment required under the scheme;

(d)   if the trader fails to make full payment of any tax assessed on him;

(e)   if the trader fails to pay the full amount of any tax due in respect of a return furnished before he joined the annual accounting scheme;

(f)   if the trader is in breach of either of the turnover tests described above but has failed to leave the scheme; or

(g)   where it is necessary for the protection of the revenue.

If an authorised trader ceases to operate the scheme of his own volition, he should account for tax in accordance with the usual rules.

There may be cash flow advantages to a trader using annual accounting, where his actual VAT liability exceeds the estimated liability. Another advantage is that default surcharge cannot be applied since only a single return is submitted each year. However, as described above, a failure to submit the annual return on time can result in authorisation to use the scheme being terminated. There is an advantage that the annual return is submitted two months after the end of the year; the normal time limit for returns is one month. On the other hand, subject to the following relaxation, VAT is paid monthly not quarterly under the scheme.

From 1 April 1996 the annual accounting scheme is further improved for businesses whose turnover is below £100,000. Such traders can make quarterly VAT payments of 20% of the previous year's net VAT liability instead of monthly payments. Furthermore, if the net liability is below £2,000 the trader can choose whether or not to make interim payments.

1.2.6 Monthly payments on account

Very large traders are liable to pay VAT monthly in advance on account of their actual liability. Returns are still due quarterly. Customs & Excise can make directions as to the manner in which these payments are made.

SI 1993/2001

A trader who does not submit monthly returns is obliged to make payments on account if either:

(a)   his total VAT liability for the previous year ending 30 September, 31 October or 30 November (whichever is the last day of his prescribed accounting period) exceeded £2 million; or

(b)   his total VAT liability exceeds £2 million in any subsequent period of one year, testing at the end of each prescribed accounting period.

The difference between tests (a) and (b) above is the periods in respect of which payments on account are required. Where test (a) is satisfied, payments on account are required for the whole of the following VAT year, commencing on 1 April, 1 May or 1 June. Where a trader falls within test (b) however, the liability to make payments on account commences from the next prescribed accounting period after that in which the £2 million threshold is exceeded.

Example

Big Ltd has a VAT year end of 30 April. In the year ended 31 October 1995, its VAT liability was £2.2 million.

Big Ltd is therefore liable to make payments on account for the whole of the year commencing 1 May 1996.

Example

Large Ltd has a VAT year end of 30 April.

The company's VAT liability for recent quarters has been:

Q/e:	Liability	Annul Total
	£	£
31.1.95	400,000	
30.4.95	300,000	
31.7.95	600,000	
31.10.95	500,000	1,800,000
31.1.96	350,000	1,750,000
30.4.96	500,000	1,950,000
31.7.96	750,000	2,100,000

Test (a) does not apply, because the liability for the y/e 31.10.95 was not more than £2 million.

Test (b) applies at q/e 31.7.96, when the previous year's liability exceeds £2 million.

Thus payments on account are required with effect from the next prescribed AP, ie. q/e 31.10.96

Payments on account are normally due at the end of the second month in the prescribed accounting period and at the end of the third month. Any further balance due should accompany the VAT return. If the payments on account exceed the total amount due for the prescribed accounting period, Customs will repay the excess, subject to any right of set-off under s.81 VATA 1994 (see para 2.4.1).

SI 1995/2518
Part IV

Example

Major Ltd is liable to make payments on account for the quarter ending 30 September 1996. The payments on account have been calculated as £250,000 (see below).

What payments/repayments are due if Major Ltd's VAT liability for the quarter amounts to either:

(a) £680,000, or

(b) £480,000?

Solution

(a) 31.8.96   -   payment of £250,000

30.9.96   -   payment of £250,000

31.10.96   -   payment of £180,000 (with return)

(b) 31.8.96 and 30.9.96 as above

31.10.96   -   repayment of £20,000 due from C & E

Where the trader is liable for payments on account by virtue of the historic threshold in (a) above, the amount of each such payment is calculated as one twenty fourth of the trader's total VAT liability in the previous year ended 30 September, 31 October or 30 November (as appropriate). Where the obligation to pay on account arises by virtue of the alternative test in (b) above, each payment is one twenty fourth of the total liability for the year in which the £2 million threshhold was exceeded. In both cases, tax on goods imported from outside the EC is excluded. Customs are required to notify the trader of the amount payable, how it has been calculated and when payment is due. In certain circumstances, Customs may reduce or increase the amount of the payments on account.

SI 1993/2001 arts 11 & 12

SI 1995/2518 Part VI

Before 1 June 1996 the monthly amount payable on account was equal to one twelfth of the annual liability. Since 1 June 1996 traders have the option to pay the actual monthly liability instead of the fixed monthly amount.

Originally traders who paid by electronic means received a 7 day period of grace for making the payment. From 1 June 1996 electronic payments by large traders are compulsory and the period of grace is withdrawn.

Originally the default surcharge system (see para 2.2.7) did not apply to payments on account. This has been amended for prescribed accounting periods ending on or after 1 June 1996 but ignoring any payments due before that date.

s.59A

If the trader's VAT liability falls to less than £1.6 million for a one year period ending after the period in (a) or (b) above, he may make a written application to Customs to be released from his duty to make the monthly payments. The trader's obligations cease only when Customs give written approval.

1.2.7   Summary

Traders generally have three monthly prescribed accounting periods. There is provision however for monthly periods, which is of particular benefit to repayment traders.

This session sets out the information which must be shown on a tax return and the accounting records a trader must keep.

Traders have one month from the end of the prescribed accounting period to furnish a return and pay the tax.

Annual accounting enables 'small' traders to submit a single return each year, but they must pay tax in ten instalments, nine of which are estimated, followed by the balance of the actual tax due which is sent with the annual return two months after the end of the year. The scheme is relaxed where the turnover falls below £100,000

Conversely, 'very large' traders have to account for net output tax monthly in advance, whilst still submitting returns quarterly.

1.3   Tax due on importation

1.3.1   General rule

The normal rule is that any VAT arising on importation (ie. from outside the EC) must be paid to the Post Office (in the case of postal imports) or the proper officer at the place of importation (in other cases) before the goods concerned can be removed from Customs control. This rule is treated as being satisfied if VAT is accounted for under the duty deferment system or postponed accounting system, described below.

CEMA 1979 s.43
SI 1986/260

1.3.2   Duty deferment system

A 'duty deferment system' is available to approved importers. In essence, duty and VAT arising on imports made in a calendar month is paid by direct debit on the 15th day of the following month. Approval is obtained by submitting an application (form C1200), a guarantee from a bank or other approved institution (form C1201) and a direct debit mandate (form C1202). An approval certificate is issued and a deferment approval number (which must be shown on import entries) allocated. Deferment is available on individual consignments only where uncollected duty and VAT does not exceed the amount guaranteed.

SI 1976/1223

1.3.3   Postponed accounting system

A 'postponed accounting system' is available to taxable persons importing goods having a value not exceeding £2,000 by post from places outside the EC. Instead of paying tax on individual consignments at the time of import, tax may be accounted for in the same manner as output tax, ie. it is included on the trader's tax return as an amount due to the Commissioners for the prescribed accounting period in which the goods were imported. The Commissioners are empowered to prevent taxable persons using this postponed accounting system.

SI 1995/2518
reg 122

1.3.4   Summary

Tax is due on imports from outside the EC at the time the goods enter the UK, subject to the duty deferment and postponed accounting systems.

1.4   Trade with other EC member states

1.4.1   EC sales statements

Where a UK taxable person despatches *goods* to persons registered for VAT in other EC member states, he is obliged to submit an EC sales statement (ECSS) to Customs, usually on a quarterly basis. 42 days are allowed for the submission of the ECSS, which must contain, inter alia, the VAT registration numbers of the customers concerned including the prefix code for the relevant member state) and the total value of goods supplied to each of those customers in the period.

SI 1995/2518
Part IV

Material inaccuracies in ECSSs and failure to submit an ECSS when required are subject to civil penalties.

ss.65 and 66

1.4.2   Supplementary declarations

Larger traders are required to submit supplementary declarations (SDs) as part of the Intrastat System for collecting statistics on intra-EC trade in goods.

SI 1992/2790

Where a trader's acquisitions and/or despatches exceed the threshold (currently £160,000) on a calendar year basis, monthly SDs must be made within 10 working days after the month end. Any failure to submit an SD is a criminal offence.

QUESTIONS

1.   What sort of trader would be advised to apply for monthly prescribed accounting periods?

2.   What is the time limit for submission of the VAT return?

3.   If VAT on imports is paid under the duty deferment system, how and when is the tax paid?

4.   Annual accounting may apply to a trader whose taxable supplies do not exceed £.......... inclusive/exclusive of VAT, in the coming year.

5.   The allocation of prescribed accounting periods to a trader is an appealable matter: true/false?

6.   Where on the VAT return is a claim for bad debt relief included?

7.   What is the maximum value of a postal import which can qualify for postponed accounting?

8.   In what circumstances is a trader required to make advance payments on account of VAT?

9.   For what period must a trader's VAT records be retained?

10.   What additional returns may a trader be required to furnish as a consequence of trading with other EC member states?

SOLUTIONS

1. One who regularly receives repayments, eg. because he makes largely zero-rated supplies. (1.2.1)

2. The return must be received by Customs within one calendar month after the end of the prescribed accounting period (1.2.4), or within two calendar months of the end of the accounting year if the trader is authorised under the annual accounting scheme. (1.2.5)

3. By direct debit on the 15th day of the month following the month of importation. (1.3.2)

4. £300,000 excluding VAT. (1.2.5)

5. False - the allocation is at Customs' discretion. (1.2.1)

6. Box 4 - input tax available for credit. (1.2.2)

7. £2,000. (1.3.3)

8. If the trader's total taxable liability:

    (a) exceeded £2 million in the previous year ended 30 September, 31 October or 30 November; or

    (b) exceeds £2 million in a subsequent one year period. (1.2.6)

9. Six years, unless Customs agree to a shorter period. (1.2.3)

10. (a) EC Sales Statement for despatches to VAT - registered customers;

    (b) Supplementary declaration for acquisitions and/or despatches (depending on the level of trade). (1.4)

By the end of this session you will be able to:

- describe the control visit procedure used to monitor the operation of the VAT system by taxable persons

- explain the penalties and interest which may be imposed by Customs

- describe the consequences of a refund of VAT

- outline the provisions which enable Customs to require security from a trader

References: VATA 1994 unless otherwise stated

2.1 Control visits

2.1.1 Introduction

Customs' officers periodically visit taxable persons to inspect their accounting records and test check the accuracy of tax returns submitted. Such 'control visits' are normally carried out by prior appointment but there are reserve powers to enter and search premises on a warrant granted by a magistrate, take samples, require traders to supply information, check the operation of a computer, open and inspect a gaming machine, and obtain documents from third parties by way of a 'production order'.

paras 7-12
Sch 11
s.10 FA 1985

A registered trader can expect his first control visit within three years of registration. The length of a control visit and the interval between each one depends on the size and complexity of the business. A trader who sends in late, incorrect or apparently inconsistent returns can expect to be visited more frequently than would otherwise be the case.

The purposes of a control visit are to:

(a)   ensure that the full amount of tax due has been properly accounted for;

(b)   discuss various aspects of the business;

(c)   examine the records and activities of the business;

(d)   discuss any VAT problems experienced by the trader; and

(e)   point out any errors found and explain how to correct them.

Despite this wide brief, a control visit cannot be regarded as an audit. The fact that the Customs' officer does not discover any errors on a control visit does not amount to a clearance that no errors exist. If underdeclarations of tax do come to light, or if excessive amounts of input tax have been claimed, the control visit will be followed by the issue of an assessment (see section 3.1 on the validity of assessments). Interest and penalties may also arise (see sections 2.2 and 2.3).

Where the trader uses the opportunity afforded by the control visit to seek the advice of Customs on particular issues, care should be taken over the extent to which the trader can rely on the advice given. The relevant rules are outlined in section 1.1.

A control visit will normally take place at the trader's main place of business, so that the officer can examine both the business records and the business activities at the same time. All of the records which the trader is obliged to keep for VAT purposes should be made available. Customs should be informed, at the time the appointment is made, if some or all of the business records are not kept at the main place of business. In that case, the trader will be told what records the officer will wish to see, so that he can make arrangements for them to be available.

In the case of records held on computer, the trader is (not surprisingly) obliged to give the officer any necessary assistance in accessing those records.

The person who is responsible for dealing with the VAT affairs of the business should be present whilst the Customs' officer is in attendance. The trader's accountant or other professional adviser may also be there.

The particular procedures followed during a control visit will vary according to the nature of the business. However, gross profit calculations and mark-up computations (see para 2.1.2 below) are likely to be carried out if cash transactions are involved.

A taxable person is liable to civil penalties calculated on a daily basis if he fails to provide information or documents demanded by the Commissioners, or if he fails to retain documents.

s.69

2.1.2 Mark-up computations

Customs' officers use a number of techniques to test the credibility of output tax figures and, as regards retailers selling goods, the most important credibility check is a 'mark-up computation'. This makes use of a known value of purchases (obtained from tax invoices retained as evidence of input tax credit) and the profit margin 'mark-ups' made on the various classes of goods sold.

The chain of calculation proceeds as follows:

(a)   ascertain the cost of each class of goods purchased in a test period;

(b)   estimate losses from pilferage, breakages, waste, etc;

(c)   calculate the mark-up on each class of goods. This is the excess of sale price over cost price (both tax-exclusive) expressed as a percentage of cost;

(d)   estimate any adjustments arising from bargain sales, discounts, etc;

(e)   calculate hypothetical sales from the above information;

(f)   compare output tax on hypothetical sales with tax declared in the test period.

Example

> Mr Meanor sells shoes, and all his sales are taxed at the standard rate. His average rate of mark-up is 25%, and he estimates that 1% of stock is lost due to pilferage, etc. A summer sale is held each year, and an estimated 15% of total purchases are sold therein at an average mark-up of 10%. Purchases for the test period amounted to £25,000 (tax exclusive), and output tax declared for that period was £3,257.

How credible is the output tax declared?

	£
Total purchases	25,000
Deduct: pilferage etc @ 1%	(250)
	£24,750
Hypothetical sales (VAT-exclusive)	
85% of £24,750 x 1.25 (ie. 25% mark-up)	26,297
15% of £24,750 x 1.10 (ie. 10% mark-up)	4,084
	£30,381
Output tax declared thereon: £30,380 @ 17^1/2%	5,317
Deduct: tax declared	(3,257)
Discrepancy	£2,060

Conclusion: Mr Meanor has not declared all of his output tax.

2.2 Penalties

2.2.1 Introduction

A *criminal prosecution* can result for such offences as: (1) fraudulent evasion, (2) furnishing false documents and (3) making false statements. These offences carry a maximum penalty of seven years imprisonment, an unlimited fine, or both when tried on indictment (ie. before the Crown Court).

s.72

Lesser VAT offences such as late registration or understating output tax or overstating input tax (or even failing to point out to Customs that an assessment raised is too low) can give rise to civil penalties. A charge to default interest may also result (see section 2.3).

2.2.2 Dishonest conduct

Dishonest conduct for the purpose of evading tax may be penalised by a civil penalty of up to 100% of the tax lost, the exact level depending largely upon the degree of co-operation given. An officer of a body corporate (eg. a director) may be made personally liable for all or part of such penalty if the conduct giving rise to it is attributable to his dishonesty. (See para 2.2.6 for details of the power to mitigate this penalty.)

s.60

s.61

Although s.60(3) VATA 1994 refers to the method of calculating the amount of VAT evaded or sought to be evaded by reference to false claims and/or false understatements by the taxpayer, that does not imply that persons who are not registered (and have therefore not made any returns) are excluded from the scope of the penalty. In the absence of returns, it was necessary simply to calculate the amount of tax evaded.

C & E Comrs v
Stevenson (1995)
STC 667

2.2.3 'Serious' misdeclaration or neglect

Misdeclarations of tax equal to or in excess of certain limits may be penalised by a civil penalty whether or not they result from dishonest conduct. The rate of penalty is 15% of the misdeclaration. This will apply where a return is inaccurate to the extent of the lesser of 30% of the relevant VAT for the period and £1,000,000. In this text, such errors are referred to as 'serious misdeclarations'. A penalty for less serious misdeclarations may apply if they occur repeatedly (see para 2.2.4 below).

s.63

Serious misdeclaration penalty ('SMP') can also apply when a trader is assessed to VAT because he has failed to make a return and fails to draw Customs' attention to the fact that the amount of tax assessed is understated. Again, the misdeclaration can only give rise to a penalty if it equals or exceeds the lesser of 30% of the relevant VAT and £1,000,000.

Where an *incorrect return* has been made, the 'relevant VAT' is the sum of the input tax and output tax that would have been shown on the return if it had been correct (called the 'gross amount of tax' or GAT). Where there is an *under-assessment*, the 'relevant VAT' is the 'true amount of tax' (or TAT) due for the period, ie. the net figure of output tax less input tax.

Example

> A trader declares output tax of £100,000 and claims input tax of £30,000 for a prescribed accounting period. It is subsequently discovered that the output tax is understated by £28,000.

The test for SMP is the lower of:

(a)   30% x (£100,000 + 28,000 + 30,000) = £47,400, and

(b)   £1 million

ie. £47,400.

Since the error is only £28,000, this is not a serious error and no SMP can arise.

Example

A trader fails to make a return for the q/e 30.6.96. On 31.8.96, Customs issue an sessment for output tax of £200,000.

The true liability for the period is:

	£
Output tax	370,000
Input tax	(80,000)
Net output tax due	£290,000

The correct position is not drawn to Customs' attention by 30.9.96, but is established on a subsequent control visit.

The under-assessment is a serious misdeclaration if it equals or exceeds the lower of:

(a)   30% x £290,000 = £87,000; and

(b)   £1 million.

ie. £87,000.

£90,000 ≥ £87,000, therefore SMP applies @ 15% x £90,000 = £13,500

A penalty may be avoided if:

(a)   there is a reasonable excuse for the conduct; or

(b)   the error is notified to Customs voluntarily.

A number of the civil penalty provisions allow for the establishment of a 'reasonable excuse' - a concept which has caused much debate. The term is not defined in statute, other than to provide that the following *cannot* constitute a reasonable excuse:

(a)   an insufficiency of funds to pay any tax due, nor

(b)   reliance on another person to perform a task.   s.71(1)

In the specific context of SMP, the principle of voluntary disclosure has received much attention. Disclosure of an error by the trader can only avoid the penalty if it is made 'at a time when he had no reason to believe that enquiries were being made by the Commissioners into his affairs'. When the penalty was first introduced, Customs maintained that if the trader had been contacted with a view to making an appointment for a control visit (see para 2.1.1), it was too late to make voluntary disclosures. Customs have now modified their approach and will allow a disclosure made after a control visit has been arranged, or even during or after the visit itself, to be treated as voluntary. This can only apply, however, where the trader can establish that the disclosure was not prompted by the control visit.

In practice, no SMP is payable if the error is disclosed during a 'period of grace', regardless of any other circumstances. The period of grace runs from the end of the prescribed accounting period in which the error is made to the due date for furnishing the return for the next prescribed accounting period.   C & E Press
Notice 26/91
19.3.91

Compensating errors in consecutive return periods do not normally attract any penalty. This may arise, for example, when a trader makes a tax point error, as a result of which his output tax is under-declared for Period 1, but this is matched by an over-declaration in Period 2. It is Customs' practice not to seek any penalty in such circumstances.

C & E Press
Notice 26/91
19.3.91

Customs will not normally impose a penalty unless the misdeclaration understating tax due in a return period exceeds £2,000. (See also para 2.3.2.)

Customs News
Release 14/92
10.3.92

Mitigation of SMP is dealt with in para 2.2.6 below.

2.2.4   Repeated misdeclarations

s.64

In cases of repeated errors, Customs can impose a penalty equal to 15% of the tax which would have been lost for a prescribed accounting period if an inaccuracy had not been discovered.

Repeated misdeclaration penalty ('RMP') is relevant only to the making of returns which either understate the trader's output tax liability or overstate his entitlement to input tax credit. It cannot apply to under-assessments (by contrast with SMP - see para 2.2.3 above).

For RMP, there is a 'material inaccuracy' (MI) in a return if the liability or credit shown thereon is incorrect to the extent of at least the lower of:

(a)   £500,000; and

(b)   10% of the 'gross amount of tax' for the period (as for SMP, ie. the correct output tax, *plus* the correct input tax).

Example

Boardman Ltd submits its VAT return for the q/e 30.6.96 showing:

	£
Output tax	550,000
Input tax	(230,000)
Net output tax due	£320,000

The correct amount of output tax is subsequently established as £640,000.

The liability is thus understated by £90,000.

This is an MI if it equals or exceeds the lower of:

(a)   £500,000; and

(b)   10% (£640,000 + 230,000) = £87,000.

ie. £87,000.

Conclusion: the return is materially inaccurate.

Once an MI has been made, Customs are empowered to issue a 'penalty liability notice' (PLN). The PLN must be issued by the end of the fourth consecutive return period after the one in which the MI is made. The period covered by the PLN is eight consecutive return periods beginning with the one in which the PLN is issued.

Example

Continuing the Boardman Ltd example above, Customs are empowered to issue a PLN at any time up to 30.6.97.

Assuming that they do so on, say, 15.11.96, the PLN will be for the period 1.10.96 to 30.9.98.

A trader is liable for a RMP for any MI occurring during the currency of the PLN, *except* the first.

Example

Continuing the same example, Boardman Ltd has further MI's in q/e 31.12.96 and 31.3.97. In the latter case, output tax is underdeclared to the extent of £65,000.

There is no RMP for q/e 31.12.96.

For q/e 31.3.97, RMP will be assessed of:

£65,000 x 15%, ie. £9,750.

Although an error which attracts an SMP liability will not also be subject to an RMP penalty it can count as a material inaccuracy for which Customs can issue a PLN or as the first MI during the currency of the PLN.

s.64(6A)

An error will not count as an MI if:

(a) the person concerned has a reasonable excuse for the inaccuracy; or

(b) full information in respect of the inaccuracy is disclosed to Customs at a time when the trader has no reason to believe that his affairs are under investigation.

This penalty may be mitigated - see para 2.2.6 below.

2.2.5 Failure to notify liability to compulsory registration

Traders liable to compulsory registration are taxable persons whether or not they take steps to register. When such a trader is late in notifying the Commissioners of his liability to registration:

(a) his registration is backdated to the date from which he was liable to be registered;

(b) he must account for output tax on his supplies and deemed supplies from that date. Credit for input tax is given if the usual recovery rules are complied with (see your Paper IIIc VAT and NIC study text; and

(c) he is liable to a late registration penalty for the period of default unless there is a *reasonable excuse* for the delay (see below).

s.67
s.71(1)

The penalty is a percentage of the net tax due for the period of default depending on the delay involved:

(a) registration no more than 9 months late   5%

(b) registration over 9 months but no more than 18 months late   10%

(c) registration over 18 months late   15%

There is a minimum penalty of £50 for late registration subject to the power of Customs or a VAT tribunal fully to mitigate any penalty (see para 2.2.6 below). Default interest (see paragraph 2.3.1) is *not* chargeable on outstanding VAT which is subject to the late registration penalty.

Example

This example is new.

David became liable to be registered for VAT from 1 August 1996 but had not realised this until just over a year later. When he informed Customs and became registered the net liability he had to account for was £7,200 covering the period from 1 August 1996 to the date of informing Customs.

David is therefore subject to a penalty of £720 (£7,200 x 10%).

On the question of 'reasonable excuse', as for other penalties, an insufficiency of funds or reliance on another person to perform any task are specifically excluded. Neither, in the case of Jo-Ann Neal, did ignorance of the law which required registration constitute a reasonable excuse. Ms Neal commenced work as a freelance model on 29 April 1985. She was then 19 years old and without any previous experience of tax, business or law. On consulting an accountant in February 1986, she was advised that her turnover for the quarter ended 30 September 1985 had exceeded the quarterly registration limit and that she was consequently liable to registration. Form VAT 1 was duly sent to the local VAT office so as to be received on 12 March 1986. The Commissioners registered Ms Neal with effect from 21 October 1985 and assessed her to a penalty for late registration. Ms Neal appealed, contending that her total ignorance of VAT law amounted to a reasonable excuse so that the penalty assessment should be withdrawn.

Neal v C & E Comrs (1988) STC 131

It was held that it is necessary to draw a distinction between ignorance of the primary rules of VAT and ignorance of other aspects of law (eg. whether a person is employed or self employed) which have a VAT consequence. The appellant's ignorance fell within the former class and she did not, therefore, have a reasonable excuse for her conduct. The penalty assessment was confirmed.

Customs leaflet 700/41/94 gives guidance concerning what might be accepted as a 'reasonable excuse' for late registration. In particular Customs identify:

(a)   compassionate circumstances, eg. the serious illness of a sole trader or member of his family;

(b)   transfer of a business as a going concern, where there was little or no break in activity and returns were made and tax paid on time under the previous owner's registration number;

(c)   doubt about liability of supplies, where correspondence has been on-going with Customs; and

(d)   doubt about employment status, where correspondence has been on-going with the Inland Revenue on whether the individual is self-employed or an employee.

It is difficult to establish a reasonable excuse, but mitigation of the penalty is potentially available (see para 2.2.6).

s.70

2.2.6 Mitigation

When the civil penalty regime was first introduced, the intention was to minimise the opportunities for any dispute as to whether a penalty should apply and, if so, its amount.

Thus, although penalties do not apply for certain non-compliance offences if the trader has a reasonable excuse for his conduct, this is difficult to establish and consequently the penalty system is often perceived as unfair for many traders caught through no deliberate attempt to delay or avoid paying over VAT.

Mitigation is however allowed for penalties imposed for:

s.70

(a)   dishonest conduct (see para 2.2.2);

s.60

(b)   serious misdeclaration (see para 2.2.3);

s.63

(c)   repeated misdeclarations (see para 2.2.4);

s.64

(d)   late notification of liability to register for VAT (see para 2.2.5);

s.67

(e)   unauthorised issue of tax invoices.

s.67

The default surcharge (see para 2.2.7) is not a mitigable penalty.

Mitigation means that both Customs, and the VAT tribunal on appeal, may reduce a penalty to whatever amount (including nil) they think proper. Note that a tribunal can reverse any reduction in penalty granted by Customs.

However, by statute none of the following may be taken in account when deciding on the amount to mitigate:

s.70(4)

(a)   an insufficiency of funds to pay the tax due or to pay the penalty;

(b)   the fact that there has been no or no significant loss of tax;

(c)   the fact that the person liable for the penalty or a person acting on his behalf has acted in good faith.

2.2.7   Default surcharge

Failure to furnish a tax return or pay tax shown to be due thereon on time are defaults which can give rise to penalties under one of two heads: a *daily penalty* (2.2.8) or *default surcharge*.

ss.59 and 69

Customs are entitled to impose a default surcharge where a VAT return or a VAT payment is submitted late, and a subsequent payment within the next 12 months is also late. As a warning the Commissioners serve a 'surcharge liability notice' after the first default. The notice specifies a 'surcharge period' commencing on the date of the notice and ending on the anniversary of the end of the accounting period of default. Default surcharge is only assessed if another default occurs within the surcharge period. The period is then further extended to the anniversary of the new default. The surcharge is 2% of the unpaid tax due in respect of the first default, 5% of the tax due in respect of the second default, rising by 5% for each further default, to a maximum of 15%.

s.59

Customs will not assess a surcharge of less than £200 unless the 10% or 15% rate applies - in which case there is a minimum charge of £30.

A surcharge liability will not apply if a nil or repayment return is submitted late, nor if tax is paid on time though the return is submitted late. Such an event will not increase the rate of surcharge for the next default in the surcharge liability period but it will trigger an extension of the period and Customs will issue a notice to show this.

Example

Y's return and payment for the quarter ended 31.12.94 is late. A surcharge liability notice is issued on 14.2.95 specifying a surcharge period of 14.2.95 - 31.12.95. Y's returns and payments for 30.9.95 and 31.3.96 are late and show tax due of £12,000 and £500 respectively. Surcharge for the period ending 30.9.95 is £240 (ie. 2% of £12,000) and for the period ending 31.3.96 is nil (ie. de minimis limit of £200 applies as 5% rate used). The surcharge period is also extended, to 30.9.96 and 31.3.97 respectively.

Y's return and payment for the quarters to 30.9.96 and 31.3.97 are late and show payments due of £13,000 and £1,100. Surcharge for the period to 30.9.96 is £1,300 (£13,000 x 10%) and for the period to 31.3.97 is £165 (£1,100 x 15% - the £200 deminimis limit does not apply at the 15% level). The surcharge period is also extended to 30.9.97 and 31.3.98.

As the surcharge liability notice is renewed on every default within twelve months of the previous default, the trader can only escape by submitting four consecutive quarterly returns on time accompanied by the full amounts of VAT due.

A default is disregarded for the purposes of the penalty if either:

(a)   the return and/or the tax due were despatched to Customs at such a time and in such a manner that it was reasonable to expect them to arrive on time. Customs have indicated that posting a return first class at least one working day prior to the due date is accepted as reasonable. Obtaining proof of posting is a sensible precaution; or

s.59(7)

(b)   the trader had a reasonable excuse for his lateness. Once again, the statutory exclusions apply, ie. an insufficiency of funds cannot be taken into account, nor can reliance on someone else to perform a task.

s.71(1)

Although it is far from easy to satisfy Customs, or, on appeal, the tribunal, that a reasonable excuse exists, case law indicates that a distinction should be drawn between the reason for the failure and the excuse. That is, if the trader's lateness can be traced not to a mere insufficiency of funds, but to some underlying cause, then a reasonable excuse may be accepted. It is necessary to show that the shortage of funds was attributable to some unforeseen and unavoidable circumstance, eg. the dishonesty of a former employee or the persistent failure of a customer, for whom the trader worked almost exclusively, to pay invoices on time.

C & E Comrs v Salevon Ltd (1989) STC 907
C & E Comrs v Steptoe (1992) STC 757

It is important to remember that default surcharge cannot be mitigated.

Where the default surcharge is not appropriate, for example if a trader submits every fifth return late, an alternative daily penalty is available.

There is a separate default surcharge system for large traders who have to make payments on account (para 1.2.6).

s.59A

2.2.8   Daily penalty

s.69

The *daily penalty* may be invoked by reference to a single default. The rate of penalty is governed by the number of failures in the two preceding years, thus:

Number of previous failures	Daily rate, greater of:
No failure in previous two years	£5 or $^1/6\%$ of tax due
One failure in previous two years	£10 or $^1/3\%$ of tax due
Two failures in previous two years	£15 or $^1/2\%$ of tax due

There is a minimum penalty of £50 and a maximum of 100 days at the appropriate rate.

A daily penalty can only be assessed, in the case of a failure to submit returns or pay tax on time, if Customs have issued a written warning of the consequences of the trader's failure to comply with his obligations.

s.76(2)

Example

X's return for the period ended 30.9.96 is furnished on 30.12.96, ie. 60 days late. The tax due is £7,500. His return for the period ended 31.3.95 was also late, but all other returns have been furnished on time. He will be assessed to a penalty of the greater of:

(a)   60 x £10 = £600; and

(b)   60 x ($^1/3\%$ of £7,500) = £1,500

ie. £1,500, provided that the appropriate written warning has been given by Customs.

2.2.9 Incorrect certificates

There are a number of situations where a person has to supply a certificate to show that zero-rating applies to a supply of land and buildings (see your Paper IIIc: VAT and NIC study text). A person giving an incorrect certificate is liable to a penalty equal to the tax thereby undercharged. The penalty can be appealed against on the grounds of reasonable excuse but is not on the list of mitigable offences.

s.62

2.2.10 Summary

A criminal prosecution for certain VAT offences can result in seven years imprisonment and / or an unlimited fine.

Under the civil penalty regime, the following penalties can be imposed.

(a)   *Dishonest conduct* - a penalty of up to 100% of the tax lost.

(b)   *Serious misdeclaration* s- a penalty of up to 15% of the tax lost where the trader does not make a voluntary disclosure may be imposed where the tax lost exceeds £2,000 and a return is inaccurate or an assessment is understated to the lesser of:

    (a)   30% of the relevant VAT for the period; and

    (b)   £1,000,000.

(b)   *Repeated misdeclaration* - a penalty of up to 15% of the tax lost where each of three or more misdeclarations out of 12 return periods is at least the lower of:

    (a)   £500,000; and

    (b)   10% of the relevant VAT.

    This penalty will only apply where a penalty liability notice has been issued and at least two of the misdeclarations have occurred during the eight periods following the issue of that notice.

(c)   *Late registration* - the penalty is a fixed percentage (either 5%, 10% or 15% depending on the lateness of the registration) of the net tax due for the period of default.

The above penalties can be mitigated, potentially to nil. If there is a 'reasonable excuse' the serious misdeclaration, repeated misdeclarations and late registration penalties do not apply at all.

A surcharge liability notice (SLN) can be issued by Customs following the late submission of a return or late payment of tax. A further late payment during the period of the SLN leads to the assessment of a *default surcharge*. The amount of the surcharge is 2%, 5%, 10% or 15% depending on the number of defaults committed. There is no mitigation, but defaults are ignored if the return and tax were despatched in good time or if there is a reasonable excuse for the failure.

The *daily penalty* can be applied in respect of a single default. The rate imposed depends upon the number of failures in the two previous years.

A penalty equal to the amount of tax undercharged can be imposed for giving an *incorrect certificate*.

2.3   Interest

2.3.1   Default interest

s.74

In law, a charge to default interest will arise when an assessment is issued to collect an underpayment of tax or when an assessment could have been issued, but the trader pays the tax before Customs in fact assess him. This is tantamount to providing for an interest charge on any late payment of VAT. The only exception is tax liable to a late registration penalty (see para 2.2.5). This is *not* subject to default interest.

Customs have indicated that in practice they will not seek to assess interest in cases where it does not represent commercial restitution. That is, a charge to interest is not appropriate where there has been no overall loss to the exchequer. An example of a situation where no assessment to interest will be made is that of a trader who makes a standard-rated supply to another VAT registered business but treats the supply as zero-rated in error. If the supplier had charged VAT, the customer would have been entitled to reclaim it as input tax and therefore there is no overall loss to the exchequer.

Customs News Release 34/94

With effect from 1 February 1995, Customs do not assess default interest on errors which are voluntarily disclosed, if the net errors amount to £2,000 or less. Para 2.3.2 below discusses the manner in which errors made by a trader should be corrected, but it is worth noting at this point that net errors of up to £2,000 do not need to be separately disclosed.

Customs News Release 9/95

At the time of publication, the rate of default interest stands at 6.25% (w.e.f. 6 February 1996). Rates are supplied in the exam paper if needed.

Default interest is also charged where an unregistered person issues an invoice which includes an amount shown as tax. That amount bears interest from the date of the invoice until payment. Default interest also applies where a person who is not registered under the flat rate farmers' scheme charges a flat rate commission on his invoices as if he were a flat rate farmer.

s.74(4)

Where an assessment is raised to collect outstanding tax, interest is calculated from a point no earlier than three years before the assessment date. This is only a cap on the starting point. Interest continues to accrue until the related tax is paid. Where tax is paid late but before the making of an assessment, the total interest period cannot exceed the three years prior to the date of payment.

2.3.2   Correction of errors on previous returns

Where a trader wishes to make a voluntary disclosure of net errors exceeding £2,000 made on previous VAT returns he must disclose this by letter to the local VAT office or use form VAT 652. Voluntary disclosure should enable the trader to avoid any misdeclaration penalty (see paras 2.2.3 and 2.2.4).

SI 1995/2518 reg 34

Net errors of £2,000 or less in total can be corrected by adjusting the VAT account and including the net amount of the adjustment in the VAT due or VAT reclaimed box on the current return. Note that the £2,000 test relates to *net errors discovered* in an accounting period, even though the errors may relate to different accounting periods.

Where a voluntary disclosure is made of net underpayments of more than £2,000, a charge to default interest is made (see paragraph 2.3.1). Since 1 February 1995, a trader who chooses to make a voluntary disclosure of a lesser net underpayment instead of merely adjusting his current return form is not charged default interest.

A voluntary disclosure must itemise under- or overpayments period by period so that the 'true amount of tax' can be adjusted for each period.

Where net errors under £2,000 are adjusted without formal disclosure, the true tax for the earlier periods remains as shown originally in the incorrect return(s). Thus once the corrections are made in this way, they become part of the true tax for the concurrent period and no further reallocation of the amounts arising from those errors can be made.

The 'true amount of tax' is relevant in deciding whether a serious misdeclaration or a material inaccuracy has been made (see paragraphs 2.2.3 and 2.2.4).

Note that the size test for method of disclosure relates to *net errors*. Thus a discovery of overstated output tax of £4,000 and also of overstated input tax of £3,000 leads to a net error of £1,000 being discovered. This can be adjusted in the VAT account.

2.3.3   Summary

Default interest will be imposed to provide commercial restitution where tax has been understated on a return and where an unregistered person issues an invoice charging VAT. Interest cannot run from a date more than three years before the date of assessment or payment.

Net errors discovered of £2,000 or less may be corrected by a trader by making an adjustment in his VAT account, which is then entered on the current return. Where the net errors are more than £2,000 a formal disclosure should be made to Customs. Default interest will be charged in respect of such disclosures.

SI 1995/2518
reg 32

2.4   Refund of overpaid tax, repayment supplement and interest

2.4.1   Refund of tax shown on VAT return

Where a tax return shows a repayment of VAT due to a trader, this will be dealt with by VAT Central Unit.

Repayment supplement is added if the Commissioners fail to issue an instruction for repayment to be made (eg. the trader receives a cheque) within 30 days following the receipt of the return, provided certain conditions are met. Repayment supplement is the greater of £50 and 5% of the repayment due.

s.79

Certain periods are left out of account in calculating the 30 day period, eg. where it is necessary to raise reasonable enquiries or correct errors. The period to leave out of account is defined as beginning when the Commissioners *first decide* it is necessary to make enquiries and ending when they satisfy themselves they have received complete answers or decide not to pursue the enquiries further, ie. including any delay on Customs' part in acting on that decision.

A right to supplement is in any event lost if the repayment shown on a return is overstated by more than the greater of £250 or 5% or the correct repayment. No supplement is available if the return giving rise to the refund is furnished later than the due date (see para 1.2.4). Thus repayment supplement is rarely available.

Example

This example is new.

> Z's return for the quarter ending 31 August 1996, received by Customs on 29 September 1996, shows a repayment due of £1,600. This results from a seasonal downturn in business but with a need to stock up for an anticipated busy autumn season. However, as Z is not normally a repayment trader, Customs decide on 5 October to make enquiries before making the repayment. Following a control visit which resulted in a £150 reduction in the amount of repayment, their enquiries are complete on 12 October but due to an administrative error, instruction to issue a repayment is not given (ie. Z does not receive the cheque) until 8 November.
>
> The total time between receipt of the return and issue of repayment order is 40 days (28 September to 8 November) which, after deducting the enquiry period of 8 days (5 to 12 October) exceeds 30 days. The adjustment of £150 is less than the greater of £250 and 5% of the correct repayment (£1,600 - £150 = £1,450 x 5% = £73). Z is therefore entitled to a repayment supplement of £73 (£1,450 x 5%).

The Commissioners may set-off any repayments of VAT and repayment supplement due to a trader against any VAT, penalty, interest or surcharge due from him.

s.81

2.4.2   Refund of overpaid tax

Where a person has paid more tax to the Commissioners than was correctly due, the person will be entitled to a refund of it on a *claim* being made. This might apply, for example, where a trader has treated certain suppliers as standard-rated, when they should have been zero-rated. On receipt of a claim the Commissioners can, however, withhold a refund if it would 'unjustly enrich' the claimant.

s.80

It is believed that Customs interpret 'unjustly enrich' as entitling them to refuse to give a refund if the refunded VAT will not in turn be distributed among the various purchasers who had borne the VAT in the first instance, so providing the claimant with a windfall gain.

Generally, claims must be made within six years of the date of overpayment. But if the overpayment results from a mistake the six year time limit for claims runs from the date the claimant discovers the mistake or (presumably earlier) the date he could with reasonable diligence have discovered it.

Customs can raise an assessment to recover refunds which were incorrectly made or which would not have been made with benefit of hindsight.

s.73(2)

2.4.3 Interest on overpaid tax arising from Customs error

A registered trader who has overpaid VAT has a statutory right to claim interest for the period of time during which he was denied the use of his money *if this arose as a result of an error on the part of Customs*. This can apply, therefore, if too much VAT was paid, or too little input tax was claimed, or if the trader was otherwise prevented from recovering VAT at the proper time.

s.78

Interest rates are not the same as those applying generally to other unpaid or overpaid taxes such as income tax. In fact they are fixed to be the same as the High Court special account rate. The current rate (since February 1993) is 8% per annum. Rates are supplied in the exam paper, if needed.

Where Customs dispute a claim to interest the trader has a right of appeal to a VAT tribunal.

A claim must be made within six years of the date on which the claimant discovered the error or could with reasonable diligence have discovered it.

2.4.4 Summary

Repayment supplement (the greater of £50 or 5% of the repayment due) is given on repayments where the return was furnished by the due date and where Customs have not issued an instruction to repay within 30 days following receipt of the return.

Overpayments of tax are refunded by Customs upon a claim being made, provided that the claimant will not be 'unjustly enriched'.

Interest can be claimed where, due to an error by Customs, too much VAT was paid, or too little input tax was claimed, or a trader was otherwise unable to recover VAT at the proper time.

2.5 Security

There are three situations in which Customs may require a person to give security:

(a) as a condition of making a VAT credit to that person, if it appears necessary for the protection of the revenue; — Sch 11 para 4(1)

(b) as a condition of allowing that person to supply goods or services by way of taxable supply, again if such action is necessary for the protection of the revenue; and — Sch 11 para 4(2)

(c) where that person has failed to act upon Customs' direction, requiring him to appoint a VAT representative. — s.48(7)

Any demand for security under (b) or (c) above is subject to a right of appeal to the tribunal. There is no appeal procedure where security is required by Customs in situation (a) above. — s.83(6)

A recent case considered the nature of the tribunal's role in an appeal against a requirement to provide security in situation (b) above. The grounds of the appellant's appeal were, broadly, that Customs decision was unreasonable in the circumstances. The tribunal found that Customs had failed to ask the appellant for financial information relevant to their decision, but that if they had done so, Customs belief that security was necessary for the protection of the revenue would have been strengthened. The High Court held, and the Court of Appeal agreed, that the approach adopted by the tribunal was incorrect. The role of the tribunal is appellate, not supervisory, so that once it had been established that Customs decision was erroneous because of a failure to take account of all relevant information, it should simply have allowed the taxpayer's appeal rather than substituting its own decision. The only exception to this rule would be a case where the decision of Customs would *inevitably* be the same, even if all the into relevant information had been considered. — John Dee Ltd v C & E Comrs (1995) STC 941

In practice, Customs will normally seek security on protection of revenue grounds if the persons concerned in a business have failed to pay VAT in the past, committed other compliance failures or been convicted of a VAT offence. Businesses run by disqualified directors or undischarged bankrupts are also likely to be subject to a requirement to give security.

The amount of the security is usually six months' estimated VAT liability (reduced to four months for traders making monthly returns). Security may be provided in cash or by guarantee from an approved financial institution, within 30 days from the date of Customs' notice.

QUESTIONS

1. X Ltd is due a repayment of VAT of £7,500 for its prescribed accounting period ended 30.9.96. The return was furnished by X Ltd on 28.10.96. The repayment is not made until 16.12 96.

   What is the total repayment due to X Ltd?

2. What is the maximum default surcharge which may be levied?

3. The rate of penalty for repeated misdeclarations is ....% of the VAT lost.

4. A trader makes a claim for refund of VAT overpaid by mistake. On what grounds may Customs restrict the refund?

5. In the quarter ended 30.6.96 a trader discovers overpayments of VAT of £400 and underpayments of VAT of £2,300 in earlier quarters. How does he correct these errors?

6. What are the consequences when a trader is late in notifying Customs of his liability to register for VAT?

7. In respect of which penalties is mitigation available?

SOLUTIONS

1. VAT   £7,500

    Repayment supplement *
    - greater of £50, and
    - £7,500 x 5% = £375
    ie.   375
                                                                              ─────────
    TOTAL REPAYMENT DUE   £7,875
                                                                              ═════════
                                                                               (2.4.1)

    * It is assumed that:

    (a)   the return is accurate to within £250/5%; and

    (b)   the repayment has not been delayed as a result of reasonable
          enquiries etc. by Customs.

2. 15% of the tax due.   (2.2.7)

3. 15% (but this can be mitigated).   (2.2.4)

4. Any refund may be restricted or refused if it 'would unjustly enrich the
    claimant'.   (2.4.2)

5. Since the net errors discovered are less than £2,000 they can be corrected
    by adjusting the VAT return for the current quarter by including the net
    sum of £1,900 in the VAT due box.   (2.3.2)

6. The consequences are:

    (a)   registration will be backdated to the date from which it was due;

    (b)   output tax on supplies and deemed supplies must be accounted for
          from the date in a); and

    (c)   a late registration penalty will be imposed (unless there is
          reasonable excuse), subject to mitigation.   (2.2.5)

7. Dishonest conduct, serious misdeclaration, repeated misdeclarations, late
    registration and unauthorised issue of tax invoices.   (2.2.6)

By the end of this session you will be able to:

- explain when an assessment may be issued and how to determine its validity

- describe when an appeal will be admitted.

References: VATA 1994 unless otherwise stated

3.1 Assessments

A Customs Officer will issue *an assessment* where it appears that a tax return has not been submitted or is incomplete or incorrect. This extends to situations where amounts of VAT have been incorrectly credited to a registered person, and where repayment has been made but was not due because registration has been cancelled. There are a number of procedural hurdles to be overcome before a VAT tribunal will recognise an assessment as validly made:

s.73(1)-(3)

(a) the assessment must be made *to the best of the Commissioners' judgement*. This means that they must consider fairly all material put before them by the trader and base their decision on it. The decision must be reasonable. So long as there is some material on which the Commissioners can act, however, they are not required to make any further investigation.

Van Boeckel v C & E Comrs (1981) STC 290

A recent case in the Court of Session has lent further support to the position, as set out in the *Van Boeckel* case. Where tax had been underdeclared for a period of 5 years, it was acceptable for the assessment to be calculated on the basis of a sample period of 3 months. It was also stated that the question of whether 'best judgement' has been exercised by the Commissioners is one of fact for the tribunal to determine. Thus traders and their representatives before the tribunal must ensure that the evidence given to the tribunal is complete;

Farnocchia and another v C & E Comrs (1994) STC 881

(b) the *time limits* must be observed, ie. the later of

s.73(6)

(i) two years after the end of the prescribed accounting period involved; or

(ii) one year after evidence justifying an assessment comes to light.

(But see additional points below);

(c) the assessment must *precisely define the period of time* to which it relates. This information need not necessarily be shown on the assessment itself.

In a decided case, the prescribed accounting periods covered by an assessment could be discerned from the accompanying letter and schedules, even though not included on the assessment. It was held by the Court of Appeal that the absence of dates from the assessment did not invalidate it; and

House (trading as P & J Autos) v C & E Comrs (1995) STI 1669

(d) the amount of the assessment must be *notified to the taxable person*. An assessment served on a partnership is deemed to be a notification to the past and present partners concerned.

Since there is no prescribed statutory form for the notification of an assessment, any document which states reasonably clearly the information required constitutes valid notification. This comprises:

(i)   the taxpayer's name;

(ii)   the amount of tax due;

(iii)   the reason for the assessment; and

(iv)   the period to which it relates.

House v C & E Comrs (see above)

There is an over-riding time limit for the issue of an assessment: an assessment must be issued not later than six years after the end of the prescribed accounting period concerned or (where an individual has died) not later than three years after his death. However, where the under-payment arises from fraud or dishonest conduct, the six year limit is increased to twenty years. Where an individual dies, an assessment may be made at any time within the three years thereafter if it would have been in time at the date of death.

s.77

In a recent case, a company had claimed credit for an amount of input tax in the quarter ended 30 June 1991. Ths supply in question however had been made in the previous quarter to 31 March 1991. It subsequently transpired that the transaction in respect of which input tax credit had been claimed was not a taxable supply at all, but instead a compensation payment outside the scope of VAT. The Commissioners made an assessment for the overclaimed input tax in June 1993. The taxpayer argued, and the Court agreed, that the assessment was out of time. The two year time limit commenced to run from the prescribed accounting period in which the entitlement to deduct the input tax *first* arose, ie. the quarter ended 31 March 1991.

C & E Comrs v Croydon Hotel & Leisure Co. Ltd. (1995) STC 855

A global assessment can be made for two or more prescribed accounting periods without allocating the amount of tax to individual periods. In that case the time limit operates from the end of the earliest period included in the assessment.

S J Grange Ltd v C & E Comrs (1979) STC 183

It is necessary to distinguish between a global assessment and a document which comprises a number of assessments for different prescribed accounting periods which happen to be notified together. In the case of a global assessment, if the earliest period is out of time then the *whole* assessment is invalid. By contrast, a document which includes a number of separate assessments can be *severed*, so that if one or more of the periods concerned is out of time, the document is invalid to that extent only - the assessments for periods within the time limit still stand. The question of whether a global assessment has been made or a number of separate assessments is one of *fact*, based upon the form in which Customs notify the trader.

C & E Comrs v Le Rififi (1995) STC 103

In a decided case, it was held that Customs could not 'convert' an assessment of overclaimed input tax into an assessment for underdeclared output tax in a different sum - a new assessment was required.

Ridgeons Bulk Ltd v C & E Comrs (1994) STC 427

3.2 Appeals

3.2.1 Right of appeal

A person has the right of appeal to a VAT and duties tribunal (referred to in this text simply as a 'tribunal') against certain Customs decisions or assessments. The appeal must be made in writing within 30 days of the date of the disputed Customs letter or assessment.

Before making the appeal to the tribunal the trader may prefer to ask Customs to reconsider their decision. If this course of action is chosen, the request should be made in writing within 30 days of the disputed letter of assessment and relevant information should be provided to enable Customs to reconsider. The trader should also ask Customs to extend the usual time limit for an appeal.

The request to Customs to reconsider their decision may result in a revised decision, in which case the trader has 30 days to appeal against this to a tribunal, provided that Customs have agreed to extend the time limit for an appeal. On the other hand, Customs may confirm their original decision. In that case, assuming again that an extension to the appeal period has been granted, the trader has 21 days from the date of the confirmation of the original decision to appeal to the tribunal.

The matters against which an appeal may be made to a tribunal include the following:

s.83

(a)   registration, or cancellation of registration;

(b)   refusal of group registration application;

(c)   assessments for VAT and/or penalties;

(d)   VAT chargeable on the supply of any goods or services;

(e)   input tax reclaimable; and

(f)   the use of special schemes including a retail scheme, cash accounting and the flat rate scheme for farmers.

3.2.2 Prerequisites for an appeal

Before an appeal will be entertained by a tribunal, the trader must have made all returns which he is required to make and paid the tax due thereon. The effect of this rule is that a trader is unable to appeal against any decision or assessment if he has outstanding returns or tax liability.

s.84(2)

For appeals in respect of certain specified matters, such as a decision relating to the amount of VAT chargeable on a supply or the assessment of a penalty, there is an additional requirement. In such cases, the trader must have either paid or deposited the tax demanded or satisfied the tribunal that he would suffer hardship if payment was made. It was decided in a Court of Appeal case that, even where an assessment covers more than one quarter, it is not open to the tribunal to fix a part payment of the total as being below the level causing hardship. Having agreed that making the full payment would result in hardship for the trader, the tribunal was required to hear the appeal without advance payment of any of the tax. The assessment had clearly been presented to the firm as a single assessment, albeit covering 25 quarters, and the tribunal could not treat it otherwise (see also section 3.1 above, regarding time limits for such assessments).

s.84(3)

Don Pasquale v
C & E Comrs
(1990) STC 206

3.2.3   Tribunal procedure

A VAT and duties tribunal will generally consist of a chairman and two other members and at least one is likely to have an accountancy background. The chairman may sit alone if it appears that the matter under dispute is a question of law only, rather than fact.

Customs are obliged to make available to the trader any documents which they intend to produce at tribunal and provide a list of any cases they wish to cite. The trader has to do likewise.

At the appeal hearing the appellant may conduct his own case or he may be represented by any person he wishes to appoint. The Commissioners of Customs and Excise (the Commissioners) may likewise be represented by any person they wish to appoint. They are usually represented by a member of their own solicitors' office.

Each party to the appeal (or their representative) is allowed to address the tribunal to give evidence and to call and cross examine witnesses. The case of the appellant is normally presented first, followed by the Commissioner. Finally, the appellant (or his representative) has a right to reply.

In a 'Tax evasion appeal' (ie. an appeal against a liability for a penalty imposed for conduct involving dishonesty or an appeal against the amount of such a penalty) the burden of proof lies with the Commissioners. This means that the Commissioners' representative, and not the appellant, will open the case. This order for the hearing will also apply where there is an appeal against both an assessment and an accompanying penalty for dishonest conduct.

It is unlikely that the tribunal will give a decision at the end of the hearing as it will normally be given in writing a few days later.

3.2.4   Further appeals against a tribunal decision

A right of appeal exists to the High Court in a case where either party is dissatisfied *on a point of law* with the decision of the tribunal. The decision of the tribunal on questions of *fact* is final. From the High Court, the appeal can proceed if necessary to the Court of Appeal and the House of Lords. It is important to recognise however that decisions of the European Court of Justice have supremacy over domestic decisions, even if the proceedings commenced in another member state.

In certain circumstances, it is possible to 'leap frog' the Court of Appeal and for the appeal to proceed directly from the High Court to the House of Lords. There is also a procedure by virtue of which an appeal against a decision of the tribunal can be heard by the Court of Appeal, by-passing the High Court. This can only apply where the point of law at issue is a question of statutory interpretation and the leave of a single judge of the Court of Appeal is required.

Certain decisions may be challenged by way of judicial review. However, the courts will be reluctant to refer a case to judicial review if some other statutory remedy is specifically provided. To be successful in an application for judicial review, the taxpayer needs to demonstrate that the case is exceptional.

R v London VAT and Duties Tribunal, ex parte Conoco Ltd (1995) STC 468

(See also 'Essential Law for the Tax Practitioner', Chapter 5.)

QUESTIONS

1. As a result of a control visit on 15.7.96, Customs obtain evidence that Bill, a trader, has understated his output tax during the prescribed accounting period ended 31 December 1994.

    What is the latest date on which a valid assessment can be made by Customs to recover the tax understated?

2. When will a Customs Officer issue an assessment?

3. What is the time limit for making an appeal against an assessment?

4. Show four matters which may be the subject of an appeal.

5. What requirements must be met before an appeal against a decision as to the VAT chargeable on a supply will be entertained by a tribunal?

SOLUTIONS

1. 14.7.97 ie. one year after the evidence of the understatement comes to light. (3.1)

2. Where it appears that a tax return:
    (a) has not been submitted;
    (b) is incomplete; or
    (c) is incorrect. (3.1)

3. 30 days. (3.2.1)

4. (a) an assessment for tax and/or penalties;
    (b) the refusal of a group registration application;
    (c) the amount of input tax reclaimable; and
    (d) the amount of VAT chargeable.
    (or other matters listed in s.83 VATA 1994). (3.2)

5. The trader must have:
    (a) paid (or deposited) the tax demanded or satisfied the tribunal that he would suffer hardship;
    (b) submitted all returns due; and
    (c) paid any tax due on the returns. (3.2)

Direct tax administration

Indirect tax administration